Translated Texts

CW00384175

This series is designed to meet the needs
history and others who wish to broa
material, but whose knowledge of Latin or Greek ...
them to do so in the original language. Many important Late Imperial and
Dark Age texts are currently unavailable in translation and it is hoped that
TTH will help to fill this gap and to complement the secondary literature in
English which already exists. The series relates principally to the period
300–800 AD and includes Late Imperial, Greek, Byzantine and Syriac texts
as well as source books illustrating a particular period or theme. Each
volume is a self-contained scholarly translation with an introductory essay
on the text and its author and notes on the text indicating major problems of
interpretation, including textual difficulties.

A full list of published titles in the Translated Texts for Historians series is available on request. The most recently published are shown below.

Antioch as a Centre of Hellenic Culture, as Observed by Libanius
Translated with an introduction and notes by A. F. NORMAN
Volume 34: 224pp., 2000, ISBN 0-85323-595-3

Neoplatonic Saints: The Lives of Plotinus and Proclus by their Students
Translated with an introduction and notes by MARK EDWARDS
Volume 35: 224pp., 2000, ISBN 0-85323-615-1

Politics, Philosophy and Empire in the Fourth Century: Select Orations of Themistius
Translated with an introduction by PETER HEATHER and DAVID MONCUR
Volume 36: 384pp., 2001, ISBN 0-85323-106-0

A Christian's Guide to Greek Culture: The Pseudo-Nonnus *Commentaries* on *Sermons* 4, 5, 39 and 43 of Gregory of Nazianzus
Translated with an introduction and notes by JENNIFER NIMMO SMITH
Volume 37: 208pp., 2001, ISBN 0-85323-917-7

Avitus of Vienne: Letters and Selected Prose
Translated with introduction and notes by DANUTA SHANZER and IAN WOOD
Volume 38: 472pp., 2002, ISBN 0-85323-588-0

Constantine and Christendom: The Oration to the Saints, The Greek and Latin Accounts of the Discovery of the Cross, The Edict of Constantine to Pope Silvester
Translated with introduction and notes by MARK EDWARDS
Volume 39: 192pp., 2003, ISBN 0-85323-648-8

Lactantius: Divine Institutes
Translated with introduction and notes by ANTHONY BOWEN and PETER GARNSEY
Volume 40: 488pp., 2003, ISBN 0-85323-988-6

Selected Letters of Libanius from the Age of Constantius and Julian
Translated with introduction and notes by SCOT BRADBURY
Volume 41: 308pp., 2004, ISBN 0-85323-509-0

Cassiodorus: Institutions of Divine and Secular Learning and On the Soul
Translated and notes by JAMES W. HALPORN; Introduction by MARK VESSEY
Volume 42: 316 pp., 2004, ISBN 0-85323-998-3

For full details of Translated Texts for Historians, including prices and ordering information, please write to the following:
All countries, except the USA and Canada: Liverpool University Press, 4 Cambridge Street, Liverpool, L69 7ZU, UK (*Tel* +44-[0]151-794 2233, *Fax* +44-[0]151-794 2235, Email J.M. Smith@liv.ac.uk, http://www.liverpool-unipress.co.uk). **USA and Canada:** University of Chicago Press, 1427 E. 60th Street, Chicago, IL, 60637, US (*Tel* 773-702-7700, *Fax* 773-702-9756, www.press.uchicago.edu)

Translated Texts for Historians
Volume 12

Selected *Variae* of Magnus Aurelius Cassiodorus Senator

The Right Honorable and Illustrious
Ex-Quaestor of the Palace,
Ex-Ordinary Consul,
Ex-Master of the Offices,
Praetorian Prefect and Patrician

Being Documents of the
Kingdom of the Ostrogoths in Italy,
Chosen to Illustrate the Life of the Author
and the History of his Family

Translated with introduction and notes by
S. J. B. BARNISH

Liverpool
University
Press

First published 1992 by
Liverpool University Press
4 Cambridge Street
Liverpool, L69 7ZU

Reprinted 2006, 2010

British Library Cataloguing-in-Publication Data
A British Library CIP Record is available
ISBN 978 0 85323 436 4

Printed and bound in the European Union by
Bell and Bain Ltd, Glasgow

CONTENTS

ACKNOWLEDGEMENTS   vii

REFERENCES AND ABBREVIATIONS   viii

INTRODUCTION

A. ITALY, A.D. 395-550   ix

B. THE *VARIAE*
    1. The Compilation   xiv
    2. The Character of the *Variae*   xvii
    3. The *Variae* as Separate Documents   xxx
    4. The *Variae* as a Historical Source:
               a Caution   xxxiii
    5. The *Variae*: Text and Editions;
       Selection, Dating and Translation   xxxiii

C. THE HOUSE OF THE CASSIODORI *(ORDO GENERIS*
                     CASSIODORORUM)

    xxxv

D. CASSIODORUS AND HIS KINDRED IN THE *VARIAE*
    1. The Family   xxxvii
    2. Cassiodorus as Diplomatic Draftsman   xxxix
    3. Cassiodorus as Quaestor   xli
    4. Cassiodorus as Consul and Senator   xlv
    5. Cassiodorus as Master of the Offices   xlvii
    6. Cassiodorus as Praetorian Prefect   l

TRANSLATED *VARIAE* WITH NOTES   1

GLOSSARY of ALLUSIONS AND
              OFFICIAL TERMS   184

SELECT BIBLIOGRAPHY   189
INDEXES   195
MAPS   203

ACKNOWLEDGEMENTS

Much of the work on these translations was carried out while I held a research fellowship at Darwin College, Cambridge, and a lecturership at Queen's College, Oxford; I must record my gratitude to the Master, Provost and Fellows. For advice on interpretation and translation, I must thank, among others, Luciana Cuppo Csaki, Raymond Davis, Karl Hölkeskamp, John Matthews, Bryan Ward-Perkins and Patrick Wormald. Angus Bowie identified the quotation from Juvenal in IX.21; he and Philip Harries gave me much advice on the wine technicalities of XII.12, after dinner one evening at Queen's. Robin Lane Fox gave a horseman's comments on my rendering of IV.1. Robin Macpherson sent me a complimentary copy of his recent study of the *Variae*, and Jill Harries let me see her article on the Quaestor of the Palace, in a fuller version than was published. Carlotta Dionisotti and Margaret Gibson scrutinised every translation, made many comments, and saved me from many errors. Lesley Smith and Neil Ferguson spent much labour and advice in assisting my word-processing.

REFERENCES AND ABBREVIATIONS

References to the *Variae* in bold type are to texts translated in this volume, e.g. **Preface**, or **VIII.33**; references in plain type are to those which are omitted.

CCSL	*Corpus Christianorum, Series Latina*
CSEL	*Corpus Scriptorum Ecclesiae Latinorum*
C. Th.	*Theodosian Code*
JRS	*Journal of Roman Studies*
MGH	*Monumenta Germaniae Historica*
MGH AA	*MGH, Auctores Antiquissimi*
PBSR	*Papers of the British School at Rome*
PLRE II	*Prosopography of the Later Roman Empire, vol. II.*
RBPh	*Revue Belge de Philologie et d'Histoire*

A. ITALY, A.D. 395-550[1]

When the emperor Theodosius I died in 395, the Roman empire was divided between his sons Honorius in the west and Arcadius in the east. Theoretically, it remained a polity united by name, law, coinage, official language, religion, and dynastic allegiance. During the fifth century, however, east and west tended increasingly to go their own ways. In the west, society was dominated by a small class of great land-owning aristocrats. Often members of the Roman Senate, which gave them identity, they were conservative in their patriotic and cultural values, but reluctant to uphold the empire against the barbarians with cash, or with the supply of recruits from their estates. Punctuating long periods of cultivated leisure with brief spells of predatory and amateurish office-holding, they came increasingly to control the great civil offices of state. Full senatorial membership, and ultimately high social status were coming to depend on tenure of those offices, civil or military, which brought the title of 'illustrious'.[2]

In the youth of Cassiodorus, Italy had seven active civilian *illustres*: in order of rank, the Praetorian Prefect of Italy, the Urban Prefect of Rome, the Quaestor of the Palace, the Master of the Offices, and the Counts of the Sacred Largesses, Private Estates, and Patrimony;[3] Gothic soldiers might hold the illustrious title, but seldom sat in the Senate. Full senators could also be created by appointment to sinecure *illustris* posts, usually as Count of the Bodyguards; also, probably, by direct nomination (*adlectio*) to the Senate. The Consulship - usually,

---

[1] For general accounts of the period, see Bury, Stein, Jones, 1964; on the Italian economy and society, Ruggini, part ii, Tabacco, ch.1, Wickham, ch.1.

[2] The Senate was the council of magistrates and ex-magistrates which had been *de facto* ruler of the Roman state from 510-49 B.C., and embodied its traditions under the emperors. The Senate of Constantinople now ranked equally with Rome's, and the term might be applied to the councils of lesser cities.

[3] For these, see glossary; VI.3-9 gives their ranking; cf. **I.4.4**.

one Consul held office in Rome, the other in Constantinople (Byzantium) - and the title of Patrician, were the two peaks of a senatorial career. The two lesser grades of the order, which by now did not imply senatorial seats, were 'distinguished' (*spectabilis*) and 'right honourable' (*clarissimus*). *Spectabiles* could vote in the provincial assemblies; the rank was achieved only by office or special nomination. (In the later Ostrogothic period, they may have entered the Senate again.) The clarissimate was achieved by special nomination, office, or inheritance in senatorial families.[4]

During the fifth century, the western empire lost much in territory and prestige, most decisively when the piratic Vandals conquered Africa, sacking Rome in 455. Soon, little more than Italy was left. The Roman army became ever more barbarian in its composition, and its commanders virtually ruled the state, with leading Italian senators as their junior partners. Of two of the latter, the Gallic senator Sidonius Apollinaris wrote in 468, 'In the most elevated rank, if we leave out of account the privileged military class, they stood easily next to the Emperor in the purple'.[5] By 500, the two chief senatorial houses seem to have been the Anicii and the Decii. The former had long been notorious for vast estates extended by the skilful and unscrupulous use of office; the latter, from 458 to 534, produced twelve Consuls and five Praetorian Prefects of Italy, in four generations. (Cf. **III.6, X.11.**) Such a record, the family of Cassiodorus, although rich and well connected, could not rival; it was, however, politically important as early as 450 (**I.3-4**).

Whatever the influence of its individual members, the western Senate had small power, and few functions as a body; it was still valued chiefly as enshrining the glorious traditions of Rome. Now and then, however, rulers might respond to its resolutions and recommendations, and it was playing an ever increasing part in papal politics (cf. **VIII.15, IX.15-16**). In the time of Cassiodorus, at least, it formally confirmed those appointments which carried full senatorial

---

[4] See Barnish, 1988, 120-3.

[5] *Ep.* 1.9.2.

rank.

In 476, the underpaid and land-hungry Germanic troops revolted. Their leader, Odoacer, killed the commander-in-chief, Orestes, and deposed his son, the usurping emperor Romulus. Settling his soldiers on the estates of northern Italy, he based himself at Ravenna, the main administrative capital, and took up the rule of the imperial rump. He preserved most of the forms and mechanisms of Roman government, nominated Consuls, and illustrious ministers, and enjoyed some support from the Senate, but was known simply as king (*rex*), using neither the imperial title, nor regalia. In fact, he hoped to be acknowledged as the viceroy of Zeno, the eastern emperor, now theoretically ruler of the whole empire. Although he gave Italy years of security, this acknowledgement was never formally bestowed. In 489, Zeno sent against him a horde of Ostrogoths, under their leader Theoderic of the Amal family. For some years, Theoderic had been playing a major part, often dangerous and destructive, in the stormy politics of the eastern empire. Consul in 484, he had been commander-in-chief, and held the title of Patrician; his master, though, was glad to get rid of him.

Overthrowing Odoacer in a long and bitter war, and replacing his barbarians by Ostrogoths on the Italian estates (I.18), Theoderic apparently followed his rival's policies, and gave fresh employment to some of his leading Roman supporters (I.4.6, I.18, II.6.2,5). Like Odoacer, Theoderic and his Ostrogoths were Arian heretics, but he long remained on good terms with the Catholic Church of Italy, then in schism with Byzantium. Like Odoacer's, Theoderic's relations with the east were troubled. His constitutional position was lengthily negotiated with Zeno and his successor Anastasius, with little satisfaction to either side.[6] He too was usually titled king; he made no

---

[6] See Jones, 1962, Thompson, ch.4; on land settlement, Barnish, 1986, against Goffart, 1980.

innovations on Roman law, but used some of the imperial regalia.[7] A
concept of twin states (*res publicae*) was sometimes employed by
diplomats in both Ravenna and Byzantium. However, the person and
regime to succeed Theoderic probably remained unclear, and he ruled
with such independence that some easterners thought of him as a
usurper. Not only did he cultivate the image of a western emperor, but,
in his times, an image of Italy as a separate, almost a national state
sometimes found expression in Roman circles.[8] In 504/5, the two *res
publicae* clashed bloodily over the control of Sirmium on the middle
Danube. The Goths were victorious, and Italy gained in security and
pride with the recovery of lost west-Roman territory. Theoderic also
employed marriage ties, and the prestige of Rome's ruler, to construct
a diplomatic framework which approached a system of alliances among
the neighbouring tribes. In 507, this was severely damaged, when
Clovis the Frank broke away, with Byzantine encouragement and naval
support. (See **I.45-46, II.38, 40-41, III.1-4, IV.1, V.1**.) At the battle
of Vouillé, he ousted the Visigoths from central Gaul, killing their king
Alaric II. Theoderic salvaged the remnants of their kingdom and
annexed Provence, ruling it as the revived Praetorian Prefecture of the
Gauls; Spain and Septimania he controlled as regent for Alaric's son
Amalaric.

Theoderic's only child was a daughter, Amalasuintha. In 515, he
married her to the Visigoth Eutharic, who claimed Amal blood; their
children were a son and daughter, Athalaric and Matasuentha. These
dynastic arrangements were approved by the emperor Justin I in
518-19, when he conferred the Consulship on Eutharic, and adopted
him as his son by arms (cf. **VIII.1**). However, Eutharic soon died, and
Theoderic's last years were darkened by quarrels with Byzantium, with
the Catholic Church, and with his allies, the Vandals settled in Africa,
who were the chief naval power in the western Mediterranean. In a
mysterious crisis, linked with eastern relations, and perhaps with the

---

[7] In the *Variae*, Cassiodorus noticeably avoids official phrases applicable only
to emperors; cf. Fridh, 1956, 110, Vidén, 136, 142.
[8] See Reydellet, ch.4.

succession problem, two probable kinsmen of Cassiodorus, the great
senator and philosopher Anicius Manlius Severinus Boethius, then
Master of the Offices, and his father-in-law Symmachus, were put to
death; Pope John I died under Theoderic's displeasure.[9]

In 526, the young Athalaric succeeded Theoderic, with his mother
as regent, an arrangement grudgingly accepted by Byzantium. Her sex
and her learning made Amalasuintha unpopular with the Goths, and the
regency was turbulent. Athalaric took to drink; and, on his death in
534, she placed as her partner on the throne her cousin Theodahad, an
unwarlike, but influential figure, who imitated both the culture and the
land-grabbing practices of the great Roman nobles (cf. X.3, X.5). He
rapidly imprisoned and murdered the queen, thus giving the emperor
Justinian an excuse to invade Italy. Justinian hoped to restore the
empire to its ancient power, and had already conquered the Vandals;
he had also supported Amalasuintha against dissident and chauvinist
Goths: his war was thus one of both vengeance and liberation, and was
assisted by some Roman senators.

Theodahad himself was soon overthrown by the soldierly non-Amal
Witigis, who married Matasuentha in 536. Witigis proved a failure in
command: Ravenna fell in 540 to the general Belisarius, and he was
taken prisoner to Constantinople. However, the Goths rebelled, finding
a brilliant leader in king Totila, and the war dragged on until 562. The
Franks expanded their power in Gaul and northern Italy, while flirting
with both sides. Italy was greatly impoverished, and the way paved for
the Lombard migration of 568. Among the casualties was the Roman
senatorial order. The western empire was not revived; Italy was
administered by the eastern emperor, after an increasingly military
pattern, and with officials of mainly eastern origin. The political
influence of the senators declined drastically, and few of the posts
which had conferred entry to the Senate were now available to them.
The Pope gradually replaced the Urban Prefect; no more Consuls were
nominated, for either Rome or Constantinople; the reign of Theoderic

---

[9] See Chadwick, 45-69, Matthews, 1981, Barnish, 1983 and 1990; further,
below, xlvii-xlix.

was looked back on as a golden age.

B. THE *VARIAE*

1. The Compilation

Our most important documents for the history of Gothic rule in Italy are the *Variae* of Cassiodorus: twelve books, comprising 468 letters, edicts and model letters (*formulae*), which the author drafted, between 506 and 538, for Theoderic, Athalaric, Amalasuintha, Theodahad, Witigis, and the Senate, and in his own person as Praetorian Prefect of Italy. In the case of those written for monarchs, he was acting as, or for, the Quaestor, chief legal expert and official publicist.[10] He apparently compiled the *Variae* in 537/8, near the harassed end of his service as Prefect, while war was raging, and Witigis was besieging the Byzantine commander Belisarius in Rome. In a long and conventionally self-deprecatory Preface, he claimed a range of motives for this work: to satisfy the demands of friends - a standard apology; to supply models of official eloquence for future administrators, himself among them; to ensure immortality for those praised in the letters; to strengthen respect for the laws; and to provide a mirror of his own character. The title *Variae* reflects the varieties of rhetorical style which the letters show. A verse couplet dedicated the collection to an unnamed rhetorician: '[Cassiodorus] Senator offers these gifts of love and duty to the master whom no gold pleases more than eloquence.'

The claims and suggestions of the Preface are a useful starting-point when considering the *Variae*. Official education is a plausible motive. Cassiodorus' later commentary on the psalms (*Expositio Psalmorum*) and his *Institutiones* show a deep concern for rhetorical training. His near contemporary John Lydus, a middle ranking career bureaucrat in Constantinople, was awarded a state

---

[10] On this office, see Honoré, 8f., 136, 201; Harries.

teaching post for his general learning and skill in Latin. In the early medieval west, formulary collections of legal and chancery documents were common; the *Variae* are an early example of the genre. An inscription from the territory of Timgad in Numidia repeats a sentence from VII.7, the formula of appointment for the Prefect of the Watch at Rome. This suggests that the collection was read and used by the provincial administrators of Justinian. A Boethius, probably related to Cassiodorus, served as Praetorian Prefect of Africa in 560.[11]

As a compilation, the *Variae* can also be read as an apology, both for the Gothic regime, and for the Roman aristocracy which had served it. (Justinian's officials were to penalise the Romans for abuses of power under the Goths.[12]) There is something almost defiant in Cassiodorus' inclusion of 67 letters from his own Prefectural administration. Perhaps, too, he was advocating either a continuing Gothic role in Italy, a revival of the western empire, or a combination of the two. About the time the *Variae* were published, he probably also collected and published his formal panegyrics on Gothic royalties.[13] While Ravenna was under siege in 540, the Goths offered the rule of the western empire to Belisarius. Many *formulae* in the *Variae* (e.g. VII.42) suggest an expectation that the Gothic administration would continue; but VI.6, at least, may describe imperial practices obsolete under the Goths. Some of the Roman senators praised in the collection probably remained loyal to the Goths; others had transferred their allegiance, and one, Fidelis, may already have been serving as Justinian's Praetorian Prefect of Italy, in rivalry with Cassiodorus.

Politically significant themes, such as the defence of Italy, relations between Goths and Franks, and diplomacy with Byzantium are also prominent. Moreover, both in general and in detail, the *Variae* may imply a critique of the growing cultural and religious intolerance of Justinian's regime. (Cf. II.27, X.26.) The emperor, furthermore, was

---

[11] *Corpus Inscriptionum Latinarum*, VIII, 2297; cf. Macpherson, 181; but both texts may be modelled on an earlier one.

[12] Procopius, *Wars* VII.i.32.

[13] On the character of these, see MacCormack, 1975, 187-91, 1981, ch.8.

at odds with the Senate of Constantinople, which probably hoped for a greater share in government, and a leading role in the choice of the emperor. Controversy of this kind may lie behind the fall of Boethius in Italy, the *Nika* riots of 532 in Constantinople, and an anonymous Greek dialogue on political science.[14] In the context of such debate, Cassiodorus gives a model of courteous relations between monarch and Senate; he depicts the Senate as a galaxy of learned, talented statesmen, which embodies the traditions of Rome; but he seldom shows it acting corporately, to devise or execute policy, and he makes it clear that it played no part in the choice of rulers for Italy.

In these political circumstances, his favourable picture of senators, tribesmen and Gothic monarchs should not be taken on trust. (He is well able to gild or ignore decay; cf. note 14 to **VIII.33.**) However, the image is far from ideal. Corruption, brutality and inefficiency among Goths and Romans, and the impotence of the monarch are often shown or hinted at, sometimes illustrating, perhaps, the political struggles of Cassiodorus and his family (**III.8, III.21, III.27-28, III.46**). A policy not of racial integration, but of an uneasy partnership, with the Goths forming Sidonius' 'privileged military class' against the civilian Romans, is also plain to view (**III.13**). Gothic rulers seem to stand above the two races, to hold an unequal balance between them, and to owe their authority to this position. (The emperors had treated the military and civilian hierarchies similarly.) Between the lines, indeed, we see these monarchs manoeuvering with difficulty to enforce their will and restrain disorder among the jostling pride and interests of Roman and Gothic barons. The land-grabbing of Theodahad is not ignored, and the drunkenness of Athalaric is hinted at; as too, perhaps, the murder of Amalasuintha (**X.5, X.20-21, XI.1.4-5**).

Cassiodorus must, however, have selected only a minority of his letters, and certain omissions are striking. Some of these may be on literary grounds. Cassiodorus must have drafted many letters of appointment for Consuls and ministers which are not included. Thus, Liberius' appointment as Praetorian Prefect of Gaul is missing; the high

---

[14] Cf. Averil Cameron, 247-53.

praise he receives elsewhere in the *Variae* (**II.16, XI.1.16f.**) suggests that the motive for this was not political. In the **Preface**, the author claims that over hasty compositions caused him embarrassment. Another factor is the composition of his public: there is much on the administration of Gaul, little on Pannonia or Spain; the Gallic and Italian aristocracies were closely linked (cf. **II.1, III.18**).

More significant is silence on the internal strife of Theoderic's last years, which brought Cassiodorus back to court as Master of the Offices, replacing his fallen kinsman Boethius. Instead, the building of a fleet to defend Italy from foreign threats is given prominence, and Boethius features only in much earlier letters. Amalasuintha's murder of her Gothic opponents, to which Cassiodorus may have owed his promotion to the Italian Prefecture, is also missing. Of such conflicts, we have only the occasional hint, although one of his major tasks must have been their favourable public presentation. Did he rewrite the letters he included?[15] For extensive political revision there was probably no time: careless syntax, incorrect titles and arrangement, and the incomplete adaptation of letters to *formulae* (e.g. **XI.36**) confirm the complaints of the **Preface**; the royal formulary books VI-VII are more carefully written.[16] Yet, like the letter collections of the younger Pliny or the elder Symmachus (written c. A.D. 100-110 and 364-402), the *Variae* were perhaps intended to coat with plaster the more conspicuous cracks in their society. Style, however, appears in the **Preface** as Cassiodorus' main concern: the study of his literary form will give a deeper understanding of his aims.

---

[15] Cf. Ward-Perkins, 116.
[16] Cf. Vidén, 140-4.

2. The Character of the *Variae*[17]

Cassiodorus gave the *Variae* a character partly formulaic, partly
timeless and literary. Some persons - especially envoys, although these
were often high in rank - are referred to not by name, but as X and Y
(*illum et illum*). Dates have been removed, save for the occasional
internal reference to the tax year (indiction), and figures for money and
commodities have often disapppeared. Official protocols, with the full
titles due to sender and recipient have been abbreviated to short rubrics
(not always accurate); presumably, this must have detracted from their
value as secretarial models. We should contrast the Merovingian
protocols in some of the *Epistulae Austrasicae*, private and official
letters, probably compiled for chancery instruction c.600. A document
which Cassiodorus' predecessor as Quaestor probably drafted in 507 is
also typical: 'King Flavius Theodericus to the Senate of the City of
Rome, Tamer of the World, Head and Restorer of Liberty'.[18] Except
in the *formulae* of VI-VII and XI.17-34, there is a very rough and
unreliable chronological arrangement, but the order of the letters is
determined partly by literary considerations: for instance, set-piece
documents, particularly diplomatic, begin and end the books.
Sometimes, though, we find a string of letters of similar date and
subject, and may surmise that portions of an official file (e.g. on the
administration of Gaul) have been included without much disturbance.

The letters differ greatly in size, content, and elaboration. In Å.
Fridh's text, the average length is some 30 lines, but the range is
between 5 and 140. Formally, the majority convey administrative
measures, legal rulings and edicts, or announcements of appointments.
The last of these usually include miniature panegyrics on the more
eminent ministers, and remarks on their offices. Resembling the
speeches of a university's Public Orator, they are literary equivalents

---

[17] On this, see especially Zimmermann, Fridh, 1956, O'Donnell, ch.3, Vidén,
ch.3-4, Macpherson, part 4; on Cassiodorus' political concepts and
terminology, Reydellet, ch.5, Teillet, ch.8.

[18] *MGH AA* XII, 392.

One of these is a formal directive sent by Theoderic to a council of
bishops set up to try Pope Symmachus; the other seems to reproduce
the words of the king on which the first was based.[55] The Quaestor of
the day improved his master's Latin and the structure of his remarks;
he eliminated biblical references, and a not very relevant historical
anecdote; in general, he produced a blander discourse, less lively and
forceful, but more coherent, and less biassed. At the same time, he
followed Theoderic's general gist, and sometimes closely echoed it. In
the same way, Tribonian's laws may express the personality of
Justinian with more elegance than the emperor could command.[56] The
Symmachus case, however, was one of great political importance, in
which the Quaestor's work would have been closely monitored; on
lesser occasions, or where flexibility was needed, he may have been
allowed a freer hand. As noted earlier, between the lines of the *Variae*,
we can sometimes read a criticism of the monarch.

Cassiodorus sometimes likens secular offices to the priesthood, and
the overall impression left by the *Variae* is of governmental liturgies,
compiled in a secular Sacramentary: their stereotyped sentiments and
instructions correspond to prayers and ritual actions, their metaphors
and digressions to pulpit oratory. Popes contemporary with Cassiodorus
did much to shape the liturgy of the Roman Church, and the age was
one of sacred texts, religious and secular: the law codes of Theodosius
II and Justinian mirror the scrolls and jewelled codexes in the mosaics
of the Ravenna churches, or the great Bible[57] produced by
Cassiodorus' monks at Vivarium.

Modern readers tend to dislike the repetitious habit of the *Variae*:
ideas are worked to death by an author who did not know when to stop.
Some ancients would have agreed: Quintilian wrote c.A.D.90, 'In our
passion for words we paraphrase what might be said in plain language,
repeat what we have already said at sufficient length, pile up a number

---

[55] *MGH AA* XII, 424f.

[56] Cf. Honoré, 26ff.

[57] The probable ancestor of the famous Anglo-Saxon *Codex Amiatinus*.

conclusive conjunctions, particles, and adverbs, words in which Latin is far richer than English. *Constat*, forms of *probari* and *videri*, and superlatives are commonplace, indeed are often almost meaningless; many words, phrases and inflections are introduced largely for the sake of rhythm and euphony. To give variety, neologisms are created, and old words given new uses. In the combination of stock phrases, or the accumulation of clauses, the syntax may become confused, and a paratactic arrangement of clauses is often preferred to a subordinate - signs, perhaps, of hasty writing and compilation.[21]

By comparison with other late Latin letters, the *Variae* make easy reading: Cassiodorus is less dry, compressed, and elliptical than Symmachus or his own contemporary, bishop Ennodius of Pavia, less recherché in vocabulary than Sidonius or Ennodius. Even so, his later *Institutiones*, a guide to the world of learning, intended partly for monastic readers, is generally plainer and more comprehensible, designed to instruct, more than to impress. The *De Anima*, appended to the *Variae*, seems to be transitional in manner as well as matter.[22]

Connoisseurs would have seen his letters as studded with rhetorical conceits and figures like a meadow jewelled with flowers. The stock vocabulary of symbols, metaphors, and abstract qualities has lately been compared to heraldic blazonry.[23] The ancients had always exploited history and nature for moral *exempla*, and this may have been especially so in late antiquity, a culture fascinated by type, symbol and allegory. The great men of the realm seem identified with virtues, vices, skills and offices (cf. **Preface, 14**); their array has as little individuality as the saints and prophets who look down in mosaic from the walls of Theoderic's church of S.Apollinare Nuovo at Ravenna. Cassiodorus' ekphrastic descriptions are often vivid and instructive - thus, **V.1** gives a remarkable word-picture of the play of light on a pattern-welded German sword. However, they lack the precision of those in Pliny's letters which lie behind their tradition, and they

---

[21] Cf. Fridh, 1956, 81f.

[22] Cf. Halporn, *CCSL* vol.96, 513ff.

[23] Cf. Roberts, ch. 2-3, Macpherson, 182.

sometimes leave us doubtful if the author has seen the object he describes. Even in the less relevant descriptions, the object, and men's response to it, are given an exemplary turn, and a moral or religious purpose seems never far away. (For instance, with **VIII.33**, contrast Pliny, *Ep.* IV.30 and VIII.8.)

Literary allusions and echoes are probably numerous. (No thorough scrutiny has yet been made, but I have noted a few instances.) Despite the many pious expressions of the *Variae*, especially those letters which the Catholic Cassiodorus drafted in his own right, rather than for Arian rulers, secular classics are more alluded to than the scriptures. In this, there is some contrast with the *De Anima*, discussed below, but the general avoidance of Christian discourse seems comparable to the non-religious *Novels* of the last western emperors. On natural disasters, Cassiodorus speaks less of divine vengeance, than of physical causes, as in **XII.25**.[24] Now and then, however, Christian miracles and morality are introduced, and may even be used to condemn traditional Roman practices (**V.42, VIII.33**). A digression addressed to the Christian philosopher Boethius combines classical and biblical allusions, and concludes with a passage of near Christian mysticism (**II.40**). While the ancient Roman title of Patrician is traced back to the priesthoods of early Rome (**VI.2**), in the next *formula* the prototype of the Praetorian Prefect is the Patriarch Joseph (**VI.3**).

On practicalities, the letters are not always very instructive: the technical exposition of law and administration features less than in the official correspondence of Symmachus (Book X, *Relationes*), or of Pliny (Book X). In one letter (**XI.14**), such is Cassiodorus' absorption in his rhetoric that the official point is all but omitted: administration has become a vestigial frame for verbal landscape-painting. Most letters, however, are quite brief; and sometimes oral messages were sent, or accounts, lists, and detailed instructions were attached in *breves*, a practice familiar from private and literary epistolography. But, in general, we do not get so sure a grasp on the diplomacy and administration of the regime as papal correspondence gives us for the

---

[24] Cf. Leopold.

sixth century Roman Church.

The late Roman upper classes linked themselves privately by elegant correspondence,[25] but it seems a strange mode for official business. Was it peculiar to Cassiodorus? His Latin is not mere bureaucratese, but it has much in common with chancery style in the late antique world. So too his moralising proems. Ancient rulers believed it important to use persuasion; and late Roman laws, which give the best comparisons to the *Variae*, often show a similar rhetorical structure: they move from the moral *arenga* to an exposition of the situation (*narratio* or *expositio*), thence to a decision (*dispositio*) and measures of enforcement (*sanctio* or *corroboratio*).[26] Examples can be conveniently studied in the imperial *Novels* and *Sirmondian Constitutions* attached to the *Theodosian Code*: some of these go straight to the point, and the *arenga* is almost lacking; others come close to rivalling the wordiest *Variae*.[27] Evidently, much depended on the time, taste and talents of the drafting officer; sometimes, perhaps, of the monarch himself; sometimes, too, on his political position. Verbose edicts of consolation to men afflicted by flood, famine or earthquake probably had a long imperial history, although Cassiodorus gives the sole surviving examples.[28] An edict of the emperor Julian, a talkative intellectual, with special need to justify himself, included an extensive essay on funerary rites; it was eventually reduced to a much briefer law.[29] The short law-code called the *Edict of Theoderic*[30] is

---

[25] Cf. Matthews, 1974.

[26] See Fridh, 1956, 39-59; Benner, 1-25; Vidén, 120-53.

[27] *Constitution* 8, an Easter-tide amnesty for prisoners, published at Constantinople in 386, may have influenced XI.40 on the same subject; cf. Macpherson, 174-9.

[28] Cf. Leopold.

[29] Julian, *Ep.* 56; *C.Th.*, IX.17.5, a.363; compare Valentinian III's Quaestor in *Novel* 23.

[30] This code is sometimes claimed as the work of the Visigoth Theoderic II (453-66); I disagree.

far more straight-forward and usefully informative than the *Edict of Athalaric* (**IX.18**). The Cassiodorian piece, though, was probably designed for a different end: not to provide a handy legal compendium for judges, but to shore up the shaky moral and political authority of the regime. Hence its rather artificial twelve-part structure, recalling the *Twelve Tables* that were the foundation of Roman law.[31]

Cassiodorus' originality lies in his elaborate use of metaphor and digression, an importation, perhaps, to the official world from sermons, secular declamations, and sermonising private letters.[32] From a tradition of private letters which goes back to Pliny, he has adopted his descriptions of scenery or natural wonders, and his miniature panegyrics; both have their parallels in the correspondence of Sidonius in late fifth century Gaul. Epistolary panegyric was also in vogue with the contemporary Byzantine bureaucracy, as shown by examples in the *De Magistratibus* of John Lydus.[33] 'A flow of the most genial impertinence', George Gissing affectionately called Cassiodorus' digressions; but there may be more to them than learned light relief.

The ascendancy of the Graeco-Roman ruling classes was based on their mastery of rhetoric and associated learning. To civilian administrators, it gave an éclat to parallel the soldier's glory.[34] East and west, this tradition was increasingly threatened, whether by social mobility, declining education, Christian values, or the contempt of warrior élites; not surprisingly, men reaffirmed it, deliberately showing its virtues in the work of government. Rhetoric, indeed, had traditionally a moral, as well as a practical function, and we shall see that the *Variae* may have been designed to educate the ruling class in the values of its role and the purposes of the state. As Cassiodorus

---

[31] Even in less rhetorical codes and edicts of the period, the laws stated may be less important than the action of stating them; cf. Wormald (2).

[32] Some of his bestiary morality is shared with the sermon-based *Hexaemeron* of St Ambrose; St Jerome gives good examples of analogy in the homiletic letter, e.g. 125.2-4.

[33] III.29f.

[34] Cf. Sidonius, *Ep.* VIII.2, Gregory of Tours, *Life of the Fathers*, ix.1.

wrote, 'the knowledge of literature is glorious, since it purifies our morals - something of prime importance for mankind; as a secondary matter, it supplies us with eloquence' (III.33.3; cf. III.6.3-5, 11.4-5, IX.21.8, 24.8). The virtues of prudence and integrity inculcated may seem tediously banal, but he occasionally reveals something of the moral dilemmas and special obligations of high office (XII.5.1-2,9, XI.16).[35]

The rule of law, as both a natural and social phenomenon, and the chief end of politics, is a common theme of the *Variae*. A key word is *civilitas*. In classical usage, this had implied a ruler's correct demeanour towards his subjects, and still did so for Sidonius and for Cassiodorus' contemporary, bishop Avitus of Vienne. In the *Variae*, as in writings of Ennodius and Pope Gelasius (492-6), it more usually denotes the duty of subjects towards each other, decent social behaviour, and respect for law; 'civilisation' and 'good order' are sometimes possible translations. By his use of natural and cultural history, Cassiodorus seems to root *civilitas* in a garden of natural law and social progress.[36]

Men of the sixth century liked to theorise about government and society,[37] and Cassiodorus gave to his picture of men at work in their secular society a theoretical dimension which combined Bible-based theology with classical philosophy. The *De Anima*, he claimed, was an afterthought; but it also formed the thirteenth book of the *Variae*, was similar in length to the others, was probably published and long joined with them in manuscript, and was allegedly composed by request of the same friends. There, the digressions of the *Variae* expand into the nature and destiny of the soul, which has made the marvellous discoveries necessary to earthly society, and perceives and understands the divinely ordered universe (XI, praef.7, *De An.* i, iv, *Expositio*

---

[35] Readers 1500 years hence may well find the high minded editorials of our more intellectual newspapers equally platitudinous!

[36] Cf. Reydellet, 193f.

[37] Cf. Averil Cameron, ch.14.

Psalmorum, cxlv.2).[38] The four cardinal virtues, which figure largely in the *Variae*, are given a social emphasis, and are complemented by a more spiritual or intellectual trio (vii). Prayer and meditation close the treatise. St Augustine's *On Order* may lie behind the concept; we might also compare the thirteen books of his *Confessions*, of which the last four turn from autobiography to associated meditation and theology. Boethius' *Consolation of Philosophy* likewise moves from political autobiography to the religious philosophy of the cosmos, and is copiously illustrated with natural analogies. In their original form, the mosaics of S.Apollinare Nuovo probably showed Theoderic's family and courtiers in solemn procession from the palace at Ravenna to the throne of Christ;[39] to this Cassiodorus gives a literary parallel.

To develop a Christian version of the rhetorical training for public life, while retaining classical elements, was a major concern for Cassiodorus.[40] In his *On the Duties of the Clergy* (c.390), St Ambrose had replaced Cicero's *On Duties*, articulating practice and ideals for the servants of God in the Latin Church. Despite the Stoic and Platonic tradition, of which Boethius was the last, belated representative,[41] Roman secular officials had always lacked an ideology of service formulated with such clarity; the *Variae* and *De Anima* seem a half deliberate response to their need.

Boethius saw it as his consular duty to translate Greek philosophy for his fellow citizens.[42] He also hoped to play the philosopher statesman at Theoderic's court, and both he and Cassiodorus may have been influenced by the orator and philosopher Themistius (317-88), counsellor to successive emperors. Roman arms had not restrained the barbarians; Roman culture might yet do so.[43] Cassiodorus celebrated

---

[38] Cf. Halporn, *CCSL* vol.96, 505, 510-13, O'Donnell, ch.4.

[39] Cf.MacCormack, 1981, 238-9.

[40] Cf. Barnish, 1989, 174-83. Ennodius 452 (*Opusc.* 6) seems a comparable project.

[41] Cf. Matthews, 1981, 35-8.

[42] *In Categorias Aristotelis* II, J.P. Migne, *Patrologia Latina* 64, c.201 B.

[43] Cf. Sidonius, *Panegyric on Avitus*, 489-518, *Ep.* VIII.2.2, 3.3.

the instruction he had given to Theoderic (**IX.24.8**). In his lost *Gothic History*, he apparently depicted a legendary sage Dicineus. This alien had given the Goths political counsel, and had taught them logic, natural philosophy, and finally religion; their understanding of nature gave them laws and moral standards. In Dicineus, did Cassiodorus idealise his own aims and achievement at the court of Ravenna?[44]

In the tenth century, the emperor Constantine Porphyrogenitus was to write of the ceremonies of his court, 'Hereby may the imperial power be exercised with due rhythm and order; may the empire thus represent the harmony and motion of the universe as it comes from its creator; and may it thus appear to our subjects in a more solemn majesty, and so be the more acceptable to them and the more admirable in their eyes...'[45] Supported by the *De Anima*, the *Variae* display this governmental mirror of the cosmos.

When not acting as Quaestor, Cassiodorus was sometimes called on to help out the Quaestor of the day with his compositions. In theory, Quaestors were men of rhetorical skill; but it seems that his talents were regarded as exceptional by successive rulers. (At a lower level, John Lydus similarly lent his talents around the Praetorian Prefecture of the East.) We have, in fact, a few documents probably drawn up by other Theoderican Quaestors which support this impresssion: the Latin is a chancery style similar to Cassiodorus's, but the letters seem much shorter and plainer than he would have made them. The rhetorical declamations of Ennodius are the work of a skilled and learned orator, and have some general resemblance to the *Variae*: for instance, a new pupil is introduced into a school of rhetoric like a new minister to the Senate. However, they show little of the Cassiodorian digressive technique, which Theoderic himself may well have enjoyed (cf.

---

[44] Jordanes, *Getica* 67-72; like a Praetorian Prefect, Dicineus was given 'almost regal power' by the king.

[45] *De Caerimoniis*, praef.D, tr. E. Barker. Compare the interpretation of the money-system [I.10], and the elaborate symbolism of chariot-races [III.51], long closely linked with imperial ceremony.

IX.24.8, and note).[46]

We should compare another Quaestor of the time, Justinian's great jurist Tribonian. The prefaces which he devised for his master's *Novels*, and which ceased when he died, often include lengthy historical digressions, reassurances to a doubtful public that radical reforms really followed Roman tradition. For the reforms themselves, though, he was probably not responsible - they were the work of Justinian and his Prefect John the Cappadocian; and some he may even have opposed.[47] Allusions to history long past are infrequent in the *Variae* - their history is contemporary - and the political thrust is rather different. The Ostrogothic rulers tried to change as little as possible. Cassiodorus could not prove them Romans, although *exempla* from Roman history may have been more frequent in their formal panegyrics. Instead, he seems to assure educated Roman gentlemen that they were not lawless, arbitrary, and uncultivated despots, that they observed natural justice, and differed from other tribesmen, who lacked their noble-savage traditions, and the educating grace of residence in Italy. Pope Gregory the Great (590-604) was to write, 'this is the difference between tribal kings and emperors of the Romans, the fact that tribal kings are lords of slaves, but emperors of the Romans lords of free men'.[48] Cassiodorus' task was to show the Goths as defenders of freedom under the law, and of civilised values, who honoured and employed gentlemen of humane education; the term 'barbarian' is never applied to them.[49] To read Theoderic's letters to the recovered provinces of Gaul and Pannonia (III.17 and 23) is to meet again the Caesar Constantius in 296, as a medallion depicts him, delivering London from

---

[46] The closest parallel may be Ennodius 8 (*Opusc.7*), a directive probably drafted for archbishop Laurentius of Milan, in 501. Also, with II.14, cf. 239 (*Dictio* 17).

[47] See Honoré, 58ff., 244f.; Maas.

[48] *Reg.Ep.* XI.4; cf. ibid. XIII.32, Wormald, 126ff.

[49] Tribonian did a similar job for his low-born emperor.

rebels and barbarians, and 'restoring the eternal light' of Rome.[50]

If the execution was the work of Cassiodorus, what of the policy? Procopius tells of cultural tension between Romans and barbarians in Italy.[51] The honours given by Theoderic to Boethius, then translating Greek philosophy into Latin, were conferred in 521-2, when Cassiodorus was out of office, and suggest royal awareness of the problem. If the *Variae* portray Theoderic, Amalaberga, Amalasuintha and Theodahad as 'philosophers in purple' - a phrase perhaps taken from Themistius[52] - the image need not have been foisted on them by Cassiodorus who helped to shape it. Many emperors had worn a double mask of soldier and intellectual, and other barbarian rulers employed Roman rhetoricians among their leading counsellors. The political, if not the cultural, tone of the reign had been set at least as early as 500, when Theoderic visited Rome in a generous and impressive but tactful triumph: citizens, clergy and senators found their religious sensibilities reassured, and their political traditions confirmed.[53] Cassiodorus enjoyed unusually long periods in high office, but these total fifteen years at most; the Ostrogothic state down to the fall of Ravenna, lasted for some forty. As with Tribonian, the influence he must have had is hard to disinter from documents in which every decision and appointment is presented, at least to the casual eye, in similar style, through all changes of political weather and regime.

One quaestor of Theoderic apparently altered a general pardon to make it still more inclusive,[54] and two non-Cassiodorian Ostrogothic documents also shed light on the independence of official draftsmen.

---

[50] Illustrated by Cornell and Matthews, 172. Compare also king Euric of the Visigoths in 476, using the declamations of his Roman counsellor Leo to restrain 'arms by laws' in his newly conquered territory (Sidonius, *Ep.* VIII.3.3).

[51] *Wars* V.i.33, ii.1: chauvinist Goths claimed that Theoderic had wisely kept his tribe illiterate; cf. Wormald (1), 97ff.

[52] IX.24.8, Themistius, *Or.* 34.viii.34; cf. Procopius, *Wars* V.iii.1, vi.10.

[53] *Anonymus Valesianus*, 65-9.

[54] Ennodius, 80.135 (*Opusc.*3).

One of these is a formal directive sent by Theoderic to a council of bishops set up to try Pope Symmachus; the other seems to reproduce the words of the king on which the first was based.[55] The Quaestor of the day improved his master's Latin and the structure of his remarks; he eliminated biblical references, and a not very relevant historical anecdote; in general, he produced a blander discourse, less lively and forceful, but more coherent, and less biassed. At the same time, he followed Theoderic's general gist, and sometimes closely echoed it. In the same way, Tribonian's laws may express the personality of Justinian with more elegance than the emperor could command.[56] The Symmachus case, however, was one of great political importance, in which the Quaestor's work would have been closely monitored; on lesser occasions, or where flexibility was needed, he may have been allowed a freer hand. As noted earlier, between the lines of the *Variae*, we can sometimes read a criticism of the monarch.

Cassiodorus sometimes likens secular offices to the priesthood, and the overall impression left by the *Variae* is of governmental liturgies, compiled in a secular Sacramentary: their stereotyped sentiments and instructions correspond to prayers and ritual actions, their metaphors and digressions to pulpit oratory. Popes contemporary with Cassiodorus did much to shape the liturgy of the Roman Church, and the age was one of sacred texts, religious and secular: the law codes of Theodosius II and Justinian mirror the scrolls and jewelled codexes in the mosaics of the Ravenna churches, or the great Bible[57] produced by Cassiodorus' monks at Vivarium.

Modern readers tend to dislike the repetitive habit of the *Variae*: ideas are worked to death by an author who did not know when to stop. Some ancients would have agreed: Quintilian wrote c.A.D.90, 'In our passion for words we paraphrase what might be said in plain language, repeat what we have already said at sufficient length, pile up a number

---

[55] *MGH AA* XII, 424f.

[56] Cf. Honoré, 26ff.

[57] The probable ancestor of the famous Anglo-Saxon *Codex Amiatinus*.

of words where one would suffice, and regard allusion as better than directness of speech.'[58] But repetition is an important liturgical element, a fact of which Cassiodorus shows some appreciation in his commentary on the Psalms. He might also be compared to a musician, composing multiple variations on a theme. With his varied repetitions, his use of paradox and antithesis, his careful, sonorous rhythms, his lengthy periods, paratactically organised, and his display of curious learning, he has his closest English counterpart in Sir Thomas Browne. Rooted in Roman liturgies of the fifth to seventh centuries, the old Book of Common Prayer also conveys the flavour of his more religious moralising and his simpler sentences (cf. **XI.2**). The style of the letters won the respect of the novelist George Gissing; while Gibbon, though outwardly contemptuous, at least paid them the compliment of paraphrase.

3. The *Variae* as Separate Documents

What congregations heard these chants of the state liturgy, as each was separately sung? One audience, of course, was the person or persons to whom they were immediately directed. An edict on simony in episcopal elections was to be engraved on marble, and placed in the atrium of St Peter's; another general edict was to be read in the Senate, then formally posted (or proclaimed) in public places and assemblies for thirty days (**IX.15-16, IX.18-20**).[59] A letter to a provincial governor regulating a country fair was to be read to the people there, then posted up (**VIII.33**). No such document would have been easily understood by an ordinary person, and the last is an essay of great literary pretensions. Doubtless, the governor was properly impressed, but we may surmise larger educated audiences. An unauthorised circulation among the educated is sometimes attested for private letters

---

[58] *Inst. Or.* VIII, praef. 24 (Loeb translation).

[59] Cf. *Anonymus Valesianus* 69: a royal address to the people of Rome engraved on bronze, and publicly displayed.

and declamations, before they were published in collections.[60] One recipient of a specially elaborate letter summoned an assembly of the cultured and eminent in his province for a formal recitation.[61] Official assemblies of provincial notables probably continued in Ostrogothic Italy, and I would guess that Cassiodorus' letters were distributed or recited at such gatherings. XII.25 was designed to reassure anxious subjects, rather than his deputy.

Some documents, at least, will probably have been publicised before they left the palace or reached the relevant official. Cassiodorus certainly did not intend the royal directives which he drafted to himself as Praetorian Prefect for his eyes only. To judge by imperial precedent, copies of edicts would routinely have been posted outside the royal residence where they had been produced. Among the duties of the Quaestor may have been the public declamation, before their despatch, of decrees and rescripts he had drafted, a practice which saved the monarch's credit if they were challenged.[62] Formal diplomatic letters may often have been recited in council; so too, perhaps, set-piece rebukes (e.g. I.2, 35) which displayed the monarch's cultivation, but which the recipient would hardly have publicised. Public shame, as well as honour, could be conveyed by letter, although learned digression might soften reproof (e.g. V.42). Many office holders, like John Lydus, must have dangled their letters of appointment before the public eye; indeed, they may have displayed them formally on their desks.[63] The letter to the honorand, and its twin to the Senate usually cover rather different ground, as if the Senate were expected to hear them both.

Moreover, some leading Goths and their followers will have been literate in Latin; and those whose style and grammar were shaky may yet have appreciated an elegant author, as did Jordanes, whose *Getica* abridged Cassiodorus' *Gothic History*. At Naples in 535, two trained

---

[60] Symmachus, *Ep.* II.12, 48; Sidonius, *Ep.* IX. 7.

[61] Synesius, *Ep.* 100/101.

[62] Procopius, *Anecdota* 14.2-3.

[63] *De Mag.* III.29f.; cf. Cornell and Matthews, 202.

rhetoricians of the city apparently persuaded a popular assembly of Goths and Romans to resist the Byzantines.[64] The *Gothic History* may likewise have been aimed at both races: to impress on blue-blooded senators, and proud Gothic chieftains the dignity and antiquity of the Amal house, whose pre-eminence was recent and precarious.[65] Probably, then, at least so long as Cassiodorus was active at court, most Roman, and some Gothic notables in state and society will have been exposed to a sequence of letters, building up the desired image of their monarchs.

What, though, of the non-élite? How far did the *Variae* resemble the ivory diptychs and silver-ware which Consuls and emperors presented to a chosen few?[66] In the **Preface**, Cassiodorus claims to have adapted his style to his audience; but, though the style does often vary, the education and status of the recipient was not always a criterion.[67] Most barbarians, and even Romans of the day would have found even the simpler letters hard to understand. (Interpreters had to be provided for a learned letter on amber [V.2], sent to Estonia!) As so often in ritual, the language and ideas are meant to be heard widely, but are intelligible mainly to a few. Goths will have depended on Romans, and the unlearned on their social betters, to interpret what concerned them; relations of dependency and respect may thereby have been strengthened or created. The Lucanian peasants at the fair of St Cyprian, whom Cassiodorus disciplined and threatened (**VIII.33**), were the distant ancestors of those whom Carlo Levi met in his exile beyond Eboli in 1935. They had received nothing from Rome except the tax collector, and radio speeches, irrelevant and incomprehensible. How much in common had the audiences of Athalaric and Mussolini?

---

[64] Procopius, *Wars* V.viii.29-42.

[65] Cf. Wallace-Hadrill, 35; Heather. The Amals are given noticeably more prominence in letters to the Senate (**IX.24.4-5, XI.1.19**) than to barbarians (e.g. **IV.1.1**).

[66] Cf. Matthews, 1975, 112, 244; Roberts, 90-111, 121, 125-9.

[67] Cf. O'Donnell, 73f., 87.

4. The *Variae* as an Historical Source: a Caution

Even where suspicious silences and overt propaganda cannot be detected, the *Variae* must be used with caution. Next to the imperial laws, they are our fullest source for the administrative workings of the late, particularly the western empire. They may, indeed, be too full a source, shedding strong light on a very restricted region and period. During the fifth century, great political changes had taken place in the west, while the volume of new legislation declined sharply, ceasing altogether in Italy from 476. Hence, we cannot always tell when features of government encountered in the *Variae* had arisen, and how far Odoacer and his successors dealt with novel situations by new arrangements. So too with administrative politics: the light cast by Cassiodorus hardly extends beyond his tenures of office. Hence, certain letters may mark new drives against private violence or official corruption, for which he and his masters should be given some credit - or they may be common form.

5. The *Variae*: Text and Editions; Selection, Dating and Translation

More than a hundred manuscripts of the *Variae* survive. Those which Th. Mommsen used in his edition (below), he divided into six classes, stemming principally from a lost archetype. This archetype may be identical with a manuscript which probably also contained the archetype of the *De Anima*, attested in a ninth century catalogue from Lorsch.[68] The *Variae* archetype came to be divided into two parts, the second commencing with letter VII.41, and wholly or partially transmitted by Classes 3-5. Class 6 is the only one to give a complete text, but it is mainly a composite, drawn from Classes 1, 4, and 5. The two best manuscripts are, for the first part, *Codex Leidensis Vulcanianus* 46 in Class 2, written at Fulda c.1170; for the second part, *Codex Bruxellensis* 10018-10019 in Class 4, also of the 12th

---

[68] Interestingly, some *De Anima* manuscripts so derived may be linked with the Palace School at Aachen; did Carolingian officials also know the *Variae*?

century. *Leidensis*, whose attractive drawings of Cassiodorus and Theoderic are reproduced in Mommsen's edition, contains I.1 to VII.41, and alone gives the dedicatory couplet. *Bruxellensis* runs from VII.42 to the end, and is the only member of its class to give VII.42-47.[69]

The *editio princeps* of the complete *Variae* appeared in 1533, the work of M. Accursius. In many libraries, the only edition available is likely to be the mediocre one of J.P. Migne, *Patrologia Latina*, vol. 69, based on that of the Maurist J. Garet (1679). Th. Mommsen's edition of 1894 (*MGH AA* XII) is a monument of scholarship, which put the text and chronology of the letters on a sound footing. It includes some additional documents relevant to Theoderic's relations with the Church of Rome, and L. Traube's edition of the fragments of Cassiodorus' panegyrics. The introduction is important for text, dates, and orthography; while the indexes, especially Traube's index of words and things, which includes remarks on textual readings, word usage, grammar and syntax, make the edition vital for research. In 1973, Å. Fridh edited the text in *CCSL*, vol.96. Based on deep study of late antique Latin, and adding a manuscript unknown to Mommsen, this edition offers some textual improvements, and cannot be ignored. It also has indexes of scriptural and other citations (to be used with caution), a bibliography, and Halporn's appended edition of the *De Anima*. However, it is marred by a throng of misprints, and the index of names and things is very inadequate, being confined to the title rubrics. The only English translation published is that of 1886 by T. Hodgkin, *The Letters of Cassiodorus*. In this, the contents of many letters are only noted; others are 'condensed.' Hodgkin was a learned authority on Ostrogothic Italy, but lacked literary sympathy for Cassiodorus, and worked from Garet's inferior text. He provided a lengthy introduction and notes, but these are frequently misleading, knowledge of the late Roman world having advanced considerably since his day. Consultation of his work is sometimes worthwhile, although

---

[69] These remarks are based on Mommsen's and Fridh's prefaces to the *Variae*, and on Halporn's to the *De Anima*.

it will often prove dangerous or frustrating.

The *Variae* have much to interest the political, social, economic, religious, and cultural historian; a selection with something for each was hard to make. To focus on Cassiodorus' career, interests, and way of life, with those of his family connections, seemed the least unsatisfactory solution; at least it fulfills one of the author's intentions. The section below, 'Cassiodorus and his Kindred in the Variae', shows why each letter was chosen for translation.

Like all translators, I have had to compromise between a rebarbatively literal rendering, and one so free that it would neither guide the student through the original, nor convey its formal qualities. I have tended to break up Cassiodorus' lengthier sentences, and have sometimes substituted the active for the passive voice. Cassiodorus commonly uses honorific plurals ('the royal we'), but does not do so with consistency, or confine them to royalty; I have altered them to the singular. In general, though, I have tried to stick closely to the text, even translating many words which were probably added more for rhythm than for meaning. The dearth of causal and conclusive expressions in English has given an inevitable and misleading monotony to the start of many sentences and clauses. Latin is also a language far more economical than English, and Cassiodorus less prolix than translation makes him seem.

In dating the *Variae*, I have used Mommsen's work as my foundation, but have sometimes had to refine or question his chronology, and have found an invaluable supplement in Krautschick's recent study.

C. THE HOUSE OF THE CASSIODORI
(THE *ORDO GENERIS CASSIODORUM*)

[This fragment is sometimes called the *Anecdoton Holderi*, after Alfred Holder, its discoverer. The work from which it was extracted must have been composed or revised at the end of Cassiodorus' secular career. In style it recalls St Jerome's *On Illustrious Men*, a catalogue of Christian writers; possibly the original was a work of similar type. In translating, I use Mommsen's text (*MGH AA* XII, v-vi). O'Donnell (appendix 1) has

recently edited it with an extensive commentary, sometimes challenging Mommsen's
readings; see also Krautschick, 78-84.]

Extracts from the little book of Cassiodorus Senator, monk, slave
of God, ex-Patrician, ex-Ordinary Consul, Quaestor and Master of
the Offices, which he wrote to Rufius Petronius Nicomachus,
ex-Ordinary Consul, Patrician, and Master of the Offices. The tree
of the Cassiodorian family: what authors arose from their stock, and
< from what men of learning they came > [70].

Symmachus, [71] Patrician and Ordinary Consul, a philosopher,
who was a modern imitator of Cato in antiquity, but surpassed the
virtues of the ancients by his holy religion. He spoke in favour of
candidates nominated to the Senate, and, imitating his ancestors, [72]
also published a Roman history in seven books.

Boethius was pre-eminent in the highest honours, and was a most
skilful orator in both tongues. [73] In thanks for the Consulship of his
sons, he praised king Theoderic in the Senate with a splendid
speech. He wrote a book on the Holy Trinity, some theological
pieces, and a book against Nestorius. He also composed a pastoral
poem. But in his work on the art of logic, that is in translating
dialectic, and in the mathematical disciplines, he was such that he
either equalled or surpassed the ancient authors.

Cassiodorus Senator was a man of great learning, and
distinguished by his many honours. While still a young man, when
he was legal adviser [*consiliarius*] to his father, the Patrician and
Praetorian Prefect Cassiodorus, and delivered a most eloquent
speech in praise of Theoderic king of the Goths, he was appointed
Quaestor by him, also Patrician and Ordinary Consul, and, at a

---

[70] The text reads *vel ex quibus eruditis*. Several emendations and additions
have been suggested; Mommsen's is *profecerint*.

[71] This Symmachus, Consul 485, is not to be confused with his ancestor, the
orator and epistolographer, Consul 391.

[72] This refers to the history of Virius Nicomachus Flavianus, Consul 394.
Both works are lost; an attempt to reconstruct Symmachus's has failed.

[73] Latin and Greek.

later date, Master of the Offices < and Praetorian Prefect. He submitted > [74] *formulae* for official documents, which he arranged in twelve books, and entitled *Variae*. At the command of king Theoderic, he wrote a history of the Goths, setting out their origin, habitations, and character in twelve books.

D. CASSIODORUS AND HIS KINDRED IN THE *VARIAE* [75]

1. The Family

The family of Cassiodorus may have originated in Syria, but, by the mid fifth century, it was established in the south of Italy. With large estates centred on the town of Squillace, it was rapidly acquiring influence in the province of Lucania-and-Bruttium, and probably of Sicily. This influence depended partly on the tenure of offices granted by the imperial government, and so on participation in the politics of Rome and Ravenna. At the same time, local power meant that such a family could not be ignored at court. Politics also created ties with older senatorial families. The grandfather of Cassiodorus supported the commander-in-chief Aetius, who, fore-shadowing Odoacer and Theoderic, dominated the western empire from 433 to 454 (**I.4.11**); another supporter was Boethius, grandfather of the philosopher Boethius, of the great house of the Anicii. The philosopher married Rusticiana, daughter of Q.Aurelius Memmius Symmachus, and

---

[74] The text reads *et praefuisset formulas dictionum*; the restoration is disputed; I have followed Mommsen's *...et praefectus praetorio. suggessit formulas dictionum...*

[75] On politics and people under Odoacer and the Ostrogoths, Sundwall is fundamental; see also Bury, ch.12-13, 18, Chadwick, ch.1, Matthews, 1981, Moorhead, 1978 and 1984, Wolfram, ch.5; for Cassiodorus and his family, see O'Donnell, ch.1-2; for the senatorial culture of the time, see Courcelle, ch.6, Momigliano, Kirkby.

Cassiodorus apparently claimed kinship with their joint family.[76] To judge by his name Aurelius, his mother may well have been a Symmachan, betrothed by her noble family to the influential minister of Odoacer (cf. **I.4.4–6**).[77] (Under Athalaric, we find the minister Opilio, probably of the Ligurian provincial aristocracy, married to a lady of the Decii, whose blue blood rivalled the Anicii.) Not only power, but local wealth was partly based on a wider society. Horse-breeding for the army in the Bruttian mountain pastures helped the family, and Cassiodorus himself once fed a Gothic force from his own resources (**I.4.17, VIII.31.5, IX.25.9**). Another contemporary Lucanian land-owner may have owed his fine villa to profits made from the state supply of pork to Rome's plebeians.[78] During the fifth century and into the early sixth, Bruttian wine seems to have found an increasing market, especially in Rome;[79] Cassiodorus may even have used his Praetorian Prefecture to advertise it at Ravenna (**XII.12**)! In all this, though, the Cassiodori may have been at a disadvantage, compared with the nobility of Rome and northern Italy. These were nearer to the court, and had a second educational centre at Milan, which was revived by the rhetor Deuterius, perhaps under official auspices; they probably filled most of the major offices during this period. **I.3-4** rehearse the family history, while granting the honorific title of Patrician to the elder Cassiodorus, probably on his retirement from the Praetorian Prefecture which he held from c.503 to 507. **VIII.31, 33, XI.39,** and **XII.12** tell us something of economy and society in Lucania-and-Bruttium, and show the author's interest in his province (compare also **XII.5** and **15**).

With Cassiodorus' father, we might compare Liberius (**II.16**). Probably a major north Italian aristocrat, he too did not belong to the

---

[76] See above, *Ordo Generis*, Cassiod., *Institutiones* I.xxiii.1, where the Proba called *parens nostra* is probably another daughter of Symmachus.

[77] But contrast Momigliano's doubts (188-91) on the closeness of the connection, in blood, politics and society.

[78] See Barnish, 1987.

[79] See Arthur.

top Roman families. A loyal minister of Odoacer, he served Theoderic as Praetorian Prefect from c.493 to 500, with the vital task of organising the Ostrogothic settlement. Both men were succeeded as Prefect by leading nobles; both were then made Patricians; and, although neither reached the Consulship, their sons may both have done so. Like Cassiodorus himself, Venantius, son of Liberius, had a literary reputation; he, though, did not enter state service, instead receiving a sinecure office which conferred illustrious rank and membership of the Senate.[80] Elegant leisure and political activity were alternatives (not always exclusive) for Roman and provincial nobles alike.

2. Cassiodorus as Diplomatic Draftsman

While the elder Cassiodorus served Theoderic as Praetorian Prefect, his young son (aged about 20) was acting as his *consiliarius*, or legal adviser and publicist, as Arator was to do for the general Tuluin (see **VIII.12**). (Unlike most of Theoderic's known Quaestors, he does not seem to have practised as a barrister.) The post allowed him to deliver a panegyric on the king, perhaps celebrating the Gothic capture of Sirmium in 504/5; his literary talents were thus brought to royal notice. The *consiliarii* of the Praetorian Prefecture were often rewarded with the title of Count of the First Rank (*comes primi ordinis*), conveying 'distinguished' status, and membership of the king's consistory council; Cassiodorus compared their task of expounding the needs of the state to the Quaestor's (VI.12.2). In 506, he was already handling Theoderic's diplomatic correspondence, either as Quaestor, or instead of the Quaestor of the day. Clovis the Frank was then growing in power and independence, and putting Gothic authority in the west under strain. The patronising 'cultural diplomacy' shown in **I.45-46** and **II.40-41** probably had Roman precedents, and seems typical of Theoderic's methods, at least in the *Variae*. It may genuinely have impressed barbarians: king Totila, receiving a letter from Belisarius -

---

[80] The accepted identification of Venantius with the Consul of 507 seems to me uncertain, as II.15-16 do not mention the office.

rewritten very much in the manner of Cassiodorus - which dissuaded him from the destruction of Rome, was deeply moved, and read it many times.[81] The courts of Clovis and Gundobad, however, were far from barbarous: both men were served by educated Roman nobles and clergy; indeed Gundobad showed a taste for sophisticated theological debate.

Such diplomacy had another face. In the late fourth century, cultural contacts between Ausonius, provincial poet and rhetorician at the imperial court, and the senatorial orator Symmachus at Rome, had helped to bind a distrustful Senate to the administration.[82] By imposing such complimentary tasks on Boethius (cf. also I.10), Cassiodorus may have been the agent of a similar détente. His ties of kinship were useful there, but perhaps not vital: in III.52, he gives a 'cultural' task in a similar manner to another senator, and it is easy to doubt how well he knew either Boethius, or the highly theoretical character of his work.[83]

Theoderic's diplomacy had its cultural imports, as well as exports, and Cassiodorus' Latinity was sometimes called on to describe the exotic gifts of barbarian tribes. In V.1, the rhetorical description of German pattern-welded swords is surprisingly vivid and accurate. To judge by the tastes of bishop Ennodius, Romans of the day are likely to have been horse-lovers; and Cassiodorus, coming from a horse-breeding family, may have found the technicalities of IV.1 rather easier to cope with.

---

[81] Procopius, *Wars* VII.xxii.8-17; what we have is fairly certainly Procopius' own composition.

[82] Cf. Matthews, 1978, 33f., 51ff., ch.3.

[83] Chadwick, 23, and Pizzani doubt Boethius' technical competence; cf. notes to I.10, I.45, II.41, for my reservations, and on Boethius' writings in Cassiodorus. Momigliano, 189f., suggests that Cassiodorus was more anxious to associate himself with Boethius and Symmachus than *vice versa*.

3. Cassiodorus as Quaestor

The imperial Quaestor controlled no finances, and had no department of his own. But, as mouthpiece, and chief adviser on a multitude of legal problems, he probably enjoyed a closer relation with the ruler than did any other of the great ministers, and his power increased during the fifth century. The senile emperor Justin I (518-27) was dominated by his Quaestor Proclus.[84] In the Ostrogothic order of precedence, the Quaestor ranked next after the Praetorian and Urban Prefects, and, as suggested by VII.42, may have come to control the king's personal bureau, an obscure institution referred to as *officium nostrum*.[85] Urbicus, probably a Quaestor of Theoderic, 'bore all the burdens of his palace'.[86] V.4 and VI.5 exemplify the Quaestor's appointment.

The Ostrogoths did not legislate, and their Quaestor was not involved in legal drafting. However, the restatement of existing laws in edictal form was partly his business, and he also handled the countless appeals and petitions to reach the king, including disputes between Gothic tribesmen. I.18, III.13, 36, IV.10, and V.29 show him at work. In this he overlapped with an officer of lower rank called the Referendary (cf. V.40-1). He had special responsibility for petitions arriving from the Roman Senate and the provincial assemblies. He was expected to have some measure of independence, and to act as guardian of the laws when the monarch was unjust, or too hasty.[87] The latter seldom rejects the appeals and petitions which feature in the *Variae*, and is usually found upholding a weaker and lowlier party

---

[84] Procopius, *Anecdota* 6.11-13.

[85] Cf. Jones, 1964, n.43 to p.255; 1974, 370f. Among other tasks, the king's bureau can be seen engaged in law enforcement, collection of rents and taxes, and the public post; it was staffed by *principes*, *scriniarii*, *comitiaci*, and *saiones*; cf. V.5-6, VII.21-2, 31, 42.

[86] Ennodius 80.135 (*Opusc.* 3); cf. ibid., 85, 168, for Leo and Laconius, counsellors of kings Euric and Gundobad.

[87] Cf. above, xxviii, on Ennodius, 80.135.

against an opponent of higher rank or power. This may be partly the result of Cassiodorus' editing, but emperors had always been expected to prove amenable to requests. Of all imperial legislators, Majorian (457-61), who had made determined efforts to protect the lesser gentry and lower orders, is most frequently cited in the *Variae*.

The Quaestor's task was complicated by Gothic rule. Roman soldiers had always enjoyed some measure of legal privilege against civilians, and so too did their barbarian successors. In the later years of the western empire, Aetius and similar generals had become more prominent in administration. Theoderic had inherited their position, and deputed civil business to his military tribal officers. Arigern and Sunhiuadus in III.13 and 36 are usurping judicial functions from the Prefect of Rome and the governor of Samnium.

The structure of late Roman government was less demarcated than it looks on paper. Emperors had frequently bypassed their ministers to communicate with their lesser nominees, and the Ostrogoths followed their example. Hence, we find Cassiodorus writing both directives to ministers, and other directives which did their job for them. (However, it does not seem that his monarchs gave orders to officials appointed by the ministers themselves, like the powerful *cancellarii* of the Praetorian Prefecture.) It is possible that the practice was increasing, since Theoderic had less territory to administer than most of his predecessors. In I.25, the king is bypassing the City Prefect of Rome; in II.20, his Praetorian Prefect.

Of the other great ministers, the Master of the Offices had, in theory, the widest range of administrative duties, including the formal conduct of diplomacy, and his work must have overlapped with the Quaestor's to some degree. The general service officers of the royal *officium*, the *comitiaci* and *saiones*, seem to have been taking over from the *agentes in rebus* of the Master's department. In the careers of Cassiodorus and others, Mastership succeeded Quaestorship; while Boethius as Master expected to have the Quaestor as his close colleague.[88]

---

[88] Cf. Sinnigen, 460f.; above, n.85; Boethius, *C.Phil.* III, prose iv.

The outbreak of war between Franks and Visigoths in 507, followed, in 508, by Theoderic's despatch of an army to Gaul, meant much work for Cassiodorus, some of it probably before his appointment as Quaestor. His services were required for diplomacy to avert the crisis (III.1-4), for the administration of the war, and for the establishment of law, and general reorganisation, in the renewed Gallic province (I.17, II.38, III.17-18, 32, 41, 44, IV.5). However, a *Vicarius*, and then a Praetorian Prefect were appointed to govern it, and the referal of problems to Ravenna probably decreased. Something similar seems to have happened in the administration of the Balkan territories taken over in 505 (cf. III.23). In III.3, a theme emerges which probably also featured in his *Gothic History*: the banding of the tribes of the post-Roman west under Rome's ruler to resist the assaults of an arrogant barbarian war-lord. Similarly, the great Aetius had united the Visigoths and many other peoples to defeat Attila at the Catalaunian Plains in 451.[89]

Disturbances in Rome which were linked with the circus factions, and involved rioting between the plebs and leading senatorial households, meant more work for the Quaestor (I.27).[90] In 500, Theoderic had solemnly affirmed his care for Senate, people and Pope, for the monuments and food-supply of Rome.[91] Cassiodorus was not the author of this policy, but his literary and cultural talents and family connections were well suited to it. Monarch and senators, especially, perhaps, those of the oldest families, were expected to work together for the city, as shown in IV.51. (On maintenance, compare I.25, III.30-1.)

Cassiodorus was a man of deep personal piety and religious interests. Do these show through in the Quaestor-drafted *Variae*? Like his tribesmen, Theoderic was divided from most Christians in Italy and the eastern empire by his Arian creed, which denied the full divinity of Christ. The support of Nicene Catholic bishops, however, was essential

---

[89] Jordanes, *Getica*, 180-224; cf. Barnish, forthcoming.

[90] On these disturbances, see Pietri.

[91] *Anonymus Valesianus* 65-7.

to the administration of his realm and the loyalty of the Romans (cf.
II.8). The Catholics themselves did not hesitate to use him as an arbiter
in their quarrels (cf. VIII.15). But religion generally figures little in the
Variae, perhaps by design. Where it does so, Theoderic emerges as the
devout but impartial protector of individuals or religious minorities
threatened by the greed or fanaticism of the Catholics or Arians (II.27,
III.7). His attitude, as readers of the collected *Variae* would have
known well, was far more tolerant than Justinian's. (Compare X.26,
for Theodahad's.) Cassiodorus himself played some part in religious
opposition to the emperor, following the reconquest.[92]

Inevitably, the Cassiodori were involved in court intrigues, which
may be reflected in the *Variae*. Letters condemn the oppressions
(III.20, 27) and inefficiency (I.35) of Faustus Niger, a great senator of
the Anician house, who probably succeeded the elder Cassiodorus as
Praetorian Prefect. His departure from office may be linked with the
recall of his predecessor to court, to serve as a councillor without
office (III.21, 28).[93] However, the difficulty of dating individual
letters, and the fact that few senators stayed long in office, make such
reconstructions of political history highly speculative. Like most leading
Romans under Theoderic, Faustus had his power base in the north of
Italy; he was a kinsman and patron of Ennodius, in whose extensive
correspondence the Cassiodori are not mentioned. Boethius was related
to both groups, but does not seem to have linked them.

---

[92] See Barnish, 1989.

[93] Cf. Hodgkin, *Letters of Cassiodorus*, 208, 212, Sundwall, 119; Martindale,
PLRE II, 456, is inclined to date III.21 before the Prefecture.

4. Cassiodorus as Consul and Senator

In 512, Cassiodorus probably retired from the Quaestorship after a lengthy tenure.[94] In 512 or 513, he was nominated Consul for 514, presumably with the assent of the emperor Anastasius (cf. II.1). He was the first of his family to reach this expensive social peak, which embodied so much of the history of Rome and the traditions of its aristocracy. Not every noble could afford it (VI.1.8, 10.2), and it was usually occupied by men like Boethius (510) and Faustus (490), from the oldest and richest senatorial houses of Rome. Inportunus (509), whom we met in I.27, in conflict with the plebs, is another example; III.6 shows the terms in which Theoderic later made him a Patrician. However, Theoderic also took the unusual step of making Consul for 511 a Gallic noble from his new territories - Felix (II.1), perhaps a relative of Ennodius. Like Cassiodorus, Felix had probably requested the honour (VI.1.8), but he seems to have found the cost of his games rather too much for him (III.39), and had no successor from his province. Chariot races (III.51), wild-beast hunts (V.42), and probably theatrical shows were expected from the Consul, not only in Rome, but at Milan. Even the Consul Maximus, of the noble Anicii, had trouble with the expenses (V.42).

In his *Chronicle*, Cassiodorus gave his Consulship credit for the final end of the Laurentian schism, which had bitterly divided Rome over the election and record of Pope Symmachus (498-514).[95] His kinsman Symmachus had probably supported the Pope; his friend Dionysius Exiguus, the anti-Pope Laurentius.[96] As Consul, he may have assisted the smooth election of the succeeding Pope Hormisdas. However, things had already quietened down in 506; and, unlike the elections of 526 and 533 (VIII.15, IX.15-16), the schism does not

---

[94] 511 is usually given; but, in view of the date of IV.50, addressed to Faustus as Prefect, which probably concerns an eruption of Vesuvius attested in 512, I would reject this.

[95] On this, see Pietri, Chadwick, ch.1, Richards, part ii, 5-6.

[96] Cf. Richards, 82, 86.

feature in the *Variae*.

At some point in his career, probably under Theoderic, Cassiodorus received the high and honorary title of Patrician, like his father before him (**I.3-4**; cf. **III.6**).[97] Like his father, and probably during the period between his Quaestorship and tenure of the Mastership of Offices, he seems to have served as governor [*corrector*] of Lucania-and-Bruttium, his native province (**XI.39.5**). Senators of the older families often held such posts, usually for one year, and exploited them to serve their connections - a matter of duty, rather than of shame - and advance their local influence and popularity (compare **XI.39, XII.5, 15**). **III.8** and **46** are *Variae* from the Quaestorship period which strongly criticise Venantius, then governor of the province. One of his victims, I would surmise, succeeded in his appeal only through the support of the Quaestor Cassiodorus. Venantius' son may well have been the Tullianus who was to muster south Italian peasants in support of the Byzantine army in 546-7, and be rewarded with a generalship.[98] We may see this house as successful rivals to the Cassiodori.

However, during most of the period from 512 to 523, Cassiodorus probably led the life of dignified freedom from public business (*otium*) proper to his class, dividing his time between Rome and his estates. As he wrote in a *formula* bestowing an honorary office, 'For what fate is happier than to till the fields and shine in the city; the fields where his own achievement delights its author, and no gain is made by deceit, while the granaries are heaped full through pleasant labour' (**VI.11.2**). Senatorial position might depend on vigorous estate management, of the kind shown in **II.21** and **III.52**. **II.24-25** and **XII.8** also illustrate the ways in which senators and major landowners could use status and influence to protect their properties from the demands of the state, and to enhance their local independence.

We should also see him as engaged in religious and historical studies, forming a friendship with the scholar-monk Dionysius Exiguus

---

[97] However, this possibly came later, on his retirement from the Prefecture of Italy, as it had for his father and Liberius; cf. Martindale, *PLRE* II, 267.

[98] Procopius, *Wars* VII.xviii.20-2, xxii.2-6, 20-1; cf. *PLRE* II, Venantius 3.

(*Institutiones* I.23.2) and other congenial churchmen at Rome, and increasing in the piety that was to dedicate the second half of his life to religious scholarship at his monastery of Vivarium on his Squillace property. (We have no record of either marriage or an heir.[99]) For some members of his class, sorcery was a traditional, if dangerous, variant on religious interests; see **IV.22**. Were his services ever demanded for senatorial delegations to Ravenna, or the drafting of senatorial letters to king or emperor? (Cf. **VIII.15** and **XI.13**.) The *Variae* show that leading senators without office were sometimes used by Theoderic for judicial or administrative tasks in the city of Rome, or in senatorial circles (**I.23, II.14, III.52**). Educational supervision of the kind entrusted to Symmachus in **IV.6** would have been very congenial to Cassiodorus - he was later to plan a Christian 'university' at Rome. Moreover, he shows us, in **IX.21**, that the Senate also had some corporate responsibility for the management of higher education in Rome.

In 519, he returned to prominence with a panegyric on Eutharic and Theoderic, delivered before the Senate (*MGH AA* XII, 465-72). He also composed his *Chronicle*, dedicated to Eutharic, and marking his consular year (*MGH AA* XI). The work is jejune, but shows an interest in cultural heroes and inventors very typical of the *Variae*; it also shows a special interest in Romano-Gothic relations. It may have suggested to Theoderic the commissioning of the twelve book *Gothic History* a few years later.

5. Cassiodorus as Master of the Offices

In 521-3, Cassiodorus' great kinsman Boethius was at the height of his career. He had ties of kinship and culture with Constantinople, and Theoderic and Justin joined to nominate his two sons as Consuls for 522; in 522/3, he was appointed Master of the Offices. By his own account, he rapidly made enemies in the attempt to check violence and

---

[99] On pressures against reproduction by the senatorial aristocracy, see Barnish, 1988, esp. 140-9.

corruption among Gothic and Roman officials. Through Roman malice especially, he was implicated in a charge of a treasonable letter to the emperor brought against a leading senator Albinus.[100] This letter may well have been connected with the succession crisis into which Eutharic's death had plunged the regime. Boethius probably exploited two roles of the Master of Offices, in diplomacy and in the arrangement of royal audiences for senators (**VI.6.2, 4**), to shield Albinus, brother of Inportunus, and extenuate his guilt. His attacker was the Referendary Cyprian, an envoy to the east, whose work at court included legal assistance to senators (**V.41**). A latent quarrel between Senate and autocrat, as old as the Roman empire, had emerged; so too newer tensions between Roman and barbarian. Theoderic's anger extended to the whole Senate, but Boethius and Symmachus are its only attested victims. While the former awaited death in prison, imperial persecution of eastern Arians created another crisis. Pope John I was sent to negotiate. Failing, he suffered the royal anger on return, and, dying soon after, was popularly regarded as a martyr.[101]

Cassiodorus was appointed to succeed Boethius, no doubt in the hope that his skill in public relations would mend broken fences. He failed to protect his kinsman, or to avert the religious crisis, but played some part in the unexpectedly smooth accession of Athalaric in 526 (**IX.25.7-11**). His *Gothic History* may well have been started in those years for purposes of tribal and dynastic propaganda.[102] Amalasuintha conciliated senatorial opinion, rehabilitating the family of Boethius, and Cassiodorus reassured the Senate that the incoming Quaestor Ambrosius would prove a 'guardian of the laws' to them (**VIII.14.2**). The preceding Quaestor had already been disgraced under Theoderic; he was probably Honoratus (**V.4**), brother of Boethius' enemy Decoratus. Relations with the emperor were even more important; see **VIII.1**.

None of the letters written while Cassiodorus was Master were

---

[100] *C.Phil.* I, prose iv; cf. *Anonymus Valesianus* 85-7.

[101] See Chadwick, 45-69, Matthews, 1981, 25-38, Barnish, 1983 and 1990.

[102] Cf. Barnish, 1984, 336-47, Heather.

composed in that capacity, but as royal mouth-piece, deputising for the Quaestor. (Had Boethius, a writer of greater genius, had the same duty?) Since the Quaestor's power was probably superior to the Master's, the fact suggests a high degree of influence at court. Letters selected from this period are, on average, markedly longer than those selected from his time as Quaestor proper, and are more apt to involve important internal and external diplomacy than administrative chores, especially after Theoderic's death. The conflicts of 523-6 do not feature, but V.40-41 and VIII.28 shed some light on two enemies of Boethius: Cyprian and the Goth Conigastus. Cassiodorus also found time to assist and eulogise his beloved home province (VIII.31; cf. 32 and 33).

The death of Pope John I meant another contested papal election, and Theoderic intervened with a divided Senate to support the candidature of Felix IV; see VIII.15. It is tempting to surmise that Cassiodorus, with his strong ecclesiastical interests, was involved in the event.

VI.6, Cassiodorus' appointment *formula* for the Master's post, may exaggerate its power.[103] It is usually held (perhaps wrongly) that Theoderic had pensioned off the imperial bodyguards, or *domestici* (cf. I.10, VI.6, note 4). As noted, the Master's *agentes in rebus* had been largely superseded by officers responsible to king and Quaestor. The Praetorian Prefect had always shared the care of the public post with the Master; in the *Variae*, he also appears as paymaster for the state weapon factories, formerly under the charge of the Master. He may also have quietly usurped some of the responsibility for provisioning Ravenna from the Master, as he had done the supply of Rome from the Urban Prefect. Of the top ministers, Praetorian Prefects and Urban Prefects received the greatest number of *Variae*; Counts of the Private Estates and Counts of the Patrimony a handful each; and Counts of the Sacred Largesses and Masters of Offices none at all, excepting their letters of appointment. Laws of the eastern empire from 439 to 527 show a broadly similar pattern of addressees.

---

[103] See Sinnigen.

Cassiodorus did not spend long in this office under Athalaric: he may have retired at the end of the 526-7 indiction. His departure is sometimes associated with the victory of a Gothic chauvinist party in the state, which resented the Roman education that Amalasuintha was giving to Athalaric;[104] but this is extremely conjectural. By late Roman standards, his four year tenure of office had been a lengthy one, and he may have stayed just long enough to see the new regime comfortably settled. His return to court in 533, as Praetorian Prefect, has similarly been linked to Amalasuintha's temporary defeat of the chauvinistic Goths opposed to her;[105] on chronological grounds, this seems a little more plausible. He reviewed his career to date, and remarked on the enemies he had overcome in achieving his new appointment in IX.24-25. In the second part of XI.1, a letter, or declamation, to the Senate thanking his benefactress, he virtually composed a full scale panegyric. His continued tenure of office after Theodahad's coup may be linked with an attempt by the king to enlist support from the friends and kinsmen of Boethius (cf. X.11).[106]

6. Cassiodorus as Praetorian Prefect

While serving in the Prefecture, Cassiodorus once again helped out the Quaestor. Lesser administrative letters are now almost absent; what we have is diplomatic correspondence, which illustrates the collapse of relations with Justinian (X.20-22, 26, 32, XI.13, XII.20); letters lauding two new rulers, and justifying a coup d'état (X.3, X.5, X.31); letters of appointment; major compositions on the reform or enforcement of existing laws; and a few other prestige documents. He also tried to smooth over deteriorating relations between Theodahad and the Senate and people of Rome (X.13, 14). The long *Edict of Athalaric* (IX.18 with 19-20) may indicate increasing corruption and lawlessness

---

[104] Cf. Sundwall, 263ff.

[105] Ibid., 272ff.

[106] Cf. Barnish, 1990, 28-31.

in a collapsing state, and so the problems faced by its chief minister. Many of the letters, especially the diplomatic pieces, seem dryer and less elaborate than those which he had written in previous offices, or, indeed, was then writing for himself as Prefect.

According to Procopius, the empress Theodora, fearing Amalasuintha as a possible rival for the affections of Justinian, prompted Theodahad to murder her, through the agency of the envoy Peter. J.B. Bury detected sinister allusions in **X.20-21** to bonds and services between Theodora, Peter and Theodahad.[107] It is surprising, though, that Cassiodorus should later have published compositions which implicated the empress in the death of the emperor's protégé, and revealed himself as an accessory after the fact. One diplomatic letter is quoted by Procopius; its wording is his own invention, but nothing with its contents appears in the *Variae*. Was it edited out by Cassiodorus, or simply drafted by another, perhaps Theodahad himself, who therein offered Justinian his personal surrender?[108]

Cassiodorus was, of course, very busy in his own ministry, described in **VI.3**, in which he had quasi-regal status, with unappellable jurisdiction, and the right to issue his own edicts. His agents in the provinces, the *cancellarii*, whom he appointed himself, seem to have been superior to the provincial governors in the control of taxation and supply (**XII.1.4**). Much of the judicial burden of the Prefecture, he claims (**XI, praef. 4**), was lifted from him by his young legal adviser (*consiliarius*) Felix, who probably provided the same services that he had given his father, long ago. As his deputy, particularly in matters of supply, he appointed Ambrosius, like him a former Quaestor (**XI.4-5, XII.25**; cf. **VIII.13-14**).[109]

Unlike **VI.3**, John Lydus's account of the Praetorian Prefecture

---

[107] Procopius, *Anecdota* 16; Bury, II, 161-9.

[108] *Wars* V.vi.15-21.

[109] Ambrosius had been Count of the Private Estates under Theoderic, and was prominent in Amalasuintha's new regime of 526. He may well be identical with a protégé of Ennodius, perhaps also of Symmachus and Boethius (Ennodius 452 [*Opusc.* 6]).

roots it in Roman history, and shows none of Cassiodorus' religious feeling; Joseph as the Prefect's biblical type goes unnoticed.[110] By publishing the De Anima with the Variae, Cassiodorus was soon to ground official ethics in Christian theology. A very religious sense of duty also appears in **XI.2**, his inaugural letter to Pope John II; but we cannot tell whether this document is routine, or if it genuinely reflects Cassiodorus' character and religious allegiances. It is interesting evidence for the growing administrative co-operation between Church and state from which the Pope was to emerge as governor of Byzantine Rome.

Among Cassiodorus' major concerns was the Joseph-like duty of relieving a famine, climatically caused, but no doubt exacerbated by war and politics, in north-eastern Italy. He also had to organise supplies for court and army, drawing much of them from the same quarter of the realm; see **XII.22, 24-27**. The plan which he and Pope Agapitus had formed for a school of Christian higher education in Rome was abandoned (*Institutiones*, I, praef.1). In his native south, law and order were apparently breaking down under the stress of war (**XII.5**); Belisarius overran the region in July to October of 536, allegedly welcomed by the Romans.[111]

During these years of growing turmoil and disaster, the taxes still had to be gathered where possible, a watchful eye kept on the Prefecture's officials, and their normal rights of pay and promotion seen to; see **XI.16, 36, XII.16**. On their counterparts in Byzantium, cost-cutting efficiency had been imposed; but, under Cassiodorus, they still enjoyed the prestige and luxury of fine papyrus paid for by the state; see **XI.38**. (Presumably they likewise continued to collect the rich fees and perquisites that were so heavy a burden for litigants.) And the Prefect still exploited the benefits he conferred by composing learned and elegant essays on the glories of Italy, including his home province; see **XI.14, 39, XII.12, 15**.

Despite the harassment of which he complains pathetically in the

---

[110] *De Magistratibus* I.14, II.6, 13-17; cf. **VI.3.1f.**; *Genesis*, ch.41.

[111] Procopius, *Wars* V.viii.1-2.

Preface to Book I, it is likely that the *Variae* were compiled before he retired from office. This event cannot be accurately dated, but may have happened while Witigis was besieging Belisarius in Rome, from March 537 to March 538. At the end of 537, he may have shared in a diplomatic mission to Belisarius (X.32, note). After retirement, he remained in Ravenna, engaged in biblical studies, and was lucky to escape the king's massacre of senatorial hostages, which happened well before the end of 537.[112] Although Witigis may have named him Patrician,[113] he was no more able to prevent it than the executions of Boethius and Symmachus. His loyalty to the Goths may well have been shattered, but it is tempting to speculate that he had some hand in their offer of the western empire to Belisarius in 540, an affair which agrees well with the politics of the *Variae*.[114] But, by now, he was turning ever more to the consolations of religion. He moved to Constantinople, probably following the fall of Ravenna, as prisoner or refugee; thereafter his work seems to have been chiefly that of a Christian *conversus* writing primarily for a religious, rather than a social élite. However, he perhaps retained that concern for the culture and morality of public men which the *Variae* and *De Anima* display.[115]

---

[112] *Expositio Psalmorum, praef.* 1-5; Procopius, *Wars* V.xxvi.1-2.

[113] Above, n.97.

[114] Procopius, *Wars* VI.xxix-xxx.

[115]See O'Donnell, ch.4-7, Barnish, 1989, esp. 175-9, Markus, 217-22; on possible political additions to the *Gothic History* at Constantinople, Momigliano, 191-6, Barnish, 1984, 347-60.

PREFACE TO BOOKS I-X[1]

1. Although I won the favour of the eloquent not by any genuine merits, but by the conversations we shared, or disinterested acts of kindness, they have been urging me to collect in one volume words poured out in my several offices to unfold the nature of items of business. Thus, future generations may appreciate both the difficulties of my labours, undertaken for the public good, and the unmercenary conduct of an upright man.

2. I have replied that their love would in fact do me harm, since writings now thought acceptable, thanks to the urgency of petitioners, would seem inept to those who read them later. I have added that they should recall the words of Flaccus [Horace, *Ars Poetica*, 390][2] who warns of the danger that hasty speech can incur. 3. You see that everyone wants a rapid response, and do you then suppose that I produce perfection? A composition which delay has not adorned with choice conceits, or which is unfolded with no subtle selection of words, is always uncouth. Speech is our common gift: it is only style that shows up the uneducated. 4. Authors are allowed nine years to write in [*Ars Poetica*, 388]: I am not even given a few hours. As soon as I begin, I am harassed and shouted at, and business, not to be too meticulous, goes on with excessive speed. One man loads me with the number of his detestable appeals; another punishes me with the mass of his miseries; others besiege me with the frenzied riot of their disputes. 5. Why do you demand the eloquence of official composition amongst all this, when I can scarcely keep up the supply of words? Even my nights are beset by complex anxieties, lest the cities should lack their food supply. This is what their inhabitants expect more than anything: their concern is not for their ears but their bellies. Hence I am forced to travel in spirit through every province, and constantly investigate my commands. It is not enough to order civil servants to do

---

[1] Cassiodorus wrote a separate preface for books XI-XII.

[2] Q.Horatius Flaccus, 65-8 B.C., a famous Roman poet, was much read in late antiquity.

something, unless the minister's diligence can be seen to enforce it. Do not, I beseech you, harm me by your affection. Persuasion that bears more risk than glory must be refused.

6. But they instead wore me down by this kind of argument: 'Everyone knows you to be the Praetorian Prefect, on whose office the public services always wait like footmen. For the army's supplies are demanded from it; without thought for the season, the people's food is requested from it; on it too is thrown a great weight merely of judicial cases. The laws, then, have placed on it a vast burden, by deciding that, for the sake of the honour, almost everything should relate to it. For what time can you steal from public toil, when all that the common good demands unites in your one breast? 7. We also mention that you are often burdened by assisting the Quaestorship, when your many ponderings deprive you of leisure time; and, as though you were a labourer in the lesser offices, the princes give you business from other ministries which the proper magistrates cannot unravel. This, however, you accomplish by selling no favour; instead, following your own father's example, you accept from petitioners only toil. Thus, by granting to suitors without a fee, you purchase all things with the gift of integrity. 8. Of course, the glorious councils of kings also have the power to occupy you for the public good during the greater part of the day, so that it would be a burden to expect from men at leisure what you evidently sustain by unceasing toil. But the fact that, under such conditions, you can produce words worth reading may serve you all the more in winning praise.

'Then, your work may inoffensively educate uncultivated men who must be trained[3] for the service of the state in conscious eloquence: those in calm waters may more happily acquire the style that you practise while tossed among the dangers of disputants. 9. Similarly - and this you cannot ignore while preserving your usual loyalty - if you allow such royal favours to pass unnoticed, you have preferred that generous haste should confer them in vain. Do not, we beg of you, recall to silence and obscurity those who were worthy to receive

---

[3] I have followed Traube's suggested emendation of *praeparatos* to *praeparandos*.

illustrious honours by your proclamation. For you took on the duty of describing them with true praise, and of painting them, in some measure, with the pigment of history. If you hand down their fame to posterity, in accordance with ancestral custom, you have nullified death for those who perished gloriously.[4] 10. Then again, you employ the king's authority to correct evil characters, you shatter the insolence of the transgressor, you restore respect to the laws. And do you still hesitate to publish what you show may have such utility?

'If I may say so, you would also be concealing the mirror of your own mind, in which every age to come might behold you. For it often happens that men beget sons unlike themselves; but it is hard to find discourse that does not conform to character. That child of one's own choosing is, then, much the more certain one, for what is born from the secret place of the heart is supposed with greater truth to be its parent's offspring. 11. Moreover, you have often spoken panegyrics to kings and queens with general applause; you have composed the history of the Goths in twelve books, anthologising their successes. Since things went well for you on those occasions, and you are already known to have published your prentice pieces in oratory, why do you hesitate to give these also to the public?'[5]

12. I am conquered - I confess it to my shame. I could not resist so many men of wisdom, when I saw myself being reproved out of love. Now forgive me, my readers; and, if there is anything rash and irregular, ascribe it rather to my advisers, since my own verdict clearly agrees with my accuser. 13. And therefore, I have put together all that I could find of my compositions made on various public affairs while I held the posts of Quaestor, Master, and Prefect. They are arranged in twelve books, so that, although the reader's attention may be stimulated by the diverse subject matter, his mind, nonetheless, shall be more effectively hurried on when he approaches the end. 14. Now I have not allowed others to endure what I have often rushed into in the

---

[4] This passage probably echoes Tacitus, *Agricola* 1.1, 46.4.

[5] The surviving fragments of the panegyrics date to 519 and the end of 536: perhaps recently published, but hardly 'prentice pieces'.

granting of honours: hasty and unpolished declamations, which are so
suddenly demanded that it seems they can hardly even be written down.
Therefore, I have included *formulae* of all posts of honour in the sixth
and seventh books, that I might thus take some belated thought for
myself, and bring speedy aid to my successors.[6]
In this way, what I said about people in the past also suits those to
come, since I have set out what is fitting not about individuals, but
about the offices themselves.

15. Now, as the title of the books, that tell-tale of the work, herald
of the contents, summary of the whole treatise, I have assigned the
name of *Variae*; for, since I had various persons to admonish, I had to
adopt more styles than one. For in one manner you must address and
persuade men glutted with much reading; in another those titillated with
a small taste; in another those who are starved of the savour of letters,
so that it may sometimes be a kind of art to avoid what would please
the learned. 16. Accordingly, it is a fine rule of our ancestors, that you
should speak with such fitness as to sway the hopes your hearers have
already conceived. For it was not in vain that the wisdom of the
ancients defined three modes of oratory: the humble, that seems to
creep along in true lowliness; the middle, which is neither swollen with
magnificence, nor thin and impoverished, but is placed between the
two, enriched with its own beauty, and contained in its own bounds;
and the third, which is raised to the highest peak of argument by choice
conceits. Clearly, different persons may thus enjoy the eloquence which
suits them; and, though it may flow from a single breast, it does so in
separate streams. For no one can be called eloquent unless he is armed
with this threefold style, and equipped like a man for any case that may
arise. 17. In addition, I sometimes address kings, sometimes ministers,
sometimes people of low rank; some of my words to them were rapidly
poured out, but others I could produce after thought. Thus, a
compilation of such diversity should rightly be entitled *Variae*. But I
hope that, as I have evidently received these modes from the ancient
rules, even so they may unlock the merits of the promised composition.

---

[6] Cassiodorus' Latin is markedly more careful in Books VI-VII; cf. Vidén, 140-4.

18. Therefore, I modestly promise to produce the humble; the middle I guarantee without dishonesty; but the high, which, because of its nobility, is appointed for solemn compositions,[7] I do not believe that I have reached. But, since I am to be read, this illegitimate defence in advance must cease. For it is unfitting to be thus disputing about myself; I should rather submit to your judgement.

[The pressure of friends, and the modesty of a reluctant author, are rhetorical commonplaces, and need not be taken at face value.]

---

[7] The MSS offer several readings; *in edita dictione* is Fridh's conjecture, followed here; Mommsen conjectures *in editiore*; one MS has *in edicto*.

I.3 KING THEODERIC TO THE ILLUSTRIOUS PATRICIAN CASSIODORUS (a.507?)

1. Although what is naturally praiseworthy enjoys its own honour; although tried integrity wields official power, since it begets high offices on the soul - for all good things are united to with their fruits, and virtue unrewarded is incredible - nonetheless, the peak of my good opinion is a lofty one, for he whom I promote is seen to be rich in outstanding merit. 2. For, if a just man's choice should be considered impartial, or a temperate man's nominee to be endowed with self-restraint, he who has earned the approval of the judge of every virtue is clearly fitted for every reward. For what greater honour can be sought than to find a witness to one's praise where there is no suspicion of prejudice? Assuredly, a ruler's verdict is formed from acts alone, and a soul strengthened by kingly power cannot stoop to flattery.

3. Of course, the actions that blended you with my consciousness must be recalled: when you realise that each deed is a pleasing fixture in my mind, you will receive the reward of your toil. Why, you were a loyal subject at the very outset of my reign: when the hearts of the provincials were going astray in those uncertain conditions, and sheer novelty allowed contempt for an untried master, you diverted from rash resistance the minds of mistrustful Sicilians, preventing their crime, and my need to punish it.[1] 4. Wholesome persuasion, not stern vengeance, put matters right. You averted a fine from a province, which, in its loyalty, deserved to avoid it. There, in military dress, you upheld the civil laws; as a judge without avarice, you weighed up both the public and the private good; neglecting your own property, making no invidious profit, you gained the riches of good character, and gave no entrance to quarrels, no room to detraction. In a land which seldom exports silence and patience, the voices of your praisers fought for you. For we know, by Tully's [Cicero's] testimony, how quarrelsome the

---

[1] The elder Cassiodorus was probably governor of Sicily, c.489/93; he was perhaps appointed by Odoacer.

Sicilians naturally are, so that it is their usual custom to accuse their governors on mere suspicion. 5. But I was not content with that glorious result: I gave you the conduct of Lucania-and-Bruttium to control [as governor], lest the fortune of your native land should not experience the good which a foreign province had earned.[2] You, though, lavished your usual loyalty, and put me under an obligation through the very gift by which I had thought to repay you everything - you increased the debt where it might have been discharged. In all things, you played the magistrate free from all error, crushing no man through spite, and exalting no man through favour and flattery. As this is a difficult achievement anywhere, in one's own country it is glorious. There it is inevitable either that kinship should lead to favour, or that prolonged disputes should arouse hatred. 6. Again, it gives me pleasure to recall the acts of your Prefecture, a most renowned blessing to the whole of Italy, in which you ordered all things with foresight, and proved how easy it is to render taxes under an honest magistrate.[3] No one grudges what he pays up under an equitable administration, since a properly ordered levy is not considered a loss. 7. Now enjoy your blessings, and receive twofold your personal profit, which you spurned with public approval. For this is a glorious gain in life, when you enjoy the praise of your fellow citizens, and your masters bear witness to your merits.

8. Stimulated, therefore, by this most lavish praise, I confer on you, as a just recompense, the honour of the Patriciate, so that what to others is a reward shall to you be merely the payment of your deserts. Most eminent of men, triumph in your praise and good fortune. You have compelled your master's heart to this confession: he must admit his gift to be really your own property. May heaven make this honour perpetual:[4] thus, although I have granted it as a recompense, I may at

---

[2] This governorship must date c.491/505.

[3] This Prefecture must date c.503/6.

[4] The accepted *Sint haec divina perpetua* does not make very good sense in context; I follow Traube's emendation of *sint* to *duint* (index, s.v. *divina*). Certain MSS read *Sint haec divino perpetrata auspicio* - 'may Providence approve the honour conferred'.

another time bestow still greater rewards on your virtues.

I.4 KING THEODERIC TO THE SENATE OF THE CITY OF ROME (date as I.3)

1. Truly I desire, fathers of the Senate, that your garland should be coloured with the flower of the various offices; I desire that the Spirit of Liberty should behold a thronged and grateful Senate. Yes, an assembly of such offices is an honour to the ruler, and all that you view with joyful satisfaction is rightly ascribed to my credit. 2. But this is my special wish: that the lamps of high honours should adorn your order, when those who have grown in power at court duly render the harvest to their fatherland. My gaze inspects these men; I rejoice to find in them a treasure of good character, in which, as if by coin portraits of honours, the kindness of my serenity is expressed.

3. Hence it is that I have rewarded the illustrious Cassiodorus, a man famous for the highest distinction in the state, with the exalted rank of Patrician: thus the honour of a great title may proclaim the merits of my servant. He is not a man borne on in the game of fortune by brittle luck, who has flitted by sudden promotions to the highest dignity; rather, since virtues are usually of gradual growth, he has ascended to the peak of glory by the regular steps of office. 4. For, as you know, his first entry to the administration was based on the foundation of the Countship of the Private Estates.[5] He did not waver there with a beginner's weakness, nor go astray through the fault of inexperience, but, on the sure footing of self-restraint, he lived an example to all. He soon received the honour of the Sacred Largesses, and grew as much in renown for his conduct as he had advanced in office. 5. Why need I tell of the good order he restored to the provinces, or mention the records of the justice he instilled into men of every condition? He lived with such integrity that he both established

---

[5] Like the Sacred Largesses, this office was apparently granted by Odoacer, between 476 and 490. The elder Cassiodorus was starting his career as one of the seven top ministers!

impartiality by his commands, and taught it by personal example. For
an uncorrupt magistrate is a ready advocate of the right: his noble
conduct shames the disreputable. For who will shun the crime whose
accomplice he sees aloft on the tribunal? When the avaricious man
condemns corruption, when the unjust decrees that the laws must be
observed, he vainly assumes the mask of feigned severity. He to whom
an untroubled conscience does not give authority lacks the spirit of
government, since excesses are held in fear only when they are thought
to offend the magistrates.

6. Trained, then, in these exercises under the preceding king
[Odoacer], he came to my palace with a well earned reputation. For
you remember - and, by now, I am reminding you of recent events -
with what moderation he sat on the Praetorian summit, when placed
there. Borne up to the height, from that position he despised the vices
of the successful all the more. 7. Indeed, no gift of fortune so elated
him, as is the way with many, that he raised himself on the actor's
boots of great power; rather, he directed all things with justice, and did
not make my favour hated in his person. He caused greater things to
be hoped for himself, while confining his greatness within the bounds
of moderation. For hence comes that most welcome harvest of proven
integrity, the fact that, although a man may have reached the heights,
all still judge him to deserve more. He well joined the royal income
with the general happiness, generous to the treasury, and just but
obliging to the tax-payers. 8. The commonwealth then experienced a
man of honour from the assembly of Romulus [the Senate]; a man who,
while making himself glorious by his self restraint, achieved something
still greater, in bequeathing to his successors a model of upright action.
For he who is able to succeed men of reputation is ashamed to do
wrong. As you are aware, then, he was terrible to public servants, mild
to the provincials, greedy of giving, too proud to receive, a hater of
crime, a lover of justice. A man who had made it his rule to refrain
from the property of others found this easy to observe. For it is a sign
of an unconquered soul to love the profit of good fame, and to hate the
gains that come from law-suits.

9. But it is those unacquainted with the noble characters of his
father and grandfather who have the right to wonder at these traits.

Truly, fame also celebrates the previous Cassiodori. Although that name may run in others, it still belongs especially to his family. An ancient stock, a race much praised, its members are honoured among civilians, outstanding among soldiers, since they have flourished alike in health and strength. 10. Now the father of this candidate held with credit the office of Tribune-and-Secretary under the emperor Valentinian [III], an honour then given to outstanding men, since only those in whom no censurable fault can be found may be chosen for the emperor's privy affairs. 11. But, since like spirits always choose each other out, he was allied by bonds of great affection to the Patrician Aetius for the service of the state - Aetius, whose counsel the master of the empire then followed in all things, because of his wisdom, and his glorious labours in the state. Together with Aetius' son Carpilio, he was therefore charged, and not in vain, with the office of envoy to that mighty warrior Attila.[6] He beheld without terror one whom the empire feared; trusting in his honesty, he despised those terrible frowns and threats, and did not hesitate to meet in argument a man who, as the prey of some mysterious madness, was patently seeking the dominion of the world. 12. He found the king arrogant; he left him pacified, and demolished his libellous accusations with such honesty that he decided to ask for favour, although it was to his advantage to have no peace with so rich a realm. By his steadfastness, Cassiodorus gave hope to frightened politicians; and those who were armed with envoys of such character were not thought unfit for war. He brought back a peace unhoped for. The benefits of his embassy are clear, since it was received as gratefully as it had been earnestly desired. 13. Soon the righteous ruler was offering him gifts of revenues, and the honour of illustrious rank. But instead, he was enriched by his native self-restraint, and, receiving an honorary office, chose the pleasures of Bruttium in place of reward. The emperor could not refuse this longed-for peace to one who had given him safety from a ferocious enemy; he released with sorrow from his service one whom he knew

---

[6] This embassy is not otherwise attested; it should date between 435 and 449. On Attila, see glossary.

he needed. 14. For grandfather Cassiodorus, distinguished by that honour of illustrious rank which could not be denied to his house, delivered Bruttium and Sicily by armed resistance from Vandal invasion: hence he deservedly held the chief place in those provinces which he defended from so savage and unpredictable an enemy. To his virtues, then, the state owed it that those inner provinces were not seized by Genseric, whose rage Rome afterwards endured.[7] 15. But the Cassiodori have also flourished with their kindred honoured in the east. For Heliodorus, who, as I saw, administered Prefectures in that state with distinction for eighteen years, was known as a member of the family.[8] It is a house glorious in either realm; joined with grace to the twin Senates, as though it were endowed with two eyes, it has shone with the purest radiance. Has any noble family anywhere spread itself wider than this one, which has earned honour in either realm?

16. This Cassiodorus himself, moreover, has lived in his province with the honour of a governor, and the tranquillity of a private person. Superior to them all in his nobility, he drew the hearts of all men to himself: those who, by their rights of freedom, could not be enslaved, were instead bound to him sweetly by successive benefits. 17. Indeed, he is also so distinguished by the wealth of his patrimony that, among other blessings, he surpasses princes in his horse-herds, and averts envy by his frequent gifts. Hence, my candidate regularly equips the Gothic army, and, improving on good principles, has preserved the inheritance he received from his parents.

18. My esteem for him has recounted all this in order, so that each of you may understand that he who resolves to live by honourable principles can renew the fame of his kindred at my court. And therefore, fathers of the Senate, since it pleases you to honour the good, and since your assent accompanies my judgement, vote

---

[7] 'Grandfather Cassiodorus' is father of the ambassador, grandfather of the new Patrician, and great-grandfather of the author. His defence of Bruttium and Sicily may have been in 440; the Vandal king Genseric sacked Rome in 455.

[8] A Heliodorus is attested as a Praetorian Prefect, or Urban Prefect of Constantinople in 468; Cassiodorus' *praefecturam* must be translated as plural; cf. *PLRE* II, 531f.

favourably for the promotion of a man who has won general goodwill. For it is more an exchange than a reward, that those who have adorned you with praiseworthy actions should be thanked with a reciprocal favour.

I.10 KING THEODERIC TO THE ILLUSTRIOUS PATRICIAN BOETHIUS (a.507-12)

1. While the whole people should be granted the common justice that wins the honour of its name by extending its equitable control equally among the great and humble, those who remain in the service of the palace still seek it with special confidence. For on men of leisure the royal generosity bestows its gifts gratuitously; but customary rewards are paid as a kind of debt to the dutiful retainer.

2. The horse and foot guards, who keep constant watch over my court, have made this complaint to me in a joint petition - the usual result of serious grievances: they do not receive *solidi* of full weight as their customary wages from X the Prefect's treasurer, and they suffer heavy losses in the number of coins. Therefore, your wisdom, trained by learned texts, is to expel this criminal falsehood from the company of truth, so that no one shall be tempted to diminish that purity.

3. For, among the world's incertitudes, this thing called arithmetic is established by a sure reasoning that we comprehend as we do the heavenly bodies. It is an intelligible pattern, a beautiful system, an integral study, an unchanging science, that both binds the heavens and preserves the earth. For is there anything that lacks measure, or transcends weight? It includes all, it rules all, and all things have their beauty because they are perceived under its standard. 4. It is a pleasure to observe how the decad [*denarius*], like the heavens, turns on itself, and is never found to be lacking. That same reckoning increases on new terms, constantly added to itself by repeating itself, so that,[9] although the decad is not exceeded, it has the power to build up large

---

[9] Fridh (1950, 72f.) rejects Mommsen's emendation of *ut* to *et*.

numbers from small. This process is many times repeated: by bending
and straightening the fingers of the hand, it is prolonged indefinitely;
and, for every time that the computation is brought back to its
beginning, it is unquestionably increased by so much.[10] The sands of
the sea, the drops of rain, the shining stars are defined by a calculable
quantity. Indeed, to the author of its being [God], every creature is
numbered, and nothing that comes into existence can be separated from
that condition.

5. And - since it is my delight to discourse with learned men on the
more mysterious elements of this discipline - although coins themselves
may seem contemptible from their common use, we should still remark
with how much reason they were marshalled by the men of old. They
decided that 6000 *denarii* should form a *solidus* with this aim, that the
shaped circle of shining metal, as if it were solar gold, should fittingly
imply the time-span of the world. But, as for the hexad [*senarius*],
which learned antiquity rightly defined as the perfect number, they
stamped it with the name of the ounce [*uncia*] which is the prime unit
of measure; and, by reckoning it twelve times, like the months, they
made up the full pound to match the courses of the year.[11] 6. O, the
inventions of the wise, the judgement of our ancestors! They discovered
something which both marks off what is necessary to human purposes,
and figuratively implies so many mysteries of nature. Rightly, then, it
is called a pound, since it is weighed[12] by such contemplation of the
world.

---

[10] This obscure passage seems to describe the origin and arithmetical uses of the decimal
base; ten was regarded with reverence in the Pythagorean tradition which influenced
Boethius.

[11] At this time, at least in Italy, 6000 silver *denarii* (= 12000 copper *nummi*) were
probably notionally reckoned to one gold *solidus*. For special occasions, a 6-*solidus*
piece, probably called a *senarius*, might be struck; this weighed 1/12 (*uncia*) of a pound
(*libra*) of gold. The hexad or six (*senarius*) was the first perfect number (i.e. number
equal to the sum of its own factors) after the monad; in a tradition going back to Philo
(fl. c.A.D.10), it was regarded with reverence. Christians sometimes held that the world
would last for 6000 years. Cassiodorus plays on the words *sol*, meaning sun, and *solidus*.

[12] *Libra* can denote a pound, or a pair of scales.

The violation, then, of such mysteries, the will so to confound certainties, surely this is a foul and cruel mangling of truth itself? Trading in goods should continue; men may buy cheap and sell dear; and the people must have reliable weights and measures, since everything is confused if frauds and purity mingle. 7. Clearly, what is granted to workers should not be pruned; rather, where honest service is exacted, let an undiminished reward be bestowed. Give a *solidus*, by all means, and reduce it again, if you can; hand over a pound, and diminish it, if you are able. Against these actions, there is an obvious defence in the very names of the things: either you render the entire sum, or you are not paying what those names refer to. You cannot in any way, you cannot designate whole units, while making criminal reductions. See to it, then, both that the ruler of the treasury obtains his just and customary perquisites, and that what I bestow on the well deserving, they receive intact.

[For one discussion of this letter and contemporary coinage, see Cuppo Csaki. Cassiodorus neither explains precisely how the abuses were achieved, nor what Boethius was meant to do about them; tampering with the scales is suggested by the text (6; cf. the much plainer language of II.25 and XI.16 on scale-frauds). Debasement of the *solidus* by mint officials was an old problem, perhaps continuing; cf. VII.32.2. The Byzantine grammarian Priscian (c.510) dedicated to Symmachus a treatise on numerical notation which includes remarks on weights and coins (*De Figuris Numerorum*, ed. H. Keil, *Grammatici Latini* III), suggesting some interest among Boethius' circle. On Boethius' arithmetical studies, see Chadwick, 71-8; his *De Arithmetica* I.1-2 shares certain themes with Cassiodorus' praise of mathematics.]

I.17 KING THEODERIC TO ALL GOTHS AND ROMANS LIVING AT DERTONA[13] (a.507-8)

1. Advised by the calculation of public utility, a care which is always a welcome burden to me, I command that the castle sited near

---

[13] Dertona (now Tortona) was the site of a state granary and major road junction, strategically located to defend Liguria from invasion over the western Alps. A number of Gothic graves have been found there.

you be strengthened, since matters of war are well ordered when planned in time of peace. Indeed, a fortification is made especially strong when reinforced by prolonged planning. Anything done in haste is evidently ill-advised, and it is a bad thing to demand building on a site when danger is already feared. 2. Then too, the heart itself cannot be ready for a deed of daring when it is troubled by various anxieties. This deed our ancestors rightly termed an expedition,[14] since a mind devoted to war should not be occupied by other thoughts. Therefore, a matter recommended by consideration of the common good should be welcomed; and it is wrong that an order clearly of special assistance to the loyal should meet with delay.

3. So, by this authority I decree that you are speedily to build yourselves houses in the aforementioned fort. You will thereby repay me: for, even as I plan for your good, I will feel that you are glorifying my reign with beautiful buildings. For it will then be the case that you will want to assemble the luxuries proper to your new homes, and you will welcome dwellings whose own architecture makes them a pleasure to you.[15] 4. What an advantage it will be to live in your own homes, while the enemy endures the harshest quarters! He will be exposed to the rains; you will be shielded by a roof; hunger will gnaw him; you will be refreshed by your stores. So, while you remain in perfect safety, your enemy will suffer the fate of the loser before the battle is fought. For clearly, in time of need, he who is not distracted among many cares will be proved the bravest. For could anyone suppose a man wise if he starts to build or lay up supplies only when he should be thinking of war?

---

[14] *Expeditio* and related words can mean a march in light order; also, a more general freedom from burdens.

[15] A move to a fort on the hill above the town (then unwalled) is probably meant; a permanent change in settlement did not result; for comparable refuges in the eastern Alps, cf. III.48 (Doss Trento above Trento), Alföldy, 91f., 214-20.

I.18 KING THEODERIC TO DOMITIANUS AND WILIA (a.507-12)

1. You who have taken up the work of proclaiming law to the people should observe and cultivate justice. For a man who is supposed to restrain others under the rule of law must not do wrong, lest he should become an example of crime, when he was chosen for a worthy task. And therefore I have taken care to answer your queries, so that you cannot go wrong through uncertainty, but only - what should never be - through the will to transgress.

2. If, after the date [489] when, by God's favour, I crossed the river Isonzo, and the realm of Italy first received me, a barbarian occupier has seized the estate of a Roman, without a warrant [*pittacium*] taken from any assigning officer [*delegator*], he is to restore it without delay to its former master. But, if he has evidently entered the property before that time, since the thirty year limitation is clearly an objection, I decree that the plaintiff's claim is to fall.[16] 3. For I want only those matters brought to judgement which I condemn as acts of seizure made in my reign, since there is no room left for idle accusations when the obscurity of many years has passed.

4. As for the case of the man who merely struck, without also killing, his brother: although he is condemned by the common law, and parricide is the only thing to surpass this defendant's tragedy, nonetheless, my humanity, which seeks out room for pity even among the impiously criminal, rules, by this authority, that a man of such ill omen shall be expelled from the province. For those who hate the society of their relatives do not deserve the company of fellow citizens, lest dark spots pollute the pleasant radiance of a stainless body.

---

[16] A *praescriptio temporis* prohibited the raising of actions after that period; cf. **II.27.2**. Lawsuits over Odoacer's settlement, in or soon after 476, are envisaged. On the Gothic settlement, see further, note to **II.16**.

I.23 KING THEODERIC TO THE ILLUSTRIOUS PATRICIANS CAELIANUS AND AGAPITUS[17] (a.509-12)

1. Since universal love for peace wins praise for the ruler, it is right that the royal glory should take care to maintain public harmony. For what does me more honour than a tranquil people, a harmonious Senate, and an entire commonwealth clothed in the seemliness of my ways?

2. Hence it is that, by this command, I decree that the magnificent Patricians Festus and Symmachus shall present in your court the case they claim to have against the illustrious Patrician Paulinus. When this has been received in legal form, and settled, if the law allows, then the Patrician Paulinus shall in turn bring forward whatever action he lays claim to against their aforementioned magnificences. I wish for no delay in the verdict on his suit either, since I would wish everything that lies between them to be decided, and nothing save the duties of affection to remain.[18]

3. Remember, therefore, that you are chosen as arbiters in so great a case; remember that my expectation demands equitable justice. You will yield me a rich fruit of gratitude if this trial proves those thought worthy to judge it to be equal to their task. For special care should be taken over men who can give clear examples to those of lesser rank. For he who fails to do away with litigation among the great unquestionably licenses the rest of society to imitate it.

---

[17] For the court of these Patricians, cf. I.27; it was perhaps an *ad hoc*, rather than a permanent tribunal.

[18] Symmachus is Boethius' father-in-law, Festus, Consul in 472, currently senior senator (*caput senatus*); Paulinus had been Consul in 498; nothing further is known of their litigation. The chronicler Malalas (384) tells how Theoderic executed lawyers who had prolonged a senatorial lawsuit for 30 years!

I.25 KING THEODERIC TO THE DISTINGUISHED SABINIANUS[19] (a.507-12)

1. It is useless to build firmly at the outset if lawlessness has the power to ruin what has been designed: for those things are strong, those things enduring, which wisdom has begun and care preserved. And therefore, greater attention must be exercised in conserving than in planning them, since a plan at its outset deserves commendation, but from preservation we gain the glory of completion.

2. Now, some time ago, for the sake of Rome's public monuments, to which it will be my unwearying aim ever to devote attention, I decreed that the depot of Licinus [*portus Licini*] should be repaired from the revenues assigned, to supply 25,000 tiles annually.[20] This should also apply to the associated depots which once belonged to that place, and which, it is reported, have now been illicitly taken over by various persons. 3. Therefore, without delay, you are to have everything returned to supplying the statutory quantity; for, although, out of reverence for them, my commands should be violated in no matter, I especially want those which beautify the city to be observed. For who would doubt that wonderful buildings are saved by this provision, and that vaults rounded with overhanging stonework are preserved by tiled roofing? Past princes should rightly owe me their praise: I have conferred long-lasting youth on their buildings, ensuring that those clouded by old age and decay shall shine out in their original freshness.

---

[19] Sabinianus may have been the state architect at Rome; cf. VII.15, which shows the post to have been theoretically under the Urban Prefect, although the king made the appointment.

[20] The *Portus Licini*, used for drying and storing new bricks or tiles, had been state property since the early 3rd century; the 25,000 are no great quantity, and may be a tax on private users; Theoderic's brick-stamps are numerous in Rome. Cf. *Corpus Inscriptionum Latinarum* XV.1, p.121, and nos.1663-70; Steinby, 114, 146ff., 153f., 157ff.

I.27 KING THEODERIC TO SPECIOSUS[21] (a.509)

1. If I am ruling the manners of foreign tribes in accordance with the law; if every land that is joined to Italy obeys the Roman code, how much more is it right for the very seat of social order [*civilitas*] to hold the laws in high reverence, so that, through this example of restraint, the beauty of high offices may shine out? For where can we look for the spirit of restraint if violence defiles the Patricians?

2. Now it has been reported to me by a complaint of the people of the Green faction - since they have resolved to come to my court, and request the usual help - that they were violently attacked by the Patrician Theodorus and the illustrious Consul Inportunus; in consequence, one of them is mourned as dead.[22] 3. If this is true, I am much moved by the savagery of the deed, that rage should arm itself and harass the harmless people whom civic affection ought to cherish. But because the condition of lesser men justly claims the ruler's aid, I command by this order that the illustrious persons named above must make no delay, but send, with you to see to it, men properly briefed, to the tribunal of Caelianus and Agapitus, both of illustrious rank.[23] Their court of inquiry must end in a careful and legal verdict.

4. But lest, perchance, men of exalted rank should be offended by the babbling of the mob, a distinction must be drawn as to such impertinence. A man who has injured a reverend senator as he passes by his insolence, cursing him when he ought to bless him, must be held responsible for a crime. But who looks for serious conduct at the public shows? A Cato never goes to the circus. 5. Anything said there by the people as they celebrate should be deemed no injury. It is a place that protects excesses. Patient acceptance of their chatter is a proven glory of princes themselves. Those who are involved in such enthusiasm

---

[21] Speciosus may have been a *comitiacus*.

[22] On the circus factions, cf. III.51.5,11; on Theodorus and Inportunus, III.6. Inportunus is the current Consul, and giver of games and races.

[23] Cf. note to I.23.

should answer me this question: if they hope that their opponents will keep quiet, they clearly desire their victory, since men break out into insults only when they are blushing for a shameful defeat. Why, then, do they choose to be angered at what they know they have certainly desired?

I.45 KING THEODERIC TO THE ILLUSTRIOUS PATRICIAN BOETHIUS (c.506)

1. I should not reject requests made by neighbouring kings to please their vanity, since a small expenditure can often purchase more than great riches. For sweetness and pleasure many times produce what weapons fail to do. May it then serve the state, even when I seem to play. For it is for this reason that I am looking for toys, to achieve a serious purpose by their means.

2. Now the lord of the Burgundians [Gundobad] has earnestly asked me to send him one time-piece which is regulated by a measured flow of water, and one whose nature it is to receive the light of the mighty sun, together with those who can operate them. So, by obtaining and enjoying these pleasures, they will experience a wonder which to me is a common-place. It is very proper that they should long to see something which has astonished them through the reports of their ambassadors.

3. I have learnt that you, clothed in your great learning, are so knowledgeable in this that arts which men practise in customary ignorance, you have drunk from the very spring of science. For, at long distance, you so entered the schools of Athens, you so mingled in your toga among their cloaked assemblies, that you turned Greek theories into Roman teaching.[24] For you have discovered with what deep thought speculative philosophy, in all its parts, is pondered, by what mental process practical reasoning, in all its divisions, is learnt, as you transmitted to Roman senators every wonder that the sons of

---

[24] Cf. Cassiodorus on himself: 'He turned Gothic origins into Roman history' (IX.25.5).

Cecrops [Athenians] have given the world. 4. For it is in your translations that Pythagoras the musician and Ptolemy the astronomer are read as Italians; that Nicomachus on arithmetic and Euclid on geometry are heard as Ausonians [Italians]; that Plato debates on metaphysics and Aristotle on logic in the Roman tongue; you have even rendered Archimedes the engineer to his native Sicilians in Latin dress.[25] And all the arts and sciences which Greek eloquence has set forth through separate men, Rome has received in her native speech by your sole authorship. Your verbal splendour has given them such brightness, the elegance of your language such distinction, that anyone acquainted with both works would prefer yours to the original.

You have entered a glorious art, marked out among the noble disciplines, through four gates of learning.[26] 5. Drawn in by authors' works, you have come to know it where it sits in the inner shrine of nature, through the light of your own genius; it is your practice to understand its problems, your purpose to demonstrate its wonders. It labours to display events that men may wonder at; altering the course of nature in a wonderful way, it takes away belief in the facts, despite displaying images to the eyes. It causes water to rise from the deep and fall headlong, a fire to move by weights; it makes organs swell with alien notes, and supplies their pipes with air from outside, so that they resound with great subtlety. 6. By its means, we see the defences of

---

[25] **Pythagoras**: philosopher, mathematician and musical theorist, fl. c.530 B.C.; he probably left no writings, but Boethius may have translated works of his school. **Ptolemy**: astronomer, musical theorist, mathematician and geographer, fl. A.D. 127/48; no Boethian translation from him survives. **Nicomachus**: a 1st/2nd c. A.D. mathematician; Boethius' *De Institutione Arithmetica* adapts his introduction to arithmetic. **Euclid**: a mathematician, fl. c.300 B.C.; fragments of Boethius' translation of his *Elements* may survive. **Plato**: a philosopher, c.429-347 B.C.; Boethius planned a complete translation of his *Dialogues*, of which nothing survives, if it was ever begun. **Aristotle**: a philosopher and scientist, 384-322 B.C.; Boethius planned, but did not finish a complete translation of his works. **Archimedes**: a Sicilian Greek mathematician and engineer, c.287-212 B.C.; no Boethian translation from him survives.

[26] *Tu artem praedictam...introisti.* Since engineering has been mentioned only briefly among many arts, I have conjecturally emended *praedictam* to *praedicatam*. On the quadrivium, cf. Boethius, *De Arithmetica, praef.* and I.1.

endangered cities suddenly arise with such solidity that machinery gives the advantage to a man who despaired at their lack of strength. Waterlogged buildings are drained while still in the sea; hard objects are disintegrated by an ingenious device. Objects of metal give out sounds: a bronze statue of Diomedes blows a deep note on the trumpet; a bronze snake hisses; model birds chatter, and those that had no natural voice are found to sing sweetly. 7. I shall say a little about the skill which imitates the heavens without sin. This has set a second sun to revolve in the sphere of Archimedes; by human ingenuity, this has constructed another circle of the Zodiac; by the light of art, this has shown how the moon recovers from its waning, and set turning by an invisible mechanism a tiny device pregnant with the world, a portable sky, a compendium of the universe, a mirror of nature which reflects the heavens.[27] Although we know the course of the stars, our eyes cheat us, and we cannot see them moving in this way: indeed, their transit is static, and you cannot see in motion what you know by true reason is passing swiftly. 8. What it is for man actually to create this device! - even to understand it may be a remarkable achievement.

Since you are adorned by your glorious acquaintance with such matters, send me, therefore, the time-pieces, at public expense, without cost to yourself. Let the first be one where a gnomon marks the day, and shows the hours by its meagre shadow [a sun-dial]. In this way a small, unmoving circle represents the revolution of the sun's amazing vastness, and equals the sun's flight, although it knows no motion. 9. If the stars were aware of it, they would be envious, and perhaps turn their courses, not to be the butt of such a joke. What has become of the great wonder of hours produced by the light, if it is a mere shadow that indicates them? Where is the glory of that unwearied rotation, if even a piece of metal fixed in a constant place can accomplish it? O the inestimable quality of a science which is mighty enough to disclose the secrets of nature, while it claims to be only playing! 10. The second time-piece must be one by which the hours are known without the sun's

---

[27] The sphere of Archimedes was a precursor of the orrery - a mechanical model of the planetary movements; cf. Cicero, *De Republica* I.21ff., Claudian, *Carmina Minora* li.

rays, and which divides the night into parts. Owing nothing to the stars, it instead turns the nature of the heavens into streams of water, and shows by their motions what revolves in the sky. With daring audacity, an invented art confers on the elements what their nature denies them.[28]

All the disciplines, the whole endeavour of the wise, seek to know the power of nature so far as they can. Only engineering tries to imitate it by contraries, and, in some things, if it is proper to say so, even seeks to surpass it. For this art, we know, made Daedalus fly; it suspends the iron Cupid without support in the temple of Diana; it daily makes dumb objects sing, inanimate live, immobile move.[29] 11. The engineer, if it is proper to say so, is almost a partner of nature, unlocking her secrets, changing what she reveals, playing with wonders, and making such exquisite counterfeits that we take for truth what is certainly artificial.

Since I know that you have diligently studied this art, you will be quick to send me the afore-mentioned time-pieces with all speed, that you may make your name known in a part of the world where otherwise you could not have come. 12. May the foreign tribes realise, thanks to you, that my noblemen are famous authorities. How often will they not believe their eyes? How often will they think this truth the delusion of a dream? And, when they have turned from their amazement, they will not dare to think themselves the equals of us, among whom, as they know, sages have thought up such devices.

[On Cassiodorus' outline of Boethius' studies and writings, see Chadwick, 102f. On late antique, especially sixth century interest in the mathematical and mechanical arts, and their prestige among the educated, see Mathew, 24-9, 67ff. Cassiodorus later constructed a sun-dial and a water-clock for his monastery (*Institutiones* I.xxx.4f.; cf. II.vii.3). Boethius' surviving works are ostentatiously theoretical, and his technical skills have

---

[28] On water-clocks, see Vitruvius, *On Architecture* IX.8.5-13, with plates M and N in F. Granger's Loeb translation; on sun-dials, ibid. IX.7 with plate L, Dilke, 70-3.

[29] Daedalus: a legendary inventor, who escaped from Crete on artificial wings. The statue of Cupid was probably suspended between opposing masses of magnetised stone in the vault.

therefore been doubted, but I am unconvinced.]

I.46 KING THEODERIC TO GUNDOBAD, KING OF THE BURGUNDIANS (date as I.45)

1. We should welcome those gifts which are evidently in great demand, since things which can gratify our desire are not to be despised. For the whole purpose of some precious objects is to gratify a want.

Therefore, I greet you with my usual friendship, and have decided to send you, by X and Y, the bearers of this letter, the time-pieces with their operators, to give pleasure to your intelligence. One is the type which seems to epitomise human ingenuity, since, as we know, it traverses the space of the entire heaven; in the other, the sun's course is known without the sun, and the length of the hours is marked off by trickling water. 2. Possess in your native country what you once saw in the city of Rome. It is proper that your friendship should enjoy my gifts, since it is also joined to me by ties of kinship.[30]

Under your rule, let Burgundy learn to scrutinise devices of the highest ingenuity, and to praise the inventions of the ancients. Through you, it lays aside its tribal way of life, and, in its regard for the wisdom of its king, it properly covets the achievements of the sages. Let it distinguish the parts of the day by their inventions; let it fix the hours with precision. 3. The order of life becomes confused if this separation is not truly known. Indeed, it is the habit of beasts to feel the hours by their bellies' hunger, and to be unsure of something obviously granted for human purposes.

---

[30] Gundobad had commanded the imperial army in 472-4; his son Sigismund had married Theoderic's daughter Areagni.

II.1 KING THEODERIC TO THE MOST PIOUS EMPEROR ANASTASIUS (a.510)

1. Solemn custom prompts me to give a name to the roll of honour, to give Rome its special glory, the Senate house its earthly distinction, so that, through the course of years, the grace of high offices may run on, and the memory of the ages be consecrated by royal generosity. May a felicitous year receive a good omen from its Consul Felix; may a period that is renowned by such a name enter the gate of days; and may the fortune of the year's beginning bless its remainder.

2. For what could you suppose more desirable than for Rome to gather her own sucklings back to her breasts, and to count the Gallic Senate amongst the assembly of the venerable name.[1] The Senate acknowledges the glory of Transalpine blood; not for the first time has it entwined its crown with the flower of Gaul's nobility. Along with the other offices, it knows how to recruit its Consulars from there. The law of time, and a pedigree rich in consular robes make Felix an hereditary bondsman of honours. For what worthy man does not know him to be felicitous in his own character, one who displayed his merits at the first opportunity, by hastening to the motherland of virtues [Rome]. Prosperity followed his good judgement; promotions came when he gained his liberty; and I was not content to leave inglorious a man who deserved to attain the chief honour of the state. 3. He clearly merits my generosity, since, while in the flower of his youth, he reined in that unstable time of life by maturity of character, and, with the rare blessing of self-restraint, when bereft of his father, he became the child of dignity. He subdued avarice, the enemy of wisdom, he rejected the enticements of vice, he trampled down the vanity of pride. So he triumphed over excess, and, by his character, publicly displayed his

---

[1]Fridh follows the MSS in reading *venerando*; I prefer the conjecture of Cujas and Mommsen, *venerandi*. 'The Gallic senate' may allude to the Council of the Gauls, or more generally to the senatorial class in Gaul.

Consulship before its time.[2]

4. Now I, who am won over by good morals, and pleased by proven honesty, bestow the consular insignia on this candidate, so that my generosity may stimulate desire for virtue; for something which is lavishly rewarded will not lack its enthusiasts. And so do you, who can be delighted in impartial goodwill by the prosperity of either commonwealth, add your support and your vote. He who is worth the elevation of such an office deserves to be chosen by the judgement of us both.

[The appointment [for 511] seems entirely the work of Theoderic, with Anastasius' assent an optional extra. Contrast the words Procopius gives to Witigis' envoys (*Wars* VI.vi.20): 'the Goths have conceded that the dignity of the Consulship should be conferred upon the Romans each year by the emperor of the East'.]

II.8 KING THEODERIC TO THE VENERABLE BISHOP SEVERUS[3] (c.508)

Who is a better choice for the laws of equity than the man who is honoured with the priesthood? In his love of justice, he can show no favour in judgement, and loving all men equally, has no place for envy. Therefore, I inform you that I have sent your holiness, through Montanarius, 1500 *solidi*, deeming the action well suited to your merits. In so far as you know any of the provincials to have suffered loss from the passage of my army in this year, you are to distribute the money to them, making an estimate of the damage; thus, no one affected by his losses will be a stranger to my bounty. For I do not intend a sum which should be rationally distributed to be given without discrimination, lest what I have plainly been compelled to send to sufferers should be bestowed without need on the uninjured.

---

[2] In the parallel letter to Felix, Theoderic praises his frugal and efficient management of his estates, perhaps with some irony (II.2.3f.).

[3] Severus was probably bishop of a city on the route from Italy to Gaul, much used by Gothic troops fighting the Franks.

II.14 KING THEODERIC TO THE PATRICIAN SYMMACHUS (a.507-12)

1. If family pieties have evidently turned to savagery, who can now bring charges in other matters? When the tragedy of crime has thundered mightily, trivial accusations are neglected; no one strives to avenge minor cases if he sees the greatest misdeeds escaping. The very nature of his role displays the ferocity of your enemy; you may often find anger in a colleague; but humanity does not permit a rebellious son to avoid punishment.

2. For what has happened to that natural influence, which the bond of kinship fastens on our children? The whelps of wild beasts follow their parents; saplings do not quarrel with the soil; a vine slip keeps to its own origin; and shall a man, once brought forth, quarrel with his own beginnings? What shall I say of those benefits that can bind even those outside our families? Children are nurtured from their infancy; for them we work; for them we seek riches; and, although each man may think his property ample for himself, when fathers continue to pursue it, they sin for the next generation rather than themselves. The grief of it! Shall we not earn the love of those for whose sake we consent to suffer death? A careful father, in the quest for foreign goods to leave to his offspring, does not shun the seas themselves, tossed by savage storms. 3. The very birds, whose life is constantly spent in feeding, do not defile their nature by so alien a stain. The stork, which is ever the herald of the returning year, dispelling the gloom of winter, and ushering in the joy of spring, gives us a fine example of family piety. For when their parents droop their wings as old age withers them, and are incapable of seeking their own food, they warm the cold limbs of their progenitors with their plumage, and revive their exhausted bodies with eatables; and, until the aged bird returns to its original vigour, the young ones repay, in a pious exchange, what they received, when little, from their parents. And therefore, by not refusing the duties of piety, they earn their lengthy life span. 4. Partridges, too, have the practice of redeeming the loss of an egg by taking from a second mother, and thus mending the

misfortune of their childlessness by adoption of an alien offspring. But soon, when the chicks begin to be strong walkers, they go out into the fields with their fosterer; then, as if summoned by the mother's voice, they instead seek out the parent of their eggs, although they were reared by others in a stolen brood. 5. What, then, is the duty of human beings, when they see that this piety is natural even to the birds?

Therefore, you are to bring before your court Romulus, who, polluted by the atrocity of his deed, disgraces the Roman name; and, if it is clear that he has laid hands on his father Martin, he shall straightway feel the vengeance of the law. For it is for this reason that I have chosen a man of your character: because you are incapable of sparing the savage, since it is a kind of piety to punish those shown to have taken part in evil deeds against the law of nature.

II.16 KING THEODERIC TO THE SENATE OF THE CITY OF ROME (c.509)

1. It is my care, fathers of the Senate, to repay an upright life, and to stimulate men of innate good qualities to better practices by the fruit of the kindness I bestow. For virtues feed on exemplary rewards, and there is no one who will not strive to scale the heights of morality when deeds praised by a knowledgeable witness are not left unrepaid.

2. Hence it is that I have raised the illustrious Venantius, resplendent both by his own and his father's merits, to the rank of Honorary Count of the Bodyguards; thus, honours conferred shall increase the glory grafted on his parentage. For you recall, fathers of the Senate, how the Patrician Liberius won praise even under my hostility. He showed such total loyalty to Odoacer as later to deserve my love, although he had done much against me as my enemy. For he did not come over to me in the mean state of a deserter, nor did he feign hatred against his proper lord, to win for himself the favour of another. With integrity, he awaited the judgement of God; nor did he permit himself to seek a king before he had lost a master. 3. So it has come about that I gladly reward him because he has loyally aided my

enemy. Under the patronage of opposing fortune, the measure of his clear disobedience at the time made him the more acceptable to me. Now, with his master almost bowed down, he was swayed by no terrors; he bore unmoved the ruin of his prince; nor could he be frightened by the new regime which even fierce tribesmen held in awe. He followed the common fortunes with wisdom, so that, while steadfastly enduring the judgement of God, he might commend himself the better to the favour of men. 4. I have proved the man's allegiance; in grief he passed over to my rule; a beaten man, he changed his loyalty, but did not bring about his own defeat.

Soon, when I gave him the office of Praetorian Prefect,[4] he administered what was entrusted to him with such integrity that any man might wonder at the guileless loyalty of one whom he knew to have been so cunning an enemy. He then, with untiring care - the hardest kind of virtue - brought in the public revenues to general approval. He increased the taxes not by adding to them, but by keeping them unchanged: income which had harmfully been dissipated, he beneficially collected with industry and intelligence. I realised that the revenues were increased; you knew nothing of extra taxes. Thus, two things were marvellously achieved: the fisc was enriched, and private advantage felt no loss.[5] 5. It is my delight to mention how, in the assignment of one-third shares [tertiae], he united both the estates and the hearts of Goths and Romans.[6] For, although neigbourhood usually causes men to quarrel, for them the sharing of property seems to have inspired harmony. For it so befell that either nation, while living in common, arrived at a single mind. Behold, a new, and wholly admirable achievement: division of the soil joined its masters in good will; losses increased the friendship of the two peoples, and a share of the land purchased a defender, so that property might be preserved

---

[4] This was held c.493-500.

[5] On tax levels, justice, efficency and actual revenue, cf. Ammianus Marcellinus XVII.3, XXI.16.17.

[6] Tertiae are probably shares of rural estates. On barbarian land settlement in Italy, see Barnish, 1986, esp. 180f.; cf. I.18. (Contrast Goffart, 1980, Wolfram, 295ff.)

secure and intact. A single law and a just discipline embraces them. For sweet affection must needs develop among those who always preserve their fixed boundaries. The Roman commonwealth owes its peace, then, not least to the aforementioned Liberius, he who has transmitted to such glorious nations the zeal for love.

6. Consider, fathers of the Senate, whether I should leave the son unrewarded, when I recall the many and mighty deeds of his father. May Heaven favour my decision: thus, as I arouse the virtues by bestowing benefits, so I may prove that honoured and upright men have increased in merit.

II.20 KING THEODERIC TO THE *SAIO* WILIGIS (a.508-12)

All men·should gladly contribute what they see may be of service to the state, since the limbs must needs feel as the whole body does. And therefore, by this command I order you to load with corn from the taxes all the ships[7] you can find at the city of Ravenna, and bring them to me, so that the state supplies, relieved by this measure, need endure no dearth and scarcity. Let Ravenna return to Liguria the supplies it usually receives from there.[8] For the province that endures my presence should find help from many sources. For my court draws with it hordes of followers; and, while benefits are swiftly bestowed, necessary supplies are demanded from the people.

II.21 KING THEODERIC TO THE DEPARTMENTAL OFFICER [*APPARITOR*] JOHN (a.507-12)

1. It is a very grave matter that a hard-working man should be defrauded of the fruit of his labour, and that one who ought to be

---

[7] Following J.Rougé (*Latomus* 21, 348-90) and Fridh, I read *sculcatorias* for Mommsen's *exculcatorias*.

[8] The court was probably at Pavia, owing to the war with Clovis.

rewarded for his industry should unjustly suffer loss. This is especially so in a case which concerns my bounty; there, no negligence is permissible, lest I should seem to have sanctioned something of no benefit.

2. Now, some time ago my bounty made over to the distinguished gentlemen Spes and Domitius[9] an area in the territory of Spoleto uselessly occupied by muddy pools, where a wide expanse of waters had submerged the kindly arable, so that no use and benefit resulted. The ground lay shipwrecked, ruined by stagnant marsh; tossed between two privations, it had not gained pure water, and had lost the glory of dry ground. 3. Since it is my desire to change all things for the better, I made it over to those mentioned above, on condition that, if this foul swamp should be drained by their labour and operations, the fields so freed should profit them. But, as reported in the petition presented by Spes' agents, the distinguished Domitius has been at fault: forgetting my command, he has tenaciously withheld expenses, and the labour of the workmen has been nullified, just as the soft surface of the ground was drained and gradually hardening, and the unfamiliar sun was warming soil long devoured and hidden by the water. 4. I will in no way allow this to be neglected, so that grudging sloth destroys a work well begun.

Therefore, your loyalty, with this moderate verdict, is to summon the aforementioned Domitius either to press on the work begun as a painstaking worker; or, if he thinks this too expensive for him, to make over his own share to the petitioners. For it is right that, if he cannot perform what he asked for, he should allow his partner in the gift to increase the glory of my reign.

[Lying halfway between Rome and Ravenna, Spoleto was much frequented by senators and courtiers. Like Decius' work (II.32), these drainage operations may have been a show-piece for the regime.]

---

[9] Inscriptions attest one Fl.Spes as a leading citizen of Spoleto in 346, and suggest that the Domitii were a noble family there in the 5th-6th centuries.

II.24 KING THEODERIC TO THE SENATE OF THE CITY OF
ROME (a.507-12)

1. It is well known that the Senate has bestowed a rule of life on
the people, for we read that you established what gives glory to the
Roman name. For this purpose you were called fathers at the very
beginning: that you might order men's lives as if they were your sons.
For your decrees have produced loyalty in the provinces, and given
laws to private persons; you have taught your subjects to obey justice
gladly in all its parts. And therefore it is unfitting that a sign of
resistance should arise where exemplary self-restraint should instead
shine out. My clemency, whose heartfelt desire it is to preserve
measure in all things, has decided to bring this matter to your notice.
Your ignorance may nourish ever more excesses, but error cannot
endure once you know of it.

2. Now, I have learnt by report from the provincial governors
sent to the magnificent Praetorian Prefect that the first period of tax
payment has been so exempted that clearly little or nothing has been
paid in by the senatorial houses. They allege that, by this difficulty, the
weak, who should have been given assistance, are ground down; for it
happens that, when the harshness of the civic tax-collectors [*exactores*]
is despised by the powerful, it turns to the weak and plays havoc
among them, and it is he who is zealous in his own payments who
instead pays another's. Moreover, they add much graver charges, that
each, according to his whim, deigns to cast something to those who ask
his taxes -- that is, all this loss is reportedly inflicted on the town
councillors -- and those whom my policy had revived for the public
service, are ruined by lawless injuries.[10]

---

[10] Cassiodorus seems to distinguish the damage inflicted by the council's tax-collectors
on those below them from that which town councillors suffer themselves when, despite
their extortions, they still fail to make up the tax deficit. The payments 'cast' are
probably in substandard coins; cf. II.25.2, Traube, index, s.v. *abicere*. The later
emperors tried repeatedly to support the councils, 'the sinews of the state', as Majorian
called them in 458 (*Novel* 7.1).

3. And therefore do you, fathers of the Senate, who owe the state an effort equal to my own, take order with such justice that, whatever any senatorial house may declare, it shall pay in three instalments to the appointed agents[11] in the provinces. 4. Or indeed, if you so wish - and this is something you have often requested as a favour - you may pay the entire sum to the treasury of the Vicar's office.[12] Thus, no town councillor shall have to labour with repeated and useless summonses, and instead lose out by your paltry payments, with the detestable result that a man who, in his loyalty, can barely support his own obligations, is weighed down in his weakness by another's burdens. 5. While maintaining official courtesy [*civilitas*], I cannot hide this fact: that, without the cruelty of war, men are borne down and stripped of their property, and perish the more, the quicker they are to serve the state. Know that I have also brought this to the attention of every provincial in an edict [**II.25**], so that he who knows himself borne down by the weight of another's obligation may be free to burst out into public notice. I know that I am giving a safeguard to the exhausted; from me they will bring back a harvest of justice.

II.25 AN EDICT OF KING THEODERIC (date as II.24)

1. Although the voice of grief is filled with protest, although losers cannot contain themselves, and an injured spirit feeds on lamentation, nonetheless, when my authority gives scope, freer speech is gained. For I hate the oppression of the wretched; I am moved even by the troubles of the uncomplaining; and what the sufferer's pretence has concealed quickly reaches my ears. Rightly so, since all men's injuries affect me, and what I experience in the losses of the poor, I see as wounding to my love.

---

[11] *destinatis procuratoribus per provincias trina illatione persolvat*: I doubt Traube's interpretation of the *procurator* (index, s.v) as a senator's agent.

[12] Like XII.8, this grants the privilege of *autopragia*, direct responsibility for one's taxes; a landlord would collect them with his rents.

2. Now I have recently learnt by report from the provincial governors, that certain houses of the very great are not fulfilling their obligations in due order. Hence it is that, when there is an effort to procure the instalment due, the larger sum is exacted from little men. Then, by the arrogance of the major tenants [*conductores*], the *solidi* due in tax are not handed over in proper order; instead, coins of bad weight are tossed to the collectors. Nor have they paid over in customary form the entire tax that they used to render. The result is that the town councillors, for whom I wish to take thought, experience heavy losses under coercion from the efforts of the tax enforcers; and - if it can be right to say so - they are even deprived of their own estates, when pressed with another's debts by the aggressive collectors of arrears [*compulsores*].

3. In order to eradicate this wrong, I have also sent instructions to the most·reverend Senate [**II.24**], and now decree by edict that any landowner or town councillor who feels himself burdened by another's obligations is to make haste to an audience with my serenity; he will know how utterly the excesses of the past have disgusted me when he sees them followed by benefits. The purpose of a just prince is, therefore, made plain to you - although it is constantly displayed by many evidences. Now either conceal with silence your grief and suffering, or open in a spirit of justice a road for your complaint. The fate of this decision will now lie in your hands; it is open to you to choose what you perceive will profit you.

II.27 KING THEODERIC TO ALL JEWS LIVING AT GENOA (a.507-12)

1. As it is my desire, when petitioned, to give a lawful consent, so I do not like the laws to be cheated through my favours, especially in that area where I believe reverence for God to be concerned. You, then, who are destitute of His grace, should not seem insolent in your pride.

Therefore, by this authority, I decree that you add only a roof to the ancient walls of your synagogue, granting permission to your requests just so far as the imperial decrees allow.[13] 2. It is unlawful for you to add any ornament, or to stray into an enlargement of the building. And you must realise that you will in no way escape the penalty of the ancient ordinance if you do not refrain from illegalities. Indeed, I give you permission to roof or strengthen the walls themselves only if you are not affected by the thirty year limitation.[14] Why do you wish for what you ought to shun? I grant leave, indeed; but, to my praise, I condemn the prayers of erring men. I cannot command your faith, for no one is forced to believe against his will.[15]

[Following the reconquest of Africa, Justinian confiscated Jewish synagogues in that province (*Novel* 37.8). At the siege of Naples in 536, the Jewish inhabitants fought bravely on the Gothic side.]

II.32 KING THEODERIC TO THE SENATE OF ROME (a.507-12)

1. I welcome dedication to the public service, fathers of the Senate, since, while proving the commendable spirit of the citizens, I find an opportunity to confer well-merited favours. For what is so like a senator as to devote zeal to the public service, that he may profit the country for which he was born?

2. Now, the magnificent Patrician Decius, compelled by love for the commonwealth, with an admirable aim, has freely requested what my power and policy could scarcely have imposed on him.[16] He has promised to drain the marsh of Decemnovium,[17] which ravages the

---

[13] Cf. Theodosius II, *Novel* 3, 3 and 5.

[14] Probably, this means 'If no-one, for thirty years, has legally challenged the right of your synagogue to exist on that site, and in that form'; cf. I.18.

[15] Cited in 1577 in a plea for religious toleration by the humanist J. Bodin.

[16] Note that the inscription below refers to the work as imposed by Theoderic; it may thereby have strengthened Decius' title to the land reclaimed.

[17] Decemnovium was the stretch of the Via Appia which ran for 19 miles north of Terracina through the notorious Pomptine (Pontine) marshes.

neighbourhood like an enemy, by opening channels. It is a notorious
desolation of the age, which, through long neglect, has formed a kind
of marshy sea, and, spreading by its waters a hostile deluge over
cultivated ground, has destroyed the kindly arable equally with shaggy
woodland. Since it began to be exposed to the marshes, the soil has
been robbed of its crops, and nourishes nothing useful beneath the
water. 3. And therefore I marvel at this man: his old-fashioned
self-confidence[18] is such that private enterprise has undertaken what
the power of the state long shunned. He, then, has promised that he
will attack this daring task with such commendable completeness that
the destructive flood will perish, but the lost ground will perish no
longer. Hence, he has requested orders from my serenity in this affair,
so that he may take on, with public authority, an outstanding work, that
will benefit all travellers.

4. But I, fathers of the Senate, to whom it is natural to assist a
good intention by helpful ordinances, enjoin by this decree that you
should send two of your number to those places at Decemnovium. By
their judgement, all the space that the mud of the marshes occupied
through stagnation of the incoming water, shall be marked by fixed
boundary stones. Thus, when the promised work reaches completion,
the ground restored will profit its deliverer, and no one will dare to
claim what he has so long been unable to defend from the invading
water.[19]

[An important inscription from Terracina records this work. *Our lord the glorious and
famous king Theoderic, victorious and triumphant, perpetual emperor ['Augustus'], born
for the good of the commonwealth, guardian of liberty and propagator of the Roman
name, tamer of the tribes, has restored the route and places of the Via Appia at
Decemnovium, that is from Tripontium to Terracina, to the public use and the safety of
travellers, by wonderful good fortune and the favour of God. Under all previous princes,*

---

[18] *priscae confidentiae virum*: for the application of such terms to old-time Roman
engineers, cf. Ammianus Marcellinus XV.4.3.

[19] By a law of 388/92 (*Code of Justinian* XI.59.8), such land might be reclaimed within
two years by its former owner, provided he paid its restorer for his work. Decius'
reclamations were to be tax free (II.33.1).

they had been flooded through marshes converging from either side. Caecina Mavortius Basilius Decius, right honourable and illustrious, former Urban Prefect, former Praetorian Prefect, former Ordinary Consul and Patrician, from the glorious house of the Decii, toiled industriously on the task imposed, and served with good fortune the most clement prince. To perpetuate the glory of such a lord, he led the waters into the sea through many new channels, and restored the ground to its all too ancient dryness, unknown to our ancestors. (Corpus Inscriptionum Latinarum, X, 6850, Inscriptiones Latinae Selectae, ed. H. Dessau, 827.) The imperial language used of Theoderic in this inscription is unique. The model emperor Trajan (98-117), to whom men compared Theoderic (*Anonymus Valesianus* 60), had rebuilt the Via Appia through the marshes, but neither letter nor inscription shows awareness of this. The route was one much travelled by senators, between Rome and the holiday resorts of Campania; cf. II.21.]

II.38 KING THEODERIC TO THE PRAETORIAN PREFECT FAUSTUS (a.508)

1. Hating the gains made for me by the misfortunes of plundered men, I hope that my wealth will increase in the treasury of pity. A levy that causes weeping damages my clemency, for a tax paid gladly is ascribed to the praise of its receiver.

2. Now, the traders of the city of Sipontum claim that they have been ruined by hostile ravaging;[20] and, since I consider that my wealth really lies in helping the needy, your illustrious magnificence will trouble those named with no levy by compulsory purchase [*coemptio*] for a continuous period of two years.[21] 3. But since there is no point in raising the fallen if another burden of payment is imposed, your highness must advise those who have lent money to the aforementioned traders, that they are to demand none of the sum credited during this two year period. So, with the help of this moratorium, they may be able to recover the money given, while their debtors' property has some breathing-space. For what does it profit a creditor to hurry himself, when he is vainly struggling to get money from ruined men?

---

[20] In 508, the emperor Anastasius sent a naval raid against the Italian coasts, presumably in support of Clovis.

[21] Cf. n. 19 to XII.22.

I am planning for them better, if, by deferment, I enable them to regain their loans.

II.40 KING THEODERIC TO THE PATRICIAN BOETHIUS (a.506)

1. Although the king of the Franks, tempted by the fame of my banquets, has earnestly requested a lyre-player from me, I have promised to fulfill his wishes for this reason only, that I know you to be skilled in musical knowledge. To choose a trained man is a task for you, who have succeeded in attaining the heights of that same discipline.

2. For what is more glorious than music, which modulates the heavenly system with its sonorous sweetness, and binds together with its virtue the concord of nature which is scattered everywhere? For any variation there may be in the whole does not depart from the pattern[22] of harmony. Through this we think with efficiency, we speak with elegance, we move with grace. Whenever, by the natural law of its discipline, it reaches our ears, it commands song. 3. The artist changes men's hearts as they listen; and, when this artful pleasure issues from the secret place of nature as the queen of the senses, in all the glory of its tones, our remaining thoughts take to flight, and it expels all else, that it may delight itself simply in being heard. Harmful melancholy he turns to pleasure; he weakens swelling rage; he makes bloodthirsty cruelty kindly, arouses sleepy sloth from its torpor, restores to the sleepless their wholesome rest, recalls lust-corrupted chastity to its moral resolve, and heals boredom of spirit which is always the enemy of good thoughts. Dangerous hatreds he turns to helpful goodwill, and, in a blessed kind of healing, drives out the passions of the heart by means of sweetest pleasures. 4. Through bodily means he softens the bodiless soul, and leads it where he wills by hearing only, while unable to control it by speech. In silence, he cries aloud through his hands; he speaks without a mouth; and, by the service of insensible matter, he is

---

[22] Mommsen and the MSS read *continentia*; Fridh *concinentia*, followed here.

strong to govern the senses.

Among men all this is achieved by means of five *toni* [scales or modes], each of which is called by the name of the region where it was discovered. Indeed, the divine compassion distributed this favour locally, even while it assuredly made its whole creation something to be praised. The Dorian *tonus* bestows wise self-restraint and establishes chastity; the Phrygian arouses strife, and inflames the will to anger; the Aeolian calms the storms of the soul, and gives sleep to those who are already at peace; the Iastian [Ionian] sharpens the wits of the dull, and, as a worker of good, gratifies the longing for heavenly things among those who are burdened by earthly desire. The Lydian was discovered as a remedy for excessive cares and weariness of the spirit: it restores it by relaxation, and refreshes it by pleasure. 5. This one a corrupt age perverted to cabaret performances, making an immoral invention out of a decent remedy. Now this fivefold number of *toni* has a threefold division. For every *tonus* has an upper and a lower range, but these are attached[23] to a middle range. And, since they cannot exist in separation, and are linked by alternating variations, an artificial musical form - that is, one discovered by the work of composers on various instruments - was conveniently found to be contained in fifteen modes. 6. To all this, human ingenuity added something greater: by learned enquiry, it formulated a certain concordant interval called, because it was drawn from every land, the diapason[24], so that this wonderful synthesis might contain all the virtues which the whole of music could possess.

By this means, Orpheus held effective sway over the dumb beasts, and invited the wandering herds to despise their pastures, and to feast instead by hearing him. Through his song, the mermen fell in love with dry land; Galatea the sea-nymph played on firm ground; the bears left

---

[23] Fridh and Mommsen follow the MSS' *dicuntur*, but Mommsen would prefer *ducunt* or *adiguntur*; I suggest *dicantur* from *dico* (1).

[24] Cassiodorus, *Institutiones*, II.v.6: the *diapason* (from the Greek *dia pasón*) he defines as an octave, one of the *symphoniae* (it is called here *harmonia*), or concordant intervals. These are 'modulations of sound from high pitch to low, or low to high'.

their beloved woods; the lions abandoned their homes in the reed-beds;[25] the prey rejoiced beside the predator. Opposing purposes were gathered in one assembly; and, as the lyre gave its promise, every beast trusted its enemies. 7. Amphion, too, the son of Dirce, is said to have built the walls of Thebes by his song and his strings, so that, when he raised men worn out by labour to the zeal for perfection, the rocks themselves were believed to quit their crags and come to him. Musaeus, also, the son of Orpheus by nature and by art, has been praised by the mighty tongue of Vergil, who tells how he was placed at the peak of blessedness among the shades, since he delighted the happy souls in the Elysian fields with the notes of his seven strings. The moral of this is that he who feasts on the savours of this art enjoys the highest reward.[26]

8. But all this was evidently achieved by the human art of manual music. Yet, as we know, the living voice has a natural rhythm: it preserves an exquisite melody when it is silent at the right moment, speaks suitably, and steps with careful elocution, on musical feet, down the path of intonation. The sweet and forceful speeches of orators were likewise invented to move men's souls, so that judges would pity the erring, and be enraged with the criminal. Whatever an eloquent man may achieve clearly belongs to the glory of this discipline. 9. To the poets also, as Terentianus bears witness, two original metres are ascribed: the heroic and iambic, the one devised to arouse, and the other to quieten men.[27] From these, various ways of delighting the souls of an audience have been born; and, as with the tones of an instrument, so in the human voice, the pregnant metres have brought forth different passions of the soul. 10. The researches of the ancients have revealed that the Sirens sang to a miracle; and, though the waves drove on the sailors, and the wind filled their sails, under the pleasant

---

[25] For lions in the reed-beds of Mesopotamia, see Ammianus Marcellinus XVIII.7.5.

[26] Orpheus, Amphion and Musaeus are all legendary Greek musicians; the Elysian Fields are a paradise of dead heroes.

[27] Terentianus Maurus: author of a poem *On Letters, Syllables and Horatian Metres*, 2nd c. A.D.

deception they preferred to run on the rocks, rather than forgo such sweetness. Only the man of Ithaca [Ulysses] escaped, who was quick to stop up the seductive hearing of his crew. Against the poisonous sweetness, that craftiest of men thought up the device of a fortunate deafness: what they could not overcome by their judgement, they conquered instead by insensibility. He, though, bound himself to the firm mast with tight knots, that he might test those famous songs with unstopped ears, and escape, in his bonds, the peril of the sweet-sounding voices, as the waters bore him on.[28]

11. But, that I may follow the example of the wise Ithacan, and pass on, let me speak of that psaltery which came down from heaven, which a man to be sung throughout the world so composed and modulated for the soul's deliverance that, by these hymns, the wounds of the mind might be healed, and God's especial grace implored. Let the world wonder at this and believe: David's lyre drove out a devil; its sound commanded the spirits; and, as the cithara played, the king [Saul] whom an inward enemy had evilly enthralled returned to his freedom.[29]

12. For, although many instruments of this delight have been discovered, nothing has been found more effective to move the soul than the sweet resonance of the hollow cithara. Hence, we suppose that the strings of the instrument were called chords because they easily move the cordial spirits. So great is the concord of the diverse notes assembled there that a string, once struck, makes its neighbour vibrate spontaneously, although itself untouched. For such is the power of harmony that it makes a lifeless object move spontaneously because it so happens that its fellow is in motion. 13. Hence different notes emerge without a tongue; hence some sweet chorus is formed from a variety of sounds: one is high through great tension, another low through a certain slackening of the string, a third mezzo, through a

---

[28] Sirens: these mythical monsters lured sailors onto the rocks by their sweet singing; Ulysses heard their song but escaped, by blocking the ears of his crew with wax, and binding himself to the mast.

[29] See 1 Samuel, xvi. 14-23.

mellow adjustment of the instrument's back. Human beings cannot achieve a unison to equal the social concord that unreasoning objects have attained. For there all notes which are tuneful or flat, harsh or most clear, and so on, are gathered, as it were, into one glory; and, as a diadem delights the eyes by the various light of its gems, so does the cithara delight the ears by its diversity of sound. 14. It is the talking loom of the Muses, with speaking wefts and singing warps, on which the plectrum shrilly weaves[30] sweet sounds. Now this instrument Mercury is said to have discovered, modelling it on the mottled tortoise. As the bringer of such benefits, astronomers have believed it should be sought among the stars, urging that music must be heavenly, since they can detect the shape of a lyre placed among the constellations. 15. Yet, the harmony of heaven cannot be fittingly described by human speech, as nature has not revealed it to human ears, but the soul knows it through reason only. For they say that we should believe that the blessedness of heaven enjoys those pleasures which have no end, and are diminished by no interruption. They maintain, indeed, that things above are absorbed by that same perception, that heavenly beings enjoy those same pleasures, and that those who are engrossed by such contemplations are constantly enfolded in blessed delights. 16. They would indeed have considered well if they had ascribed the cause of heavenly blessedness not to sounds, but to the Creator. With Him there is truly perpetual joy, an eternity that abides for ever with no weariness; and the mere sight of God creates unsurpassable blessedness. This sight in truth bestows everlasting life, and heaps up pleasures; as no creature can exist without it, so without it, unchangeable joy cannot be had.

17. But, now that I have had the pleasure of this digression - for I am always glad of learned discussion with experts - let your wisdom select the superior cithara-player who has, as I said, been requested of me. He will perform a feat like that of Orpheus, when his sweet sound

---

[30] Mommsen reads *tegitur*; Fridh *texitur*.

tames the savage hearts of the barbarians.[31] And the obligation will be repaid with a suitable reward, since you are both obeying my command, and accomplishing what will increase your own reputation.

[The more technical part of this letter has small resemblance to Boethius' *De Musica*. (So too the related *Institutiones* II.v.) However, its relation of music to bodily and cosmic harmony, and its identification of the verbal arts as part of music seem comparable. *De Musica* I.34 treats practical music-making with contempt - perhaps assumed, for Boethius was a fine poet - but values highly the discipline of musical criticism; cf. Caldwell, 144-8.]

II.41 KING THEODERIC TO LUDUIN [CLOVIS], KING OF THE FRANKS (date as II.40)[32]

1. I take pleasure in my marriage kinship with your courageous spirit, since you have aroused the long idle Frankish race to new wars, and, by your victorious right arm, have subdued the Alamannic peoples, who have yielded to a stronger power.[33] But, since crimes should always be avenged on the authors of treachery, and the punishable fault of chieftains should not be requited on the commons, restrain your attack on the exhausted remnants. Those who, as you see, have taken refuge in the protection of your kindred, deserve to escape, by the law of friendship.[34] Forgive those frightened men who are

---

[31] Boethius remarks in *De Musica* I.1, 'For the fiercer tribes are pleased by the harsher modes of the Goths, but gentle tribes by moderate modes; in our days, though, the last is most unusual.'

[32] Relations between Theoderic and Clovis were clearly not yet at crisis point. II.40-1 should then be dated well before the battle of Vouillé in 507. The chronology of Clovis' wars with the Alamanni is controversial; see Van de Vyver, and, recently, Wood, 262f., James, 84f. From archaeological evidence, the defeated Alamanni had been in close contact with Italy; Theoderic settled them in Italy, on reclaimed marshland (Ennodius, 263.72f. [*Opusc*.1]).

[33] Fridh reads *causis fortioribus inclinatos*; Mommsen *caesis...* I have here followed Fridh's translation (1968, 29ff.), but it seems to me uncertain.

[34] Theoderic was married to Audefleda, sister of Clovis.

hidden within my borders. 2. It is a memorable triumph so to have terrified the warlike Alaman that you are forcing him to beg for the gift of life. Let it suffice that that king has fallen, along with the pride of a race; let it suffice to have subdued a countless nation, part with death, part with slavery. For if you go to war with the remnants, it will not be believed that you have already beaten them all.

Accept the advice of one long experienced in such affairs: those wars of mine have turned out well which were carried through with moderation at the end. For it is the man who knows how to exercise restraint in all things that is habitually the victor; and the happiness of good fortune is more apt to favour those who do not become too hard and severe. Submit gently, then, to my guiding spirit, since, by common example, kinship has the habit of yielding to itself. So you will be seen to gratify my requests, and you will have no anxiety over what you know affects me.

3. Therefore, I greet you, as is right, with honour and affection, and, with my usual love, have sent X and Y as envoys to your excellency. Through them, I may obtain news of your welfare, and also the fulfillment of my request. There are, indeed, some things which I have thought of for your benefit: these I have entrusted to the bearers to be delivered to you by word of mouth, that thus you may be made more prudent, and steadily obtain the full results of your longed-for victory. Indeed, your prosperity is my glory, and I believe that the whole realm of Italy benefits whenever I hear of your success. 4. I have also despatched the cithara-player whom you asked for, one who, by mouth and hands and harmonious song, may delight the glory of your mightiness. As you judged that he should be sent urgently, I believe that he will prove welcome to you.

III.1 KING THEODERIC TO ALARIC, KING OF THE VISIGOTHS (a.507, early/mid.)

1. Although the countless numbers of your clan gives you confidence in your strength, although you recall that the power of Attila yielded to Visigothic might,[1] nevertheless, the hearts of a warlike people grow soft during a long peace. Therefore, beware of suddenly putting on the hazard men who have assuredly had no experience in war for many years. 2. Battle terrifies those who are unused to it, and they will have no confidence in a sudden clash, unless experience gives it in advance. Do not let some blind resentment carry you away. Self-restraint is fore-sighted, and a preserver of tribes; rage, though, often precipitates a crisis; and only when justice can no longer find a place with one's opponent, is it then useful to appeal to arms.

3. Wait, therefore, until I send my envoys to the Frankish king [Clovis], so that the judgement of friends may terminate your dispute. For I wish nothing to arise between two of my marriage kinsmen[2] which may, perhaps, cause one of them to be the loser. There has been no slaughter of your clansmen to inflame you; no occupied province is deeply incensing you; the quarrel is still trivial, a matter of words. You will very easily settle it if you do not enrage yourself by war. Though you are my relative, let me set against you the notable tribes allied to me, and justice too, which strengthens kings and quickly puts to flight those minds which it finds are so armed against it. 4. And so, giving first the honour of my greeting, I have seen fit to send you X and Y as my envoys. They will convey my instructions, as requisite, and, with your approval, will hasten on to my brother Gundobad and the other kings, lest you should be harassed by the incitements of those who maliciously rejoice in another's war. May Providence prevent that wickedness from overcoming you. I judge your enemy to be our

---

[1] In 451, at the battle of the Catalaunian Plains; see Jordanes, *Getica* 180-217, probably deriving from Cassiodorus.

[2] Theoderic was married to Audefleda, sister of Clovis, and had married his daughter Theodegotha to Alaric.

common trouble. For he who strives against you will find in me his due opponent.

III.2   KING THEODERIC TO GUNDOBAD, KING OF THE BURGUNDIANS (date as III.1)

1. It is very wrong to see a clash of wills among royalties who are dear to us, and to look on, hiding our feelings, in the hope that some misfortune will arise for one of them. If our kinsmen go bloodily to war while we allow it, our malice will be to blame. From me you hold every pledge of high affection; the two of us are united; if you do anything wrong on your own account, you sin gravely by causing me sorrow. 2. It is our part to restrain by reason young men of royal power; for, if they feel that their evil ambitions genuinely displease us, they will be unable to retain their rash purposes. Heated by the energy of youth they may be, but they will respect their elders. Let them realise that we are opposed to their quarrels, and are resolved that neither should overstep the mark. For harsh words are our duty, lest our kinsmen should push matters to extremes.

3. Therefore, I have seen fit to despatch X and Y as envoys to your fraternity, with the aim of sending further, and in company with the tribes allied to me, to the king of the Franks, if my son Alaric approves. So, the dispute being carried on between them may be terminated by friendly and reasonable mediation. For it befits such mighty kings not to seek out regrettable quarrels among themselves, with the result of injuring us too, by their own mischances. 4. Therefore, let your fraternity labour, with my assistance, to restore their concord; for no-one will believe that they have gone to war without our wish unless it is very clear that our battle has been rather to prevent a fight. Now I have entrusted to the bearers of this letter some oral messages to be given you, that thus your wisdom may set all in order; by God's help, it usually achieves those things which it studiously reflects on.

[Gundobad eventually supported Clovis in the war.]

III.3 KING THEODERIC TO THE KING OF THE THORINGI;
ALSO TO THE KINGS OF THE HERULI AND WARNI[3]
(date as III.1)

1. The common consensus should take action against pride, as something always hateful to God. For the man who deliberately and wickedly seeks to destroy a famous race is not resolved to deal justly with others. Contempt of truth is the worst of customs. If an arrogant man happens to be victorious in an evil war, he thinks that everything will give way to him.

2. And so do you, who are roused by the consciousness of virtue, and stimulated by reflection on this detestable aggression, send your envoys, along with mine and my brother king Gundobad's, to Luduin [Clovis] the king of the Franks. He must either give thought to justice, hold back from war with the Visigoths, and appeal to international law, or else face the attack of all those whose arbitration he has seen fit to despise. What more can he ask for, when pure justice is offered him? I will declare my feelings openly: he who decides to act without law is resolved to shake the realms of all. 3. But it is better that a dangerous design should be checked at its outset; thus what might have meant war for each of us may be achieved without effort for us all.

For remember the goodwill of Euric in former days [466-84]: how often and with how many gifts he aided you, how often he averted from you wars that neighbouring tribes were threatening. Return the favour to his son [Alaric], although you are aware that it is also for your own benefit. For, if the enemy should inflict some defeat on so great a kingdom, there can be no doubt that he will dare to move against you.

4. Therefore, greeting your excellency in this letter, I have

---

[3] The Heruli and Warni are probably the western branches of those tribes, between the lower Rhine and Elbe.

entrusted a verbal message for you to X and Y, the bearers of this letter. Thus, a common agreement may bind you, who, by God's help, are following my resolve, and you may take this action abroad, lest you should fight in your own territories.

III.4 KING THEODERIC TO LUDUIN [CLOVIS], KING OF THE FRANKS (date as III.1)

1. The holy laws of kinship have purposed to take root among monarchs for this reason: that their tranquil spirit may bring the peace which peoples long for. For this is something sacred, which it is not right to violate by any conflict. For what hostages will ensure good faith, if it cannot be entrusted to the affections? Let rulers be allied by family, so that separate nations may glory in a common policy, and tribal purposes join together, united, as it were, through special channels of concord.

2. In view of all this, I am astonished that your spirit has been so roused by trivial causes that you mean to engage in a most grim conflict with my son, king Alaric, with the result that many who fear you are gladdened by your clash. You are both kings of leading tribes, both in the prime of life. You will shake your kingdoms severely, if you give rivalries their head, and come to blows. Your courage should not become an unforeseen disaster for your country, since the jealousy of kings over light causes is a great matter, and a heavy catastrophe for their peoples. 3. I will say what I feel frankly, and with affection: it is a headstrong character that mobilises forthwith at the first embassy. Claims on your relatives should be made through chosen arbitrators. For, with such men as you decide to make mediators, generosity will be their pleasure. What might you yourself think of me, if you knew I had ignored your dispute? Let there be no war, in which one of you will be defeated and come to grief. Throw down the steel, you who are planning to shame me by fighting. 4. I forcibly prohibit you, with the

authority of a father and a friend.[4] He who sees fit to despise such warnings - not that I expect this - will feel the enmity of myself and my allies.

Therefore, I have decided to send X and Y as envoys to your excellency; and I have also sent my letters, by them, to your brother and my son, king Alaric, that no foreigner's ill-will may in any way sow quarrels between you.[5] Rather, you should remain at peace, and terminate what quarrels there are by the mediation of your friends. 5. I have also sent you an oral message by those envoys, so that the tribes which long flourished peacefully under your forebears may not be ruined by a sudden shock. You should trust one whom you know to rejoice in your advantage, for it is certain that a man who directs another into dangerous courses can be no honest counsellor.

III.6 KING THEODERIC TO THE SENATE OF THE CITY OF ROME (a.510-12)

1. Welcome indeed is my task, fathers of the Senate, when I raise new men to high honours. It is a pleasure to plant those of foreign stock in the lap of Liberty [the Senate], so that the senatorial hall shows the leafage of different virtues. For a multitude of such character adorns the assembly, and a throng of those honoured gives a joyful aspect to the state. But I find it much more gratifying when I return to office those who are born from the actual glory of the Senate, since, in your case, my assessments are easy; bestowing merits with life itself, you pass down virtues that can be assumed in advance. Ancestry itself is already glorious; praise is born with nobility; for you, life and honour have the same beginning. For the fullest honour of the Senate, which others scarcely attain in maturity, you acquire by birth.

2. Although this is my honest opinion of you in general, with the result that senatorial gratitude unites the spirit of your order, it is the

---

[4] Cf. Vergil, *Aeneid* VI.826-35.
[5] Does this allude to Gundobad, or to the emperor Anastasius? Cf. III.1.4.

blood of the Decii that especially dazzles the eyes of my serenity. For
so many successive years, it has shone out with the brightness of
consistent virtue; and, though glory is a rarity, no variation can be
detected in so long a family tree. This noble strain has produced great
men through the ages of its existence; mediocrities can never be born
to it; all its offspring are distinguished, and - a hard achievement - they
are both choice and numerous. See how a fourfold glory springs from
a single seed, an honour to the citizens, a glory to their family, an
increase to the Senate.[6] They blaze out in their common merits, but
you can still find one to praise for his personal qualities.

3. Consider how this young man pleases us by his physical grace,
but still more by the beauty of his mind. His looks recall the glory of
his blood; his face declares the nature of his soul; and by the fair
weather of his body, he dispels clouds from the mind. At the same
time, he has adorned these natural goods with the insignia of learning,
so that, sharpened on the whetstone of the great arts, he may shine the
more in the sanctuary of the intellect. From the books of themen of old
he has learnt of the ancient Decii, a noble race, still living through their
glorious deaths.[7] 4. Certainly, he was lucky in his toil at his studies:
it was his fortune to learn the poetry of the past through his ancestors,
and to educate his young breast from the first in the glory of his
forbears. It is a pleasure to recall how, during a great display, the gaze
of the entire school was turned to him: on hearing the ancestor, they
quickly looked at his heir, hoping to endorse, through the latter's
resemblance, what they had heard the progenitor say. 5. For, as an

---

[6] The four Decian brothers were Albinus, probably Theoderic's first consular nominee
(490), Avienus, Consul in 503, Theodorus, Consul in 505, and Inportunus, Consul in
509. They were the sons of Caecina Decius Maximus Basilius, Odoacer's first consular
nominee (480), and Praetorian Prefect of Italy in 483, and probably nephews of the
Decius of II.32. Albinus and Theodorus were also Praetorian Prefects under Theoderic.
Cf. Moorhead, 1984.

[7] In legend, three generations of Decian generals ritually devoted themselves to death for
victory (340, 295, 279 B.C.); the late Roman Decii claimed descent from them. The
display described below presumably included a recitation of Livy, VIII.9, X.28, or some
other text on the early Decii.

unworthy posterity rejects the praises of its forebears, so a distinguished one confirms the eulogies of its ancestors. We believe in all that we read about the Decii, since a contemporary vein of virtue has taught us the glory of the ancients, and the flame of genius is rekindled in the workshop of a school of rhetoric.

He was educated, indeed, by these examples, but he was reared, with still better results, by domestic discipline. 6. For, on losing the comfort of her husband, his glorious mother took up the burden of rule; neither the heavy care of an estate, nor the guardianship of so many sons could dismay her. She fed and nurtured them; she increased their estates; she adorned them with honours; and for every young man she produced for the family, she gave a Consular to the Senate. My judgement, which investigates morals, has, then, looked into these achievements; it seeks out even the good of domestic virtue, that it may bestow public honours on those praised in private.

7. And therefore, fathers of the Senate, I have conferred on the illustrious and magnificent Inportunus the lofty rank of the Patriciate, that, even as your assembly springs from the chance of birth, so it may be increased by the insignia of office. Show favour to your kinsman, join your votes; yours is the offspring I am honouring. You will assuredly have reason to congratulate yourselves if, from love of your kin, you make my judgement public; and a debt discharged from natural love will be deemed as credited to my commands.

III.7   KING THEODERIC TO THE VENERABLE IANUARIUS, BISHOP OF SALONA (a.507-12)

1. I indeed require that all men should honour justice and comply with it, but especially those who are so elevated by the honours of God's service that, while they are far removed from earthly avarice, they come very close to heavenly grace.

Now John has assailed me with the deplorable charge that your holiness received from him sixty vessels of oil to fill the lamps [of your church], whose price he asks to be duly paid to him. Assuredly, a vow is good, but only if no wrong is mingled with it. 2. For, although justice should be maintained in all dealings, it is especially necessary in those things which are offered to the divine inspection: we should not suppose that, if God accepts fraudulent oblations, He is ignorant of their origins.

And therefore, if you know this petitioner's complaint to be true, give thought to the justice which you proclaim from the sacred law, and have his legal dues paid without delay. Thus, no one shall lament that you, who should instead give aid, have caused him loss. Take heed, then, that you, who never err in great matters, should not now appear - may it never happen - to sin in small ones.

III.8 KING THEODERIC TO THE DISTINGUISHED VENANTIUS, GOVERNOR OF LUCANIA-AND-BRUTTIUM (a.507-12)

1. Justice counsels us to claim from each man what he is evidently charged with, and to demand the public taxes without delay, lest negligence should create a burden for the debtor. For, if indulgence should find its way into official admonitions, contempt will inevitably entangle every payer. And, in a way, compassion gives birth to cruelty, if you are later forced to make exactions from those whom you have failed to admonish. It is, then, a useful task to issue advance warnings, since the opportunity for error is removed, and the place for crime abolished.[8]

2. Now I have learnt by the report of the illustrious Count of the Sacred Largesses that the exaction of the *bini et terni* tax was assigned to you some time ago, in accordance with ancient custom. I therefore advise you by this pronouncement that you should fulfill the allotted time, in accordance with the authority of the instructions to collect

---

[8] Against Mommsen's *emundatur*, Fridh, followed here, retains the MSS' *emendatur*.

[*canonicaria*].[9] Otherwise, any loss the public taxes may suffer, you will be forced to make good from your own property, as you neither held such a command in reverence, nor fulfilled your promise.

III.13 KING THEODERIC TO THE DISTINGUISHED SUNHIUADUS (a.507-12)

1. Your long and laborious services, and the many proofs of your tested faith furnish me with this decision: you who have governed your own soul shall now be placed in charge of other men's morals, and give good order to a province, since, as a private person, you loved self-restraint. For it is he who has studied to conduct himself fittingly that can rule well over others. So, moved by the appeal of the Samnites, I have thought to help them in their troubles by the remedy of commanding your distinction to go out and end their disputes.

2. Now use this opportunity: strive to respond to so favourable a judgement by honourable practices, and show yourself well fitted to my commands, since you formerly pleased me of your own accord. Therefore, within the province of Samnium, terminate according to the laws any case that may arise between Roman and Goths, or Goth and Romans.[10] Those whom I single-mindedly wish to defend, I do not permit to live by separate laws. You will therefore decide for the common good what agrees with justice, since he who thinks on equity alone is no respecter of persons.

---

[9] This tax, the 'twos and threes,' may be fees and collection costs for the basic land tax, to the value of 2½ *solidi*, but more probably it is a name for the *canon vestium* tax from which the army was clothed; see Zimmermann, 222f., Jones, 1964, 468; collection was supervised by the king's *officium*. For an example of a *canonicaria* see XII.16.

[10] Probably since the early empire, cases involving soldiers had been heard in military courts; the Goths had succeeded to the position of Roman soldiers. VII.3 directs the counts commanding Gothic city garrisons to hear cases between Goths and Romans with the help of a Roman adviser; c.f. VIII.28.

III.17 KING THEODERIC TO ALL THE PROVINCIALS OF THE GAULS (c.510)

1. You who have been restored to it after many years should gladly obey Roman custom, for it is gratifying to return to that state from which your ancestors assuredly took their rise. And therefore, as men by God's favour recalled to ancient liberty, clothe yourselves in the morals of the toga, cast off barbarism, throw aside savagery of mind, for it is wrong for you, in my just times, to live by alien ways.

2. Hence, pondering your needs with my innate benevolence, I have decided to send - fortunately, let us hope - the distinguished Gemellus, Vicar of the Prefect, a man of proven loyalty and industry, to settle the province. I trust that he will be incapable of doing any wrong, as he is aware that sinners displease me deeply. 3. Therefore, you have my commands to obey his ordinances, since I believe that his decisions will be to your benefit.

Little by little, you must take on law-abiding habits. A virtuous innovation should not be troublesome. For what can be better than for men to trust in the laws alone, and to have no fear of future chances? The public laws are the surest comforts of human life; they help the weak, and rein in the powerful. 4. Love them, since your security comes, and your good conscience grows from them. For the barbarians live at their own will, where he who can get what pleases him more often finds his own death. Now show yourselves secure in your riches: let ancestral treasures long hidden away be brought to light. For a man is the more noble, the more he gleams both with upright character and with shining wealth. 5. For it is for this reason that I have sent you a Vicar of the Prefecture: that I may be seen to have despatched a rule of civil life along with such an office. Enjoy now what once you only heard of. Realise that human beings are valued less for bodily strength than for wisdom, and that those who can furnish justice to others prosper deservedly.

[Despite these claims for the restoration of Roman law and civilian rule, the province remained under military control. Gemellus was outranked by at least one of Theoderic's Gothic generals (Marabadus, probably Count of Marseilles), with whom he had to

co-operate in legal matters (IV.12, 46). We should not suppose that Gaul had been in a
state of total anarchy under the Visigoths.]

III.18 KING THEODERIC TO THE DISTINGUISHED GEMELLUS
(c.510)

1. Favours are deserved by those who have preferred my clemency,
so that I may prove the rightness of their judgement by their personal
gains. But, if such men should be provided for by official generosity,
how much more fitting is it for them to possess their own? For this is
the plain and common gift of justice.

2. Now the distinguished Magnus, rejecting association with the
enemy, and remembering his birth, has returned to the Roman empire,
his own country. Allegedly, it has happened that his wealth may have
been ruined by his absence. And therefore, I decree by this order that
anything belonging to him in any way, whether in land, or in town
slaves, or in country slaves, which he can prove to be now lost, he is
to recover without delay. By my authority, he is to retain all the rights
of ownership that he had, and is to suffer no challenge over property
long in his possession, since my purpose is to bestow new wealth on
him as well.

[The order conforms to the laws of *postliminium*, which guaranteed their rights and
property to returning captives. Magnus probably belonged to a leading Gallo-Roman
family, and may have been related to bishop Ennodius of Pavia. His rank suggests that
Theoderic had already honoured him; compare Felix, II.1, perhaps also a connection.]

III.20 KING THEODERIC TO THE *SAIO* TRIWILA AND THE
DEPARTMENTAL OFFICER [*APPARITOR*]
FERROCINCTUS (a.507-12)

1. Among those glorious cares of state, which, with God's help, I
revolve in ceaseless thought, the relief of the humble is dear to my
heart, that I may raise up against the power of the proud the barrier of

my devoted love. I, whose principle it is to tread down what is proud, will allow no act of insolence. 2. Now I have been moved by the grievous disaster of Castorius, on whom, up to now, the deadly malice of various men has pressed. It has given an opportunity for a salutary decree, so that the help of my devotion may avail more than the evil cunning of the wicked. And therefore I decree that, if the magnificent Prefect Faustus has burdened the property of Castorius with his titles of ownership, or has seized it by an act of private usurpation, the occupier must quickly be forced by you to return him that estate, along with another of equal value. So I may take thought for one afflicted by cruel losses, and afford him the remedy of my devotion. 3. But should an intermediary be discovered in this audacious deed, who is found to be too poor for these commands, bring him to me bound in chains, so that he whose estate does not suffice for vengeance may satisfy me with his suffering. Thus may the assault of an evil mind now cease in confusion, lest it seem to attack not so much Castorius as my own will. 4. But if, at any subsequent opportunity, that notorious plotter [Faustus] should try to harm the aforementioned Castorius, he is immediately to be smitten with a fine of fifty pounds of gold; and may the agony be worse than torture, to view uninjured the man he had hoped to see in distress.

Behold a deed which will immediately restrain and chasten all men of power: the Praetorian Prefect is forbidden to run wild to the injury of the humble, and he to whom I rise from my seat in honour loses the power to hurt the wretched. Hence, let all appreciate the love of justice that delights me, since it is my will to diminish even the power of my magistrates, that I may increase in the blessings of a good conscience.

III.21 KING THEODERIC TO THE ILLUSTRIOUS FAUSTUS[11] (c.512?)

1. It is the custom of humankind that change should have great power; and, although magnificence may be our usual way of life, everything that satiates breeds distaste. Therefore, constantly dwelling, as you are, within the sacred walls [of Rome], you request that leave of absence should be granted you, for your personal benefit. This is not because so noble a residence irks you, but so that your new return may be the sweeter.

And therefore, my love bestows on your illustrious greatness four months' leave of withdrawal to your province, on condition that you hasten to return to your own house, when they have expired.[12] Thus, the residence of Rome, the most glorious place on earth, which I mean to be crowded with vast throngs, may not grow thinly populated. I judge that this decision is also well suited to you, since a Roman senator will lament it when he is delayed elsewhere. For where will you find that pleasure in your kindred? Where can you look on public buildings of such beauty? It is a kind of sin for those who can have their fixed dwellings in Rome to make it long a stranger to them.

---

[11] This letter has been linked to the fall from office of Faustus Niger (see introduction), but it may be addressed to another great senator, Anicius Acilius Aginantius Faustus, nicknamed Albus. Faustus Niger probably remained in office well into 512; cf. *PLRE* II, s.v. Faustus 9.

[12] Rome (or Constantinople) was a senator's official domicile, and special leave (*commeatus*) was required for absence, at least in theory; cf. IV.48, *Code of Justinian* XII.1.15.

III.23 KING THEODERIC TO THE ILLUSTRIOUS COUNT COLOSSEUS[13] (a.507-12)

1. It is a pleasure to assign control to the proven, since the selector's judgement rejoices over them, while people's property is in safe hands when entrusted to the approved. For, as I choose an acceptable man, so I take care that the acceptable should be outstanding.

2. Set out, therefore, with good omens at your appointment, and girt with the honour of the illustrious belt, to Pannonia Sirmiensis, the former seat of the Goths.[14] Defend the province entrusted to you by arms, order it by the law: thus, knowing that it once happily obeyed my kindred, it may receive its former defenders with joy. 3. You know the upright conduct by which you may commend yourself to me. Your sole means of pleasing is to imitate my actions. Cherish justice; defend innocence by virtue, so that, among the evil customs of the various peoples, you may display the justice of the Goths. They have always maintained a praiseworthy mean, since they have acquired the wisdom of the Romans, and have inherited the uprightness of the tribes. Do away with the accursed customs that have arisen: law-suits should be conducted by words rather than by weapons; to lose a case must not mean death; he who retains another's property should repay the theft, and not his life; civil accusations must not carry off more than war destroys; men should raise their shields against the enemy, not their kindred. 4. And, lest poverty should chance to hurl a man on his death, you must nobly pay a price for such persons: you will receive a rich reward of favour from me if you can establish a civil way of life there, and a reward truly worthy of my governors, if the magistrate suffers

---

[13] Despite his Roman-sounding name, Colosseus was apparently a Goth, probably holding the rank of Provincial Count (cf. VII.1), and governing a tough frontier province with full civil, as well as military powers.

[14] The Ostrogoths were settled in the Pannonian provinces from 456/7 to 473.

loss to give life to a doomed man.[15] Therefore, my customs must be implanted in savage minds, until the violent spirit grows accustomed to a decent way of life.[16]

III.27 KING THEODERIC TO THE DISTINGUISHED JOHN, GOVERNOR OF CAMPANIA (a.507-12)

1. It is the principle of kingly love and duty to cut away opportunity from unjust hatreds, and to check the pride of armed power by reverence for its commands. The offences of a superior are indeed a trouble to the lowly, since he wins praise when he takes vengeance on lesser men. Hence, long tossed about by many persecutions, you have fled with reason to the remedy of my pity, lest private hatred should be glutted on you under the pretext of public discipline, alleging that the most exalted [Praetorian] Prefecture is a terror to you.

2. But I, who wish the offices I bestow to serve justice, not pain, wall you in with my protection [tuitio] against illicit attacks. Thus, with the royal majesty a barrier, the rage of frenzied souls will be shattered on its cliffs, and insolence that is checked and harmless will instead be its own punishment. For a man can be called a judge only so long as he is thought to be just, since a name won by equity cannot be kept by pride.

3. It remains, now, that you should fulfill the office of governor which you have assumed, and devote yourself with industry and loyalty to the public services that your predecessors are known to have performed. The more you enjoy my protection, the more you should hasten to be ruled by self restraint. For, if you rejoice in the knowledge that the Praetorian Prefect has been removed from harming you, who are demonstrably his subordinate, what do you think you will suffer if

---

[15] In III.24, the Romans of Pannonia are reproached for settling law-suits by single-combat; this apparently resulted from the fees due in the governor's court.

[16] Fridh follows the MSS in reading velle vivere; Mommsen, followed here, emends to belle vivere.

you do wrong?[17]

III.28 KING THEODERIC TO THE ILLUSTRIOUS PATRICIAN CASSIODORUS (c.512?)

1. I always welcome the sight of those who have won a place in my heart by glorious deeds, since men who have been tested by me in the practice of virtue have given a perpetual pledge of their love. Therefore, by these commands, I summon your mightiness, tested in my glorious service, to my court: honoured by you, it will increase in obedience to the king, while you yourself will prosper as I behold you. 2. For it is right that you who notably brought distinction to my reign should be sought out. You honoured the palace by your integrity; you bestowed deep peace on the people. This is why your achievement was well known to everyone - because he who placed you in power was ignorant of it. Those summoned to your tribunal, though, looked on their judge without any fear of loss; because you were never sold for a bribe, you were priced more highly by all. Who will not long to see a man whom I have publicly favoured? For I, who have endeavoured to suppress another councillor,[18] have praised you before my palace. Direct your steps here, speed your arrival in haste. He who is confident in the support of his prince should come with eagerness.

III.30 KING THEODERIC TO THE ILLUSTRIOUS ARGOLICUS, PREFECT OF THE CITY OF ROME (a.510-11)

1. Care for the city of Rome keeps perpetual watch over my mind. For, of the proper subjects for my thought, what is worthier than to maintain the repairs of that place which clearly preserves the glory of my state? Hence, your illustrious sublimity must know that I have

---

[17] This Prefect is usually identified with Faustus Niger; cf. III.20.
[18] Perhaps Faustus Niger.

despatched the distinguished John, for the sake of the glorious sewers of the city of Rome, which cause such amazement to beholders that they surpass the wonders of other cities.[19] 2. There you may see rivers enclosed, so to speak, in hollow hills, and flowing through huge plastered tunnels; you may see men sailing the swift waters in the boats prepared - with great care, lest they suffer a seafarer's shipwreck in the headlong torrent. Hence, Rome, we may grasp your outstanding greatness. For what city can dare to rival your towers, when even your foundations have no parallel? And therefore, I order you to give the help of your bureau to the aforementioned John, since I wish those in public office to fulfill my ordinances, removing the hands of those private persons which are so daringly plunged into illegalities.

III.31 KING THEODERIC TO THE SENATE OF THE CITY OF ROME (date as III.30)

1. Although it is my desire to spend unceasing care on the entire commonwealth, although, by God's favour, I strive to restore all things to their original condition, the improvement of the city of Rome still binds me to a special concern; there whatever is spent on adornment is furnished for the joy of all.

Now my sense of duty, which cannot ignore corrupt actions, has been informed, by reports from many men, that hateful misappropriators have taken over a number of things to the damage of the city of Rome, so that the place to which I wish to give the greatest attention is suffering from their unlawful cunning. 2. Hence, I am bringing my ordinances to your notice, since I believe that your city's losses cause you special displeasure. Now, it is said that the water of the aqueducts, which should be protected with the greatest attention, has been diverted to power water-mills and irrigate gardens, through concern for private profit. This practice should hardly be adopted in the

---

[19] Rome's sewers were flushed by the surplus from the water system. Taken with III.31, this letter suggests that John's mission was caused chiefly by a shortage in this supply.

countryside; its occurrence in that city is a lamentable disgrace.[20]

3. And because I may not go beyond legal right in correcting this kind of thing, lest I demolish the towers of the laws while intending to benefit buildings, if the man responsible for this wicked action is supported by the thirty year limitation,[21] he is to receive a proper price and sell his error [back to the city]. Thus, the damage that he does to public buildings shall be carried no further; otherwise, what I now correct with generosity, I shall henceforth avenge with the greatest severity. 4. But if anything of this kind has been attempted in a recent case of misappropriation, it shall be unhesitatingly eliminated. For the general utility must be preferred to the corrupt wishes of an individual; even in just causes it can seldom be opposed.

But, as to the slaves assigned to the service of the aqueducts by the forethought of princes, I have learnt that they have passed into private ownership. Bronze, moreover, - no small weight of it - and soft lead, which is very vulnerable to theft, are reported to have been removed from the adornments of the public buildings, although their inventors dedicated them to the service of the ages. For bronze was discovered by Ionos the king of Thessaly; lead by Midas the ruler of Phrygia. And how lamentable it is that I should incur a reputation for negligence where others won fame for their forethought. Furthermore, temples and public places which, at the request of many, I assigned for repair, have instead been given over to demolition.[22]

5. And, since the correction of evils gives me joy, I have despatched the distinguished John, chosen by my justice, to inquire into those matters which I noted above, lest silence should seem to grant permission. Thus, everything shall be examined in order, and explained

---

[20] Such abuses, like misappropriation of the slaves (below) were as old as the aqueduct system; for legislation and maintenance in late antiquity, see *C.Th.* XV.2, Ward-Perkins, 42, 47f., ch.7.

[21] Cf. I.18.2, II.27.2.

[22] In 458, Majorian legislated against similar problems (*Novel* 4), including the destruction of buildings to give materials for the repair of others; see, in general, Ward-Perkins, ch.3.

to me by the service of a report, so that I may decide after the manner of my justice what should be done about individual objects or their appropriators. Now give your attention, apply your care, so that you may be seen to carry out with readiness an inquiry that you ought to have requested.

III.32 KING THEODERIC TO THE DISTINGUISHED GEMELLUS (a.510-11)

1. Assuredly, I do not forget the services of loyal men, but what they rendered me in hard times, they recover in better fortune. Now, to the men of Arles, who held firm to my side and endured the hardship of a glorious siege, my humanity remits the taxes for the fourth indiction [510-11], in such a way that, at a future time, they shall revert to their usual obligation.[23] Thus, I shall make an evident recompense to the well deserving, while their customary loyalty will not be denied when occasion offers. 2. Let those who preferred to hunger for me in pinching times eat their fill in freedom; let those rejoice who faithfully endured sorrow. He who could barely avoid the last extremity should not be anxious about his taxes; I look for those from men at peace, not men under siege. For what can you demand from the owner of a farm which you know he has not tilled? They have already given me precious revenue from their fidelity. It is unjust that those who have offered the glories of their honour should render up vile money.

---

[23] Arles was besieged by the Franks and Burgundians, probably in 507-8, until relieved by Theoderic's forces.

III.36 KING THEODERIC TO THE ILLUSTRIOUS COUNT ARIGERN[24] (a. 507-9)

1. It is the principle of my loving duty not to deny a hearing to pitiable lamentations, especially since it is my practice to refer everything to the laws, so that the plaintiff may deserve the result, while the defeated party cannot complain that he has been the victim of bias.

Well now, Firminus claims he has a case against the magnificent Patrician Venantius,[25] and his statements of it have frequently been rejected by that person. 2. And, since power is always suspect in law-suits - for the will to harm is supposed because the ability is evident - I command that, with due reverence, the aforementioned individual shall be warned by you to promise, under legal guarantee, to send a briefed person to my court. He may be able to provide an answer to the charges of Firminus before the judges appointed on my initiative. Should he prove to have slandered the magnificent Venantius, that plaintiff will answer for his insolence.

III.39 KING THEODERIC TO THE ILLUSTRIOUS CONSUL FELIX (a.511)

1. Reason and justice persuade me to preserve the traditional custom towards those who serve the public entertainment, especially when the custom is the Consul's. Obviously, he aims to be praised for his liberality; the office should not appear to promise one thing, while the senator intends to do another. Hence, when munificence is expected, it is not right that a miser should be discovered, since the darkness of tight-fistedness casts a shadow on the public fame of a Consul. 2. Therefore, your illustrious mightiness shall know that I have been

---

[24] One of the only two Ostrogoths known to have sat in the Senate, Arigern twice supervised law and order in Rome for several years; cf. **IV.22.4**.

[25] Probably the Decian Basilius Venantius, Consul 508, cousin of Inportunus.

approached by the Milanese charioteers. In your time of office, they have been deprived of those rewards which antique custom had granted them, although that time should make munificence a law. Hence, if their claims are flawed by no dishonesty, your sublimity should conform to the ancient practice, which, by special privilege, demands gifts as if they were debts. You must not withhold what you know has traditionally been bestowed.

III.41 KING THEODERIC TO THE DISTINGUISHED GEMELLUS (c.510)

1. Everything that is ordered with equity becomes bearable, since a burden evenly shared certainly does not weigh down the subjects. For only a very small part affects the individual, although the whole includes everyone.

2. Now the grain which my forethought has sent from Italy for the needs of the army, lest an exhausted province should be damaged by its provision, must be transported from the granaries at Marseilles to the forts sited on the river Durance.[26] 3. I command, therefore, that the task of moving the aforementioned grain is to be borne in common; taken on by all men's energy, it will thus be quickly carried out.

III.44 KING THEODERIC TO ALL THE LANDOWNERS OF ARLES (c.510, winter)

Although the prime task may be to revive injured inhabitants, and to display the sign of pity chiefly towards human beings, nonetheless, my humanity has combined two things: I am taking thought for the citizens with generous assistance, and I am hastening to restore to splendour the ancient monuments. For so it will come about that, while the city's fortune is founded on its citizens, it shall also be displayed by

---

[26] The forts probably guarded the frontier with the Burgundians.

the beauty of its buildings.

Therefore, I have sent a certain quantity of money to repair the walls and aged towers of Arles. I have also had victuals made ready, which are intended to assist your supplies, and are to be sent to you when the sailing season favours. Now lift up your hearts, and, restored through my promise, and keeping the hope of future supplies, have confidence by God's favour; for my words hold as much as any granary.

III.46 KING THEODERIC TO ADEODATUS (a.507-12)

1. The case of a criminal defendant is material for the prince's glory, for there would be no place for pity if opportunities did not arise from wrong-doing. For what could a salutary decree achieve if sound morals were to order all things? A thirsty drought demands the gift of soaking rain. Only when it is sick does the body's condition need the health-giving hands of healers. So, when we are overcome by weakness, it is proper to apply remedies. Therefore, in harsh cases, praiseworthy mitigation should be brought to bear, with due regard to justice, so that I neither permit the vengeance to surpass the sin, nor allow crime to exult, unpunished by the laws.

2. Now, in your petition you have alleged that you were oppressed by the bitter hatred of the distinguished Venantius, governor of Lucania-and-Bruttium. Afflicted by rotting long in prison, you were forced to confess to the rape of the young virgin Valeriana, as it was easier to seek the hope of a quick death than to bear the cruelties of torture. For, in extreme suffering, the prayer of the groaning man is to perish rather than to live, since the hateful feeling of pain excludes the love of sweet life. You also add what justice wholly forbids, that you were deprived of the frequently requested advocacy of legal defenders, although your opponents, distinguished for their talents, were able to tie you in the nooses of the law despite your innocence. 3. While this appeal was entering the mind of my pity with effect, and was gradually bending it towards the claims of mercy, a report arrived, sent from the

governor of Bruttium. In rhetorical style, it crushed this private allegation, by denying that credence should be given to a deceitful appellant against the assurance of the public court.

4. Therefore, I soften the harshness of the penalty with my leniency, decreeing that, from the day this decision is published, you will suffer six months exile, in such a way that no one, after my decision, may charge you with infamy by any construction, since it is right that the prince should wipe away the spots that appear on a tainted reputation. But, when this time has passed, you are to be restored to your native district and all your property, and you are to have all your original legal rights; for I decree that you, whom I mean to detain in temporary exile, are not to groan with the brand of disgrace. At the same time, I threaten a fine of three pounds of gold against anyone who tries to violate my present decision, either by resisting, or by otherwise interpreting it. 5. But, since I do not wish this decree to affect the innocent, lest a man should have no benefit from his own ignorance, by present authority I free from fear those who may have been unconsciously involved, at any time or place, in the same case. For he who does not have a criminal conscience is like a man with an alibi.

[This ruling may have been devised to save Venantius' face; also to protect Adeodatus by removing him from the province while Venantius was still governor. If so, it illustrates the limitations of royal power.]

III.51 KING THEODERIC TO THE PRAETORIAN PREFECT FAUSTUS (a.507-12)

1. The rarer good faith and honest character are among public performers, the more precious is any commendable feeling that may be shown among them. For a man likes to discover something worthy of praise where he had not thought to find it.

Now, some time ago, my judgement bestowed a reasonable salary on Thomas the charioteer, an immigrant from the east, until I should have tested his skill and character. But, since he has become the champion in this contest, and has willingly left his own country, and

chosen to support the seat of my rule, I have decided to confirm him
in the monthly allowance; otherwise, his pay from me would still be
uncertain, although I know that he preferred the realm of Italy. 2. For
he, in his many victories, has 'flitted on the lips' of many, riding more
on popularity than on chariots. He took up a constantly defeated faction
of the people; and those to whom he had himself caused grief, he
strove to make happy again, now overcoming the drivers by skill, now
surpassing them in the speed of his horses. From the frequency of his
triumphs, he was called a sorcerer - and among charioteers, it is seen
as a great honour to attain to such accusations. For, when victory
cannot be attributed to the quality of the horses, it is inevitably ascribed
to magical cheating.

3. Racing is a spectacle that drives out dignified manners: it invites
frivolous quarrels, it drains away honesty, and is a gushing spring of
strife. Antiquity, indeed, held it to be sacred, but a quarrelsome
posterity has made it a scandal. For the first to hold races, it is said,
was Oenomaus, in Elis, a city of Asia.[27] Later, Romulus, when
carrying off the Sabine women, gave Italy the show in a rustic guise,
as no buildings for it had yet been founded.

4. But Augustus, the lord of the world, raised a work equal to his
power, and laid out a construction [the Circus Maximus] in the
Murcian valley that is a marvel even to the Romans. A vast mass,
firmly girded in by hills [the Palatine and Aventine], encloses a space
which contains images of the universe. Hence, they placed twelve gates
for the twelve signs of the zodiac. These are opened suddenly and
together, by ropes let down from small herms, showing that everything,
as men suppose, is done with forethought, there where a carven head
is seen at work.[28] 5. The colours, moreover, are designed as a
fourfold image of the seasons: the Green is dedicated to the fertility of
spring, the Blue to the clouds of winter, the Red to fiery summer, and

---

[27] Oenomaus, legendary king of Elis in the Greek Peloponnese, held lethal chariot races
against his daughter's suitors; Asia may be a mistake for Achaea (Greece), or Apia (the
Peloponnese).

[28] A herm is a four-sided pillar, topped by a head or bust.

the White to the frosts of autumn. Thus, the entire year is indicated, passing, as it were, through the twelve signs. This is done so that the works of nature may be mimicked by the ordered fantasy of the public shows. 6. The two-horse chariot was invented as an imitation of the moon, the four-horse of the sun. The out-riders' horses, on which the circus attendants announce the heats to be run, imitate the speed of the morning star, the sun's fore-runner. Thus it came about that, while they believed they were honouring the stars, they profaned their faith by this absurd representation. 7. Not far from the gates, a white line has been drawn, straight as a ruler, to either parapet: when the four-horse chariots set out, their contest begins from that point, lest, while they try to smash each other in their excessive speed, the people should lose the pleasure of its spectacle.[29] The whole race is run with seven goals, an image of the week's recurring seven days. The goals themselves, like the zodiacal divisions, have three peaks, around which the swift four-horse chariots wheel like the sun. 8. They[30] signify the limits of east and west. The central cisterns [the Euripus] give an image of the glassy sea; hence, marine dolphins there pour in the waters. Moreover, lofty obelisks are raised to the heights of heaven; yes, and the taller is dedicated to the sun, the lower to the moon, while the mysteries of the ancients are marked on them by Chaldaean signs [hieroglyphs], as though by letters. The backbone [spina] of the course represents the fate of unhappy captives, when Roman generals, trampling the backs of their enemies, obtained the joyful reward of their labours.

9. Now the napkin [mappa], which is seen to give the signal for the races, came into use by this chance. When Nero[31] was prolonging his dinner, and the people, greedy for the spectacle, was making its customary demand for haste, he ordered that the napkin he was using to wipe his hands should be thrown from the window, to give

---

[29] Humphrey, 85: a break line 'at which the chariots were allowed to leave their lanes and head for the inside position'.

[30] I have followed Meyer's conjectural emendation of Eoae to eae.

[31] Emperor, 54-68; 'contorniate' medallions, struck for the games in late imperial Rome, sometimes commemorate his public displays and love of racing.

permission for the requested contest. Hence, the practice that the display of the napkin should be seen as a sure promise of races to come.

10. The circus gets its name from a circuit; the races are, so to speak, sword-circlings [*circenses quasi circu-enses*]: this is because, in primitive antiquity, which had not yet transferred its shows to splendid buildings, they were held in green meadows, among swords and streams. Nor is it by chance that the rule of the contest is for a decision in twentyfour heats, as the hours of day and night are assuredly summed up in this number. Nor should it be thought a meaningless device that the circuits of the goals are marked by the taking down[32] of eggs, since that very act, pregnant with many superstitious beliefs, asserts, as an egg does, that it will give birth to something. And therefore, you may understand that the flighty and inconstant behaviour, which men have ascribed to mother birds, is born thence.

11. It would be a long task to describe all the other features of the Roman circus, since they all seem to relate to separate reasons. However, this I declare to be altogether remarkable: the fact that here, more than at other shows, dignity is forgotten, and men's minds are carried away in frenzy. The Green chariot wins: a section of the people laments; the Blue leads, and, in their place,[33] a part of the city is struck with grief. They hurl frantic insults, and achieve nothing; they suffer nothing, but are gravely wounded; and they engage in vain quarrels as if the state of their endangered country were in question. 12. It is right to think that all this was dedicated to a mass superstition, when there is so clear a departure from decent behaviour.

Compelled by pressure from the people, I cherish the institution: such gatherings are what they pray for, while they delight in rejecting serious thoughts. 13. For few men are controlled by reason, and few are pleased by a right purpose. The mob, rather, is led to what was

---

[32] I have followed Mommsen's reading, *ereptionibus*; Fridh has *erectionibus*.

[33] I have followed Fridh in retaining *potius*. Mommsen conjectures *ocius*; Meyer *protinus*; Alan Cameron (1973), supported by Accursius, prefers *potior* - see his 96, n.3, for discussion.

plainly invented for oblivion of its cares. For it supposes that whatever serves its pleasure must also be linked to the happiness of the age. Therefore, let us grant the expenses, and not be forever giving from rational considerations. Sometimes it is useful to play the fool, and so control the joys the people long for.

[Chariot races had close associations with imperial ceremony, and ancient links with solar cult. On circus design and symbolism, see Humphrey, esp. 84-91, 264f., 265ff., 281, 288, 290; on the Circus Maximus in general, ch.3-5; on the circus of Constantinople, Dagron, ch.11. Dudley, 213f., translates a poem on the symbolism (*Anthologia Latina*, no.377, ed. Baehrens). Cassiodorus' contempt for the race-goers' enthusiasm is conventional; his words may owe something to Juvenal, *Satire* XI.197-201, and Ammianus Marcellinus, XXVIII.4.29-31.]

III.52 KING THEODERIC TO THE ILLUSTRIOUS CONSULARIS[34] (a.507-12)

1. As I have learnt from the all too bitter submission of the suppliants, a boundary dispute has arisen between the distinguished gentlemen Leontius and Paschasius, with the result that they have decided to vindicate the bounds of their estates not by the laws, but by force. This amazes me, that something which must be defined by the witness either of boundary stones, mountain ridges, river banks, or of artificial marker ditches and other evident signs, has been so hotly contested in law. 2. What would they do if they held land in regions of Egypt where, when the flood rises, the vast waters of the Nile erode the boundary marks, where mud covers everything and the surface of the ground is made indistinguishable? Hence, they should not resort to weapons, even if the lawsuit set in motion should fail, defeated by lack of reparation. For this matter is carefully sorted out by geometrical figures and the surveyor's art, just as every word is specified by letters.

---

[34] On this letter and surveying in late antiquity, see Dilke, 44ff. Consularis is otherwise unknown.

3. As to geometry, now, it is recorded that the Chaldaeans first discovered it, since they are the most intelligent and painstaking race of men. Building up the general theory of this discipline, they showed that it is useful in both astronomy, music, mechanics, architecture, medicine, and in the art of logic, or in anything that can be defined by general figures; so much so that, without it, nothing in these can attain certainty. 4. Later, the Egyptians, not dissimilar in their burning spirit, transferred geometry to the measurement of land and to restoring the shapes of boundaries, because of the rising of the Nile, which they experience every year in a prayed-for inundation; thus, art made clear what was once exposed to lawsuits and confusion.[35]

5. Therefore, your mightiness is likewise to recruit a highly skilled land-surveyor [*agrimensor*] - his name is derived from his art. Using visible markers, he will make known everything which clear reasoning has separated. For, if, by sure reasoning, that wonderful discipline can achieve the separation of unenclosed land, how much more should it make known everything which must already be enclosed in its own boundaries?

6. For, in the time of Augustus, the Roman world was divided into fields, and registered by census, so that no one should be unsure of the property which he held with the duty of paying tax. 7. Heron, a writer on mensuration, reduced this to a written doctrine, so that the student can learn from his reading what he must fully demonstrate to the naked eye.[36] Those skilled in this art may perceive what public opinion feels about them. For those disciplines that are famed throughout the world do not enjoy such honour: you lecture[37] on arithmetic - the hall is empty; geometry, in so far as[38] it discourses on the heavens, is

---

[35] See Dilke, 19-22.

[36] On Augustan surveys, here linked with provincial censuses, see Dilke, 37ff.; on Heron of Alexandria, who may have written under Nero (54-68), 40, 54, 76-9.

[37] Mommsen reads *indicas*; Traube and Fridh, followed here, with stronger MSS support, *dicas*; see Fridh, 1968, 45f.

[38] Mommsen reads *cum tantum*; Fridh, followed here, *cum tamen*; on the use of *tamen*, and on celestial geometry, see Fridh, 1968, 47-50.

expounded to students only; astronomy and music are learnt for the
sake of knowledge alone. 8. But, when a boundary case arises, it is
entrusted to a land-surveyor, to put an end to shameless quarrels. Of
necessity, he is the judge of his own art; his law-court is abandoned
fields; you might think him a man possessed, as you see him walking
the winding paths. For he seeks his evidence among rough woods and
thickets; he does not walk as all men do; his route and his reading are
one. He points out what he tells you; he proves what he has learnt; his
footsteps clarify the rights of the disputants; and, like a vast river, he
takes land from some, and gives fields to others.[39]

9. Therefore, supported by my authority, choose a man of such skill
that, after his verdict, the parties may blush to continue with their
brazen litigation. Thus, the rights of owners, for whom it is essential
to cultivate their own land, may not be confused.

---

[39] This may echo Lucan, *De Bello Civili* VI.276f.; Lucan (A.D. 39-65) was a favourite
poet of Boethius.

IV.1 KING THEODERIC TO HERMINAFRID, KING OF THE THORINGI (a.506-12)

1. In my desire to add you to my kinship, I unite you, by God's favour, to the beloved pledge of my niece. Thus may you, who are descended from a royal stock, shine forth still more widely in the splendour of the Amal blood. I send you the glory of a court and home, the increase of a kindred, a loyal and comforting counsellor, a most sweet and charming wife. With you, she will lawfully play a ruler's part, and she will discipline your nation with a better way of life. 2. Fortunate Thoringia will possess what Italy has reared, a woman learned in letters, schooled in moral character, glorious not only for her lineage, but equally for her feminine dignity. So, your country will be famous for her character, no less than for its victories.

3. Therefore, greeting you with proper affection, I acknowledge the arrival of your envoys, and the receipt of the destined price - the purchase is, in fact, priceless, but international custom requires it - horses of silver colouring, such as befit a marriage. Their chests and legs properly and handsomely swell out in muscle; their sides are the right breadth; their bellies are short; their heads suggest a stag's, and they imitate the speed of the animal they resemble. These horses are very well fed, and thus gentle, swift from their great size, good to look at, pleasant to ride. For they are soft-paced; they do not tire their riders by foolish prancing; one rests, rather than toils, when riding them; and, being broken in to a pleasant and equable pace, they are trained to a steady and enduring speed.

4. But you are aware that this herd, for all its nobility, is surpassed, like the trained wild animals and the other remarkable gifts that you have sent, since she who adorns the glory of royal power rightly outdoes them all. I too have sent you such gifts as the royal rank requires; but I have made over nothing to equal the union I have formed between you and a woman of such distinction. May divine favour attend your marriage, that, as friendship has allied us, so may family love bind our posterity.

[The bride is Amalaberga, daughter, by an unknown husband, of Theoderic's sister Amalafrida (now married to the Vandal king Trasamund), and sister of Theodahad. With her education, compare Amalasuintha's, XI.1.6. In his *Getica* (21), Jordanes, perhaps using Cassiodorus' *Gothic History*, notes the fine horses of the Thuringi.]

IV.5 KING THEODERIC TO THE LOYAL [*VIR DEVOTUS*] COUNT AMABILIS (c.510)

1. It is well known that my commands advance the good of the loyal; no-one should receive them as a burden. Now, in the region of Gaul, I am aware that there is a dearth of food-stuffs, something to which commerce makes haste in its constant alertness, so that it may sell for a higher price what was bought for a lower. It so happens that my forethought will both satisfy the sellers and rescue those in need. 2. And therefore, by this authority, your loyalty shall know that the shippers [*navicularii*[1]] of Campania, Lucania, and Tuscia must commit themselves to wealthy guarantors, to set out with food-stuffs, for Gaul only, with licence to dispose of them as may be agreed between buyer and seller. 3. It is a great convenience to deal with the needy, since famine gives no heed to anything, in order to make good its wants. For he who sells when solicited seems almost to make a gift, even when he serves his own profit. To go with merchandise to the well supplied means a struggle; but he who can bring food-stuffs to the hungry, prices them at his own judgement.

IV.6 KING THEODERIC TO THE ILLUSTRIOUS PATRICIAN SYMMACHUS (a. 507-12)

1. I who give thought to justice, even without solicitation, gladly welcome the reasonable petitions of suppliants. For what is more proper than for inviolate equity to preserve my state, even as arms

---

[1] Hereditary members of shipping guilds organised for the service of the state.

protect it? (And this I ponder carefully, by day and night).

Now, the distinguished Valerianus, a resident of the city of Syracuse, who has brought his children to the city of Rome for their education, has asked leave to return to his own home. 2. By my command, your illustrious magnificence is to detain those children, and cause them to remain in the before-mentioned city; they are not to leave unless my word is uttered. For thus, they will gain advancement in learning, while respect for my command is preserved. 3. A man should not feel as a burden a gift that he ought to pray for. All should enjoy Rome, that fertile mother of eloquence, that vast temple of every virtue, that city which cannot be called an alien place. This clear fact should be plainly appreciated: he on whom such a residence is conferred is assuredly favoured.

[Bishop Ennodius of Pavia similarly entrusted youthful protégés to leading men and women, including Symmachus, for their education in Rome, and had problems with their discipline; see, e.g., 225, 405, 452 (*Ep.* V.9, VIII.28, *Opusc.*6).]

IV.10 KING THEODERIC TO THE DISTINGUISHED JOHN, GOVERNOR OF CAMPANIA (a. 507-12)

1. It is a vile deed to licence private hatreds among the public laws; nor should the unthinking fury of men's spirits be surrendered to their own wills. Indeed, what pleases the angry is especially prejudicial. The wrathful have no feeling for justice, for, once stirred up, they rage for vengeance, they look for no moderation in their affairs. For this reason, holy reverence for the laws was discovered, so that nothing should be done by violence, nothing at one's own will. For how does the tranquillity of peace differ from the confusion of war, if law-suits are ended by force?

2. Now I have learnt from a complaint of the provincials of Campania and Samnium that many, forgetting the good order of the times, have taken themselves to the practice of distraint. And, as though my edict were forgotten, the wrongful license has increased

among the people.[2] To this, they have added a much more grievous complaint: some are forced to pay the debts of others, and the only plausible justification seems to be some link of neighbourhood between them and the debtor. This is a scandalously mistaken view. Siblings conduct their law-suits separately; a son is free from his father's obligations, if he is not his heir; a wife is not held liable for her husband's debts, unless by the bonds of inheritance; and now unconnected persons are being impudently forced to pay, although the laws may absolve the kindred. So far, my ignorance may have allowed this to happen; now there must be a legal remedy, one that can reach my attention.

3. Therefore, your distinction, understanding the force of my edict, must bring it to the public attention that he who happens to seize by the practice of distraint property which he should claim by legal process, is to lose his case; nor is it lawful for anyone to appropriate a pledge at his own will, unless it happens to be obligated to him.[3] If, indeed, he should choose to distrain on one man instead of another - merely to mention the practice is a crime - he is to make double restitution to the man on whom he used violence; for fines do most to check wrongdoing, and those who have abandoned shame think only of their losses. But he whom the disgraceful patronage of poverty absolves from restitution is to be chastised by the penalty of cudgelling, according to the character of the perpetrated crime. For what I do not permit, I do not allow to go unpunished.

IV.22 KING THEODERIC TO THE ILLUSTRIOUS ARGOLICUS, PREFECT OF THE CITY OF ROME (a.510-11)

1. Unbearable is the transgression that attempts to injure the majesty of heaven; forgetful of piety, it follows a cruel road of error. For what place for pardon can he expect who has spurned the reverend author of

---

[2] Cf. *Edict of Theoderic*, cap. 123; distraint had to be authorised by a judge.

[3] I.e. only property specifically pledged may be taken by the creditor; cf. *Edict*, cap.124.

his being? A ritual that is now profane must depart from the midst of
us; this punishable muttering by men's souls must fall silent. It is not
lawful to practise magic arts in Christian times.
    2. Now, by the official report of your mightiness, I have learnt that
Basilius and Praetextatus, who have long been polluted by the infection
of the sinister art, have been indicted for your examination by the
charge of certain individuals.[4] In this affair, you assert that you look
to my verdict, so that what is commanded by my pious authority may
be strengthened. 3. But I, who am incapable of departing from the
laws, to whom it is natural to maintain a regular justice in all things,
decree by this authority that you shall try this case by legal
examination, together with five senators: namely the magnificent
Patricians Symmachus, Decius, Volusianus and Caelianus, and the
illustrious Maximianus.[5] And, keeping to every legal procedure, ensure
that, if the accusation brought should be proved, it is also punished by
the penalty of the laws themselves, so that hidden and secret culprits,
whom our uncertain knowledge cannot bring before the laws, may be
deterred by this kind of punishment from such sins.
    I have sent instructions about this affair to the illustrious count
Arigern: he is to restrain a violent defence by anyone, and, if the
accused conceal themselves, to bring them to your court. Sitting with
you in this case, he is to allow neither the innocent to be oppressed,
nor criminals to evade the laws.[6]

---

[4] Basilius and Praetextatus were probably of noble blood: the former bears a Decian
name; the latter may well descend from the great pagan senator Vettius Agorius
Praetextatus (d.384).

[5] A court of five senatorial judges (*iudicium quinqevirale*, originally chosen by lot),
presided over by the Urban Prefect (and here a Gothic count) was decreed for senators
on criminal charges in 376, following a notorious hunt for senatorial sorcerers (*C. Th.*
IX.1.13). It was perhaps used to try Boethius on charges of treason and sorcery. See
Matthews, 1975, 56-66, Stein, 71, n.2, 257f., Barnish, 1983, 593f. For Decius, see
II.32.

[6] On Arigern, see note on III.45. The accused had escaped from custody (IV.23).
According to Pope Gregory the Great (*Dialogues*, I.4), Basilius hid in a monastery.
Detected and returned to Rome, he was burnt alive in a popular lynching.

IV.51 KING THEODERIC TO THE PATRICIAN SYMMACHUS
(a.507-12)

1. Since you have taken such care for private building as to create public works of a sort in your own dwelling, it is right that you should be known as he who maintains in its wonders Rome, which you have embellished by the beauty of your houses. You are an outstanding founder, and a great adorner of buildings, since each springs from wisdom - good design, and the tasteful decoration of existing works. 2. For the praise you won by extending Rome into its suburbs is well known: should a man enter those buildings, he does not feel that he looks on them outside the city, save when he notices that he stands among the pleasures of the countryside as well. Of antiquity, you are the most careful imitator; of modern works, the noblest founder. Your buildings proclaim your character, for the devotee of such work must be rich in sensibility.

3. And therefore, I have decided that the fabric of the Theatre [of Pompey], yielding to the pressure of its vast weight, should be strengthened by your counsel. Thus, what your ancestors evidently bestowed for the glory of their country will not seem to decay under their nobler descendants.[7] What can old age not disintegrate, when it has shaken so strong a work? You might think it would be easier for the mountains to fall than to shake that solidity. For that very mass is so entirely formed from vast blocks that, but for the added craftsmanship, it too might be thought the work of nature. 4. I might perhaps have neglected the building, if I had not happened to see it: those arched vaults, with their overhanging stonework and invisible jointing, are so beautifully shaped that you would suppose them the caverns of a lofty mountain, rather than anything made by hands. The ancients made the site equal to so great a population, intending those who held the lordship of the world to enjoy a unique building of

---

[7] Pompey the Great: a Roman general, 106-48 B.C.; his Theatre, completed in 55 B.C., had been extensively restored by the emperor Honorius in A.D. 395/402. Did the Symmachi claim descent from Pompey, or had they previously repaired the Theatre?

entertainment.

5. But because my discourse is clearly with a man of learning, it will be a pleasure to recount why, as we read, uncultivated antiquity originated these monuments. When farmers, on the holidays, celebrated the rites of various deities in groves and villages, the Athenians were the first to raise this rustic beginning into an urban spectacle. To the place where they looked on, they gave the Greek name of theatre, since the gathered throng, separated from the bystanders, could look on with no hindrance.[8] 6. But the back-drop of the theatre was called the *scaena* from the deep shade of the grove where, at the start of spring, the shepherds sang various songs. Musical performances flourished there, and the precepts of a wise age. But it gradually came about that the respectable arts, shunning the company of depraved men, withdrew from that venue out of modesty.

7. Tragedy owes its name to the impressive voice of the actor: fortified by echo-chambers, it produces such a sound that you would hardly think it issued from a human being. Tragedy in fact stands on goats' feet, for any shepherd winning favour by such a voice was rewarded with the gift of a goat.[9] Comedy is named from villages; for a village is called a *comus*, and is where the rustic actors made fun of human doings in merry songs. To these were added the speaking hands of dancers, their fingers that are tongues, their clamorous silence, their silent exposition. The Muse Polymnia is said to have discovered this, showing that humans could declare their meaning even without speech. Now the Muses, in the eastern tongue, are so called as if *Homousae* [beings of the same essence] because, like the virtues, they depend on one another. They are depicted with light and pointed feathers on their foreheads since their perceptions are borne up on swift thought, and contemplate the loftiest matters.

9. Again, there is the pantomime actor, who derives his name from

---

[8] Cf. Isidore, *Etymologiae*, XV.ii.35: 'But the theatre is named from the spectacle, *apo tes theorias*, because, in it, the people, standing above and looking on, watches the stage plays.'

[9] Cassiodorus conventionally derives tragedy from the Greek *tragos* and *aoide*, goat-song.

manifold imitations.[10] When first he comes on stage, lured by applause, bands of musicians, skilled in various instruments, support him. Then the hand of meaning expounds the song to the eyes of melody, and, by a code of gestures, as if by letters, it instructs the spectator's sight; summaries are read in it, and, without writing, it performs what writing has set forth. The same body portrays Hercules and Venus;[11] it displays a woman in a man; it creates a king and a soldier; it renders an old man and a young: you would thus imagine that in one man there were many, differentiated by such a variety of impersonation. 10. The mime, too, which is now merely an object of scorn, was devised with so much care by Philistio, that its performances were set down in writing: a world boiling with consuming cares might thus be cooled by its humour.[12] 11. And what of the ringing of the *acetabula*?[13] Why mention that sweet sound modulated by a range of strokes? It yields such pleasure that, of all the senses, men think their hearing is the highest gift conferred on them.

The succeeding age corrupted the inventions of the ancients by mingling obscenities; their headlong minds drove towards bodily lusts an art devised to give decent pleasure. 12. As with other observances, the Romans uselessly imported these practices to their state, and founded that building - the fruit of lofty thought, and a marvellous greatness of soul. From it, we suppose, Pompey was really called the Great, and not undeservedly.

And therefore, whether such a fabric should be held together by socketed rods, or whether it should be renewed and reconstructed, I

---

[10] Such pantomimists performed solo. Through balletic dancing, changes of mask and costume, and stylised gestures, they gave a sequence of character sketches, usually from mythology. Musicians accompanied them, and singers supplied a narrative.

[11] Hercules (Heracles): a demi-god, the classical Super-Man. Venus (Aphrodite): the goddess of love.

[12] Philistio: a famous writer of mimes (now lost), born A.D.6. According to Ennodius (452.19 [*Opusc*.6]), Symmachus had too much literary taste to be interested in the mime, which was usually a burlesque mixture of drama and other entertainment, often satirical or obscene.

[13] An instrument like the glockenspiel, but with metal cups instead of bars.

have taken care to assign you expenses from my treasury. Thus, you may gain reputation from so excellent a work, while, in my reign, antiquity is fittingly renewed.

V.1 KING THEODERIC TO THE KING OF THE WARNI (a.523-6)

1. Along with sable furs, and slave-boys who shine with the fair colour of barbarians, your fraternity has sent me swords, so sharp that they can cut even through armour, more costly than gold for their steel. Polished splendour glows from them, and reflects in complete clarity the faces of their admirers; their edges converge on the point with such equality that you would think they were cast in the furnace, rather than shaped by files. The centre of the blade is hollowed into a beautiful groove wrinkled with serpentine patterns: there such a variety of shadows plays together that you would suppose the gleaming metal to be a tapestry of various tints. 2. All this your grindstone has diligently sharpened, your shining sand has carefully scoured, to make the steely light into a kind of mirror for men. By nature's generosity, your country is so rich in this sand that it gives you a special reputation in this work. For their beauty the swords might be thought the work of Vulcan, he who fashioned implements of such grace that men believed the work of his hands to be not mortal, but divine.[1]

3. Therefore, paying you the greeting of friendship which I owe, by X and Y our envoys, I acknowledge that I have received your weapons with joy, weapons which have conveyed your concern for the blessings of peace. In consideration for your expenses, I send you an exchange for the gift, which should prove as acceptable to you as yours were welcome to me. May Providence grant concord, that, as we carry on this pleasant intercourse, we may unite the hearts of our peoples, and, as we show concern for one another, we may be linked by mutual obligations.

[On this letter, see Ellis Davidson, 39, 106-9. When he drafted it, Cassiodorus was probably Master of the Offices (VI.6) with a special duty of receiving envoys. The implication of luxury trade by reciprocal exchange between rulers is of interest.]

---

[1] By the method of euhemerism (much used by Christians), the smith-god, Vulcan, is here represented as a deified human. The sand may be *kieselguhr*, found on the Lüneburg Heath; this helps to locate the Warni.

V.4 KING THEODERIC TO THE SENATE OF THE CITY OF ROME (a.524, Sept.1st)

1. It is certain, fathers of the Senate, that your council flourishes with men of wisdom, but the presence amongst you of literary distinction is clearly also an outstanding feature. For I judge all those whom I promote to the high rank of Quaestor to be men of the greatest learning, as befits the interpreters of the laws and sharers of my counsels. The office is not to be achieved by riches, nor by birth alone; but only education joined with wisdom can claim it. For, while in the case of other honours I confer benefits, from this I always receive them. Not surprisingly, it has a happy portion in my cares; it enters the doorway of my meditations; it is acquainted with the breast in which the cares of state are pondered.

2. Consider how the sharer in such secrets should be esteemed. Legal skill is demanded from him; in him the prayers of petitioners meet; and, what is more precious than any treasure, the fame of my good order [*civilitas*] rests in his hands. With an upright Quaestor, the character of the innocent is safe; only the plans of scoundrels are made anxious; and, when the wicked cannot hope for secret thefts, devotion to sound morals is advanced. 3. The Quaestor guards his rights for every man. In money matters he is self-restrained, but lavish in justice, unable to deceive, and ever ready to assist. He serves the mind of the prince, a fact which surpasses all else - the man without an equal must speak through his mouth. He who, under my authority, can render this office free from corruption, and a home for virtue, must surely deserve to be your colleague. For you know the stock from which he so proudly comes.

4. Hence you remember Decoratus, toiling as a barrister, and the integrity with which he allied himself to every worthy man. He was a faithful advocate in your cases. Insisting on essentials, he brought the spirit of a judge to the lawyers' bench. His triumphs were frequent and deserved, since he examined with intelligence the material to be brought forward. For those who first correct themselves, acting as their own judge, will never suffer shame. Inferior in rank, he made himself

a patron to former Consuls; and, although he was not your equal in
honours, it is told that a Patrician was his client in a famous case. 5.
It is all too rare a thing, fathers of the Senate, to speak firmly, and not
to stammer when you have much to say. Decoratus most certainly had
this ability, and you have proved it before my judgement seat. For, in
his day, what man struggling to pass through the reefs of law-suits,
could afford to ignore him as a pilot for his case? He who did not seek
his help soon had small use for the law.

I am not now bewailing his untimely end: from this man's fertile
stem a sibling has sprouted. For, when the brother who formerly
overshadowed him was removed by nature, he spread the leafage of his
own fame through the wide air. 6. He who grew up as the leader by
birth ripened soon and duly, and yielded a harvest from his seed; but
that noble stock has saved in the successor the fruit which it lost in his
predecessor. This family is like that precious branch which, in Vergil's
poem, is always springing; for when this 'is torn away, another golden
bough replaces it, and the shoot bears leaves of the same metal'
[*Aeneid* VI,143f.]. Assuredly, this man too has nurtured eloquence by
advocacy. Yielding to his brother a reputation in Rome, he preferred
to take part in the affairs of Spoleto: a hard task, the more so as it was
severed from your wisdom. For it was a very easy achievement to
assert the cause of justice among men of high character, but very
difficult when provincials were behaving with erratic freedom. 7. It
seems that he urged the restraints of law, where even the very judges
are often carried away by wicked avarice; the more they seem to
themselves great men among little, the less they brook opposition to
their will. In such conditions, it is difficult to champion the laws, and
the force of much persuasion is needed to recall a venal judge to the
right path.

Adopt my assessment, then, fathers of the Senate, and be glad to
take Honoratus to your bosom, on his promotion to the high office of
Quaestor. For he who has deservedly been found equal to such an
honour is worthy of your love.

[Boethius despised Decoratus, and refused to hold office with him; probably, Honoratus
was later discharged from the Quaestorship in disgrace (VIII.13.3, *C.Phil.* III, prose iv)!

The epitaph of a Decoratus from Spoleto celebrates his noble birth, justice, hospitality,
and charitable generosity.]

V.29 KING THEODERIC TO THE ILLUSTRIOUS NEUDIS
(a.523-6)

1. The petition Anduit poured out has indeed moved me; but the
lost glory of his eyesight renders the man still more pitiable, since a
calamity that we see must affect us more than one that we hear of. For
he who lives in perpetual night has hastened to gain my assistance with
the help of borrowed eyesight, that he might at least taste the sweet
clemency of one whom he could not see. For he cries out that the
condition of slavery, unknown to his family, has been imposed on him
by Gudila and Oppa, although he long followed my army in freedom.
2. I am amazed that such a man should be dragged into servitude, one
who should have been discarded by a genuine master. It is a strange
kind of malpractice to pursue a man you might shudder at, and to call
a slave one whom, with God in mind, you ought to serve. Now he adds
that false charges of this kind were removed from him by the enquiry
of Count Pitzias, a man of high repute.[2] But now, bowed down by the
weight of his infirmity, he cannot defend his freedom with his right
arm, which is the proven help and patron of the brave.

3. But I, whose special task it is to preserve an impartial justice
between equals and unequals, decree by this command that, if he has
proved himself free in the court of the afore-mentioned late Pitzias, you
are immediately to make his slanderers withdraw. Nor may those who
should have condemned their own intentions, when they were first
defeated in law, dare to harass him any further with compulsions
foreign to his status.

[Migrant barbarian tribes tended to attract recruits from the Roman lower classes; this
may explain the challenge to Anduit's free status, a status partly dependent on his service

---

[2] Pitzias commanded a Gothic army against the Gepids and Byzantines in the Balkans in
504-5; presumably, Neudis is likewise a Gothic general.

as a Gothic warrior; cf. Wolfram, 300ff.]

V.40 KING THEODERIC TO CYPRIAN, COUNT OF THE SACRED LARGESSES (a.524, Sept.1st)

1. I rejoice that I often bestow benefits beyond the petitioners' desires, that sometimes - a most difficult feat - I surpass the prayers of human ambition; but the deeds I more gladly embrace are those where I glory in acting with good cause. Long, indeed, must he be weighed, to whom the scales are entrusted;[3] and he who deserves the prince's love must be of such character as the law itself decrees. Precious stones are prized when set in the gleam of gold, and take on the grace of beauty, since they are defiled by no ignoble contact. 2. So, good deserts, allied to high honours, are assisted by mutual glory, and the appearance of a single object gains in beauty from the loveliness that is joined with it.

Now in your case, I have not trusted to purchased praise, or gossiping fame - you have often satisfied my scrutiny. For you stated the confused wranglings of appellants in most clear and analytical reports; those who could not express their own grievances won their suits when commended by your pleading; and, lest any wrongful partiality should be suspected, you reported the requests of petitioners in their own presence.[4] 3. The requests of disputants met in your mouth, and you satisfied either party, winning impartial praise - the hardest kind of favour, and an achievement which has put even orators in the shade. For their task is to declare the wishes of one party after long thought; you always had to state either side of a case suddenly brought to you. There is also the most honourable burden of the royal presence, under which you served so well that what men can hardly

---

[3] This probably refers to the responsibility of the Count of the Sacred Largesses for the coinage.

[4] This refers to Cyprian's duties as Referendary (VIII.21.4, *Anonymus Valesianus* 85); V.41 makes his presentation of cases seem less formal!

obtain from their judges by elaborate rhetoric, you procured from the
king by simple statements. 4. No wonder my serenity's verdict was
furnished for the public good, since it endured no delay in hearing the
case. For a suit stated by you was soon understood. And why should
the end of the case be delayed when you were concluding your report
with brevity and clarity? You, I trust, have learnt to judge by serving
my justice: thus, in the most effective kind of training, you have been
taught by action, rather than by reading. 5. Schooled, therefore, in
such practice, you took on the duty of an embassy to the east
[Constantinople], and were despatched to men truly of the highest
expertise. In their company, though, you were troubled by no
nervousness, since, after my presence, nothing could amaze you. Since
you are trained in three languages, Greece found nothing new to show
you; nor did she surpass you in the cunning in which she excels.[5]

6. To your merits is added a loyalty more precious than all praise,
which God loves and mortals revere. For, among the gusty storms of
the world, how will human frailty control itself, if a steadfast mind
does not attend our actions? This preserves friendship among partners;
it serves rulers with simple integrity; to the majesty of heaven it pays
the reverence of pious trust; and, should you look more widely for the
blessing that belongs to such a virtue, all that lives well is unchangeable
in loyalty.

7. Take up then, with God's favour, the honour of the Sacred
Largesses, for the third indiction [524-5]. Conduct yourself as befits
your birth. So far, you have deserved my gift of high honours; now act
so that I may likewise confer on you still higher favours.

---

[5] The three languages are Latin, Greek, and Gothic; VIII.21.6f. tells us that Cyprian's
children were brought up in the royal palace to speak Gothic and practise barbarian
weapon-skills. Some argue that Cassiodorus' Greek was poor; and, although he used
Gothic tales in his *History*, it is doubtful if he knew Gothic. Cyprian's embassy cannot
be dated; it may be connected with the charge of treason which he brought against
Albinus, and subsequently Boethius.

V.41 KING THEODERIC TO THE SENATE OF THE CITY OF ROME (date as V.40)

1. Although princely generosity has often brought your candidates to birth, and my kindness is as fertile as nature for you, you now assuredly have a man whom it befits me to choose and you to receive. As the promotion I gave him was fortunate, so his union with your assembly by the law of honours will be glorious. In this, though, the Senate is the luckier: even a raw recruit may serve me, but it receives only a man already found worthy of honour. 2. Rightly, then, is your order judged to be outstanding, composed, as it always is, of tried men. For its portals are not opened to the vulgar: only such men are allowed to enter as are likewise seen to leave it.

Receive, then, a colleague whom my palace has long tried and tested. He has served the royal utterances with such confidence that many times he expounded my commands as I watched and praised. 3. You certainly know what I am speaking of. For which of you was excluded from Cyprian's service? For the man who sought his help soon received my favours. He often obtained during my horse rides what used to be transacted in the solemn councils [*consistoria*] of former days. For, when I wished to relieve a mind exhausted with cares of state, I would turn to horse exercise, that the body's strength and energy might be refreshed by the very change of activity. Then, this agreeable reporter would present many cases to me, and his statement was welcome to the judge's wearied mind. Thus, while this kindly artist in doing favours was presenting his cases, a mind inflamed with greed of beneficence was refreshed. 4. The candidate, then, held to his allegiance, and so served my spirit that no resentment of mine gave him trouble. I was often enraged with unjust cases, but the reporter's tongue could give no offence; sometimes I condemned the business, while pleased by its advocate; and, strong in the favour he possessed, he many times withstood the onset of my anger.

5. He is glorious, moreover, for no upstart family. For, as you remember, his father was Opilio, a man picked out for palatine service even in a degraded reign [Odoacer's]. He could have grown much

greater had not his loyalty lain fallow in the barren season of a parsimonious giver of rewards. For what could an impoverished benefactor confer? But, if he did not enrich him, he distinguished him, since, when the state is poor, to earn even the lesser gifts means a wealth of high praise. 6. This man has surpassed his forebears by the good fortune of the age he lives in; and the fact that his elevation was higher must be credited to my reign. Indeed, the difference between the rulers measures the promotion of their subjects.[6]

Therefore, fathers of the Senate, I have exalted to the height of the Sacred Largesses Cyprian, shining out with his own merits and the splendour of his family. Thus, your number may be increased, while the devotion of my servants is stimulated. Consider, reverend fathers, my feeling for your order, when I commend with many intercessions those whom I have decided to add to your number.

V.42   KING THEODERIC TO THE ILLUSTRIOUS CONSUL MAXIMUS[7] (a.523)

1. If those who wrestle with oiled and supple limbs call forth the consular munificence, if organ players are rewarded in return for their performance, if the song we delight in wins its fee, what gift should be spent on the huntsman who strives by his death to please the spectators? His blood gives them joy; trapped by an unhappy destiny, he hastens to please a people who hope that he will not escape. A hateful performance, a wretched struggle, to fight with wild beasts which he knows that he will find the stronger. His only confidence lies in his tricks, his one hope in deception. 2. If he fails to escape the beasts,

---

[6] Apparently, Cyprian's father Opilio never reached the rank here given to his son; he therefore cannot be identified (as is usual) with a Count of the Sacred Largesses under Odoacer, who fathered two more holders of that office under Theoderic and Athalaric, one called Opilio (VIII.16-17). The latter Opilio probably shared in the denunciation of Boethius.

[7] On Maximus, see note to X.11.

sometimes he may not find a tomb: while a man is still living, his body perishes, and, before he becomes a corpse, he is savagely devoured. Once caught, he is a tit-bit for his enemy, and, alas, he gluts the animal he longs to kill.

Such a show, ennobled by its building, but most base in its performance, was invented in honour of the goddess Scythian Diana, who rejoiced in the spilling of blood. 3. O the error, the wretched deceit, to desire to worship her who was placated by human death! The prayers of countrymen, made in woods and groves, and dedicated to hunting, first, and by a lying fantasy, formed this three-fold goddess: they asserted that she was the Moon in heaven, the Mistress [Diana] in the woods, Proserpine among the shades. But perhaps it was only as the potentate of Hell[8] that they thought of her without a lie, when, deceived by such falsehood, they and their errors passed living into deep darkness. 4. This cruel game, this bloody pleasure, this - so to speak - human bestiality was first introduced into their civic cult by the Athenians. Divine justice allowed it, so that the invention of a false religion's vanity might be degraded by a public show. 5. The building [the Colosseum] was conceived by the power of imperial Titus, spending a river of gold, to display the chief of cities.[9] And since a viewing place is called in Greek a theatre, which is a hemisphere, when two are, as it were, joined into one, it must rightly be termed an amphitheatre. Its arena is shaped like an egg: thus there is a fit space for runners, and the spectators may see the more easily, since its vast circle has gathered them all in.

---

[8] Cassiodorus here echoes Vergil, *Aeneid* VI.247, less conspicuously than later (11). 1-4 also owe much to the Christian poet Prudentius's *Against Symmachus*, I.351-401, written c.395.

[9] The text is very uncertain: a lacuna is possible, but I have adopted Mommsen's suggestion of *patuisset* for *potuisset*. Titus was emperor, 79-81, and completed the Colosseum; inscriptions from its reserved seats record many late fifth century senators.

6. They go, then, to sights which humanity should shun.[10] The first hunter, trusting to a brittle pole, runs on the mouths of the beasts, and seems, in the eagerness of his charge, to desire the death he hopes to avoid. They rush together with equal speed, predator and prey; he can win safety only by encountering the one he hopes to escape. Then the man's bent limbs are tossed into the air like flimsy cloths by a lofty spring of his body; a kind of embodied bow is suspended above the beast; and, as it delays its descent, the wild beast's charge passes beneath it. 7. In the following way, an animal which is duped may seem less savage: one man trusts in angled screens, fitted in a rotating four-part apparatus. He escapes by not retreating; he retreats by keeping close; he pursues his pursuer, bringing himself close up with his knees, to escape the mouths of the bears.[11] Draped on his stomach over a slender spar, a second lures on the deadly beast, and can find no way of surviving without peril. 8. Another shuts himself up against the fiercest animal in a portable wall of canes, like the hedgehog, which suddenly sheltering in its own back, hides by gathering itself together; and, though it runs nowhere, its body is nowhere to be seen. For as the one is rolled into a ball and defended by its natural spines when an enemy comes, so the other, enclosed in wattle-work stitched together, is made the stronger by frail canes. 9. Others, from an arrangement, so to speak, of three little gates, dare to arouse the wrath prepared for them. On the open arena, they hide behind latticed doors, now showing their faces, now their backs, so that it is a wonder they can escape, as you watch them dodging among the teeth and claws of the lions. 10. One man is delivered to the beasts on a rolling wheel; another is lifted up on it, so that he is snatched from danger. So this device, formed on the model of the faithless world, feeds some with

---

[10] The following feats and contraptions are mostly depicted on ivory consular diptychs of the early 5th to early 6th centuries; see Volbach, photographs 8-11, 17, 21, 59. These carvings and Cassiodorus' text do much to explain each other; his lively vignette of the pole-vaulter may, indeed, have been influenced by them.

[11] A four-leaved screen of bars revolved around its central pole. The man, in the angle between two leaves, rotated the screen with arms and knees, following the beast round as it tried to get at him.

hope, tortures others with fear, but smiles on all in turn, that it may deceive them. 11. To wander in speech among so many perils and chances is a long journey. But I should fittingly add what the Mantuan said of the shades below: 'who could describe all the types of crime, or run through all the names of torments?' [Vergil, *Aeneid* VI.625f.]

But to you, whose duty it is to show such sights to the people, I give this command: open your hand, pour out the rewards, that you may give the wretches an answer to their prayers. If not, it is an act of extreme extortion to withhold the ritual gifts, while commanding hateful deaths. 12. And so, whatever, by ancient generosity, has become a long-standing custom, you are to bestow on the petitioner without delay. For there is the guilt of manslaughter in being tight-fisted to those whom your games have lured into death. Alas for the grievous error of the world! If there were any perception of the right, as much wealth ought to be given for the lives of mortal men as is now poured out on human deaths.

[Theoderic's apparent disapproval of these hunting shows (*venationes*) was typical of the later emperors, and generally of educated men in the ancient world. (Cf. III.51, on racing.) In 498, Anastasius banned them, at least partly on humanitarian grounds, but consular diptychs make it clear that the prohibition did not last. However, the displays died out during the sixth century in both east and west. Cf. Alan Cameron, 1973, 228ff., 242; Ward-Perkins, 111-16.]

VI.3 FORMULA OF APPOINTMENT TO THE PRAETORIAN PREFECTURE

1. If the origin of any post of honour deserves praise, if a good beginning can give glory to what comes after, the Praetorian Prefecture may take pride in a founder who was clearly both of highest wisdom before the world, and most acceptable before God. For when Pharaoh king of Egypt was warned by unprecedented dreams of the peril of future famine, and human counsel could not explain such a vision, the blessed Joseph was discovered, who could both truthfully predict the future, and providently rescue an endangered people.[1] 2. He first consecrated the insignia of this dignity; he mounted the official carriage as an object of reverence; he was raised to this peak of glory that his wisdom might bestow on the populace what the power of their ruler could not provide. For even now the Prefect is hailed as Father of the Realm on the model of that patriarch; even today the herald's voice is sounding Joseph's name, advising the magistrate to resemble him - it is right that he to whom such power has been entrusted should be constantly and delicately admonished.

3. For this dignity and my own [the monarch's] position have certain rights in common. For it summons men living at a distance to its court without legal limitation; it imposes large fines on wrong-doers; it distributes public moneys at will; it bestows travel warrants with like power; it confiscates unclaimed property; it punishes the misdeeds of provincial governors; it pronounces judgement by word of mouth. What is not entrusted to the Prefect, when his very speech is a verdict? He can almost establish laws, since the awe he inspires can settle cases without appeal. 4. On his entry to the palace, he is adored, as I am, by large numbers; and so high an office permits a practice that would mean a treason charge for others. Hence, no office equals his power. In every case, he may judge as a substitute for the ruler. No servant of the state is legally privileged against the authority of his court, save officials of the commander-in-chief. (I suppose that the ancients

---

[1] See Genesis, xli.

conceded something to those who waged war for the commonwealth.)
He may also flog the town-councillors, whom the laws call 'a lesser
Senate'.

5. Among his staff, he holds special rights, and issues commands
to men of such standing that even provincial governors dare not defy
them in anything. His staff is evidently esteemed, effective, well
instructed, of strong and resolute character; they so carry out their
orders that commands will suffer no delays. To those who have
completed their service, the Prefect grants the rank of
Tribune-and-Secretary, and makes his officers the equals of those who
mingle with the leading courtiers, and are subject to my gaze.

6. I confirm his decisions with pleasure; reverence for him so
constrains me too that I readily carry out what I know that he has
decreed. Deservedly so, since he supports the palace with his supplies,
procures rations for our servants, furnishes victuals to the magistrates
as well, and, by his ordinances, satisfies the gluttony of tribal envoys.
And, although other offices have demarcated duties, his handles almost
everything that is dealt with under my just and moderate rule.

7. To conclude, I place on your shoulders from this indiction, as is
fitting, this fairest weight of every kind of care, an action that should
prove beneficial to me and useful to the state. May you bear the burden
by your virtuous character, and strive to act with all loyalty. The more
this office is fettered by many anxieties, the more it triumphs, winning
the highest praise. And therefore, may such a light of glory rest on
your actions that it both shines in my palace, and gleams in the remote
provinces. May your prudence equal your power; may the four virtues
wait on your conscience.[2] Know that your tribunal is built so high that,
when seated there, you will think no mean and despicable thoughts.
Take heed to what you should say, since so many will receive it. 9.
The public archives should record what no reader will blush at. A
worthy magistrate has no part in crime; unless he is constantly engaged
in noble works, he is blamed even for his idleness. For, if we recall
that aforementioned and most holy founder, to discharge with fitness

---

[2] Cf. Cassiodorus, *De Anima* vii, lines 1-15.

the office of Praetorian Prefect is a kind of priesthood.

VI.5 FORMULA OF APPOINTMENT TO THE QUAESTORSHIP

1. If honours gain in distinction the more they enjoy my gaze, if the ruler's frequent presence shows his affection, so no magistrate can be more glorious than he who is admitted to a share in my counsels. For to others I entrust the procurement of the public revenues, to others the hearing of law-suits, to others the rights of my estates. The Quaestorship I value as the words of my tongue, and take it whole-heartedly to myself. 2. Of necessity, this office is linked intimately to my thoughts, that it may speak in its own words what it knows as my sentiments; it discards its own will and judgement, and so absorbs the purpose of my mind that you would think its discourse really came from me. How hard it is for the subject to assume the speech of the ruler, to be able to express what may be supposed my own, and, advanced to public honour, to create a noble lie. 3. Think of the honour and responsibility you have in equal measure. If I am in any doubt, I ask the Quaestor, who is a treasury of public reputation, a store-room of the laws, ever ready for the unexpected; and, as Tully [Cicero], the master of eloquence puts it, nothing 'seems more remarkable than the ability, by speech, to hold men's minds, to attract their inclinations, to drive them whither, or to lead them whence he wills' [*De Oratore* I.30]. For, if it is the proper part of the orator to speak with gravity and style that he may move the minds of the judges, how much more eloquent must he be who is known to admonish the people with their prince's mouth that they should love the right, hate the wrong, praise good men without ceasing, and zealously denounce the evil. So, punishment may be given a holiday where the power of eloquence prevails. He must imitate the ancients with intelligence; he must correct the morals of others, and preserve his own with due integrity.

4. Finally, the Quaestor must be such a man as it befits to bear the image of a prince. For if, as is often the case, I should chance to hear

a case from documents, how great will be the authority of that tongue
which can prime the royal wits under the public eye? Legal skill and
cautious speech must accompany him, so that no one shall criticise
what the prince may happen to decide. Moreover, he will need a
resolute spirit, so that no bribes and no threats may carry him from the
path of justice. 5. For, in the preservation of equity, I, who should still
be obeyed, suffer myself to be contradicted.[3] But take heed to bring
forward such legal learning that you may expound all things fitly on
request. Other offices, indeed, may seek the help of legal assessors, but
yours gives its counsels to the prince.

And therefore, prompted by the fame of your wisdom and
eloquence, for this indiction, I allot you, by God's favour, the
Quaestorship, the glory of letters, the temple of social order [*civilitas*],
the begetter of every honour, the home of self-restraint, and seat of all
virtues; so act that you strive to be equal to the duties just described.
6. For to you, the provinces transmit their petitions; from you, the
Senate seeks the aid of the laws; from you experts request the justice
they have learnt; and you must satisfy all those who may demand legal
help from me. But, while doing all this, you must be carried away by
no pride, gnawed by no grudge, never pleased by the misfortunes of
others, since what is hateful to the prince cannot be right for the
Quaestor. Wield a prince's power with a subject's rank. Ennobled as
my mouth-piece, so speak that you may still think yourself due to
render account before my judgement seat, where a man will either be
condemned and receive his reward, or be praised and gain the glory of
his upright ways.

---

[3] *et nobis patimur contradici, cui etiam oportet oboediri*: Fridh supposes a lacuna after
etiam, and suggests *prava iubenti*. For a Quaestor contradicting his threatening emperor,
see Ammianus Marcellinus, XXVIII.1.25.

VI.6 FORMULA OF APPOINTMENT TO THE RANK OF MASTER [OF THE OFFICES]

1. Whoever receives the name of Master takes up an honour to be held in reverence; for this title is always derived from its bearer's expertise, and we know from the name what we should believe of his character. Naturally, the discipline of the palace belongs to him: he lulls the stormy character of insolent guardsmen with the calming breeze of his moderation.[4] He harmonises so many ranks without the smallest confusion, and sustains in his own person the common burden, which most men see as divided. Thus, he fulfills the authority of his title, and honours the government by his actions.

2. Through him, senators on arrival are presented to my sight: he prompts the nervous, he controls the talkative; in fact, he usually inserts his ôwn remarks, so that I hear everything in proper form. His promise of a royal audience can be trusted; he wins glory in bestowing my conversation; he is, as it were, the morning star of the court. For, just as it promises the coming of day, so he confers the countenance of my serenity on those who long for it. Moreover, with complete security I place in the bosom of his attention a vast weight of legal cases, so that I may be relieved by his loyal efforts, and devote the greater energy to public affairs.

3. But he also guards with diligent severity the serviceable swiftness of the post-horses, which are kept always at the gallop: thus, with the help of speed, he advances my labours which he aids by his counsel. 4. Through him, foreign tribesmen are given hospitality to the glory of my state; and those who were sorrowing when he received them depart with reluctance. Through him, indeed, I am forewarned of the arrival of envoys, even when they are in haste; through him travel warrants are sent out in my name, and to this man so vital a matter is chiefly

---

[4] The theory (see introduction) that the guards (*domestici*) had been pensioned off is based on (a) Procopius, *Anecdota* xxvi.27f.; (b) the appearance in the *Variae* of the *comitiva domesticorum* as a sinecure (cf. II.16.2). But Procopius refers only to guards stationed at Rome; I.10 seems to imply that the *domestici* served for their pay.

entrusted.

5. Antiquity, moreover, weighing up his labours, has conferred on him a very great power, that no provincial governor should take up authority unless he has decreed it. It has subordinated the judgements of others to his opinion, so that the appointment bestowed by another is referred to him. He does not have, though, the trouble of tax collection, but he enjoys the blessing of the power he has obtained in wide fields - in order, I suppose, that a rank created to help the prince should pluck its flowers from different official prerogatives. 6. At his own judgement, he also appoints the assessors of food prices in the royal city [Ravenna], and creates a magistrate for business of such necessity. For he brings joy to the people and credit to my rule when he sets over the public supplies men of such calibre that the grumbling populace is well fed, and raises no riots.

7. His staff, furthermore, is dignified with such a privilege of rank that he who has completed the duties of his service is honoured with the title of *princeps*, and those who gave you their humble obedience astonishingly take the chief place among the personnel of the Urban and Praetorian Prefectures. Thus, a sort of injustice is done with legal sanction in the favour shown to this great office, since the man who has served elsewhere is placed over the duties of others. 8. The Master's chief assistant [*adiutor*] is also admitted to my presence, so that, by a kind of substituted kindness, I may distinguish the supporter of the man who gives me such faithful help.

So, for the nth indiction, with fitting gravity, I entrust to your control this office, distinguished by so many prerogatives, and so rich in insignia; thus you may be seen to act the Master in all you come to do. For if, which God forbid, such wisdom as yours should sin, there is no help left for human nature.

VII.42 FORMULA FOR AN EDICT ADDRESSED TO THE QUAESTOR, DIRECTING THE MAN WHO HAS BEEN GRANTED A *SAIO* TO PROVIDE A GUARANTEE

1. I have learnt that the *saiones*, whom I have decided to allot in all good will, have often been involved in serious disputes. My generosity - the grief of it! - has been corrupted; and, when the malice of petitioners has transferred them to uses other than those for which my remedies assigned them, disaster has instead arisen from this medicine. Hence, I must check pestilent intentions with a health-giving remedy, lest, while my care and devotion draw me to acts of justice and beneficence, I should submit to the most inequitable intrigues.

2. And therefore, by a proclaimed edict I lay down this: anyone who wishes, from compelling necessity, and against violent attacks, to obtain a *saio* must pledge himself to my bureau [*officium*] with the penal bond of a guarantee. If the *saio* he has obtained should transgress my instructions by his punishable instigation, he himself is to pay so many pounds of gold as penalty, and must promise to repay any loss his opponent may suffer, whether as fee [to the *saio*] or travel expenses. 3. For, when I wish to suppress lawless spirits, I should not be a burden to the innocent. But the *saio* who, of his own will has transgressed the measure of my instructions, must know that he will be deprived of his donative, and - something more serious than any loss - may incur peril from my disfavour. Nor will anything further be entrusted to the man who has emerged as the violator of my command, whose executor he should have been.

VIII.1 KING ATHALARIC TO THE EMPEROR JUSTIN
(a.526, after Aug.30th)

1. I would be justly blamed, most benevolent of princes, if I were to ask in a lukewarm way for your peace, which my forebears, as is known, demanded with so burning a desire. In what respect would I be a worthy heir, if I were found to be unequal to my predecessors in so glorious a concern? The purple-clad rank of my ancestors has done less to distinguish me, the royal throne to exalt me, than the far-reaching power[1] of your favour to ennoble me. For, if I know that I possess it completely, then I am confident that all is well in my realm.
2. But, as it is the glory of your piety to cherish those whose fathers you loved - for no-one is believed to have given harmless and sincere affection to the old unless he demonstrably approves their posterity - let hatreds be shut up with men entombed. May anger perish with the violent; affection should not die with those held dear, but you should treat with the greater goodwill one who cannot be blamed for his kingdom's quarrels. Consider what the heir of worthy men deserves from you. 3. You exalted my grandfather [Theoderic] in your city to the Consul's ivory chair; in Italy you distinguished my father [Eutharic] with the Consul's robe of office. And, through desire for concord, he was adopted as your son by arms, although he was almost your equal in age.[2]

The name of son, which you bestowed on my elders, you will grant more fittingly to a lad. Your love should now take up a father's role; for, by the laws of nature, the offspring of your son cannot be held an alien to you. 4. And therefore, I seek peace not as a stranger, but as close kindred, since you gave me a grandson's favour when you bestowed on my father the joy of adoption. I have assumed a royal inheritance: let me find a place in your thoughts also. To me, it matters

---

[1] Mommsen conjectures *patens* for *potens*; Fridh retains the MSS reading.

[2] Eutharic was probably designated, not just acknowledged, as Consul by Justin; contrast II.1. Adoption by arms implied the inferior status of the adoptee; cf. IV.2, Procopius, *Wars* I.xi.22. Theodoric was made Consul by the emperor Zeno in 484.

more than my lordship to have the goodwill of so great a ruler. May, then, the first days of my reign deserve the help of an aged prince; let my boyhood procure the guardianship [*tuitio*] of your favour; and I who am sustained by such a protection will not be wholly bereft of kin. 5. Let my realm be tied to you by the bonds of gratitude. You will reign more effectively in a region where you sway all things by love.

Therefore, I have seen fit to send X and Y as envoys to your serenity, so that you may accord me your friendship on those agreements, those terms which your glorious predecessors are known to have had with the lord my grandfather, of divine memory. Perhaps I deserve even more good faith from you because my age cannot make me suspect, and it is known that my family is not alien. By my aforementioned envoys, I have sent some oral messages for your most serene ears; and may you, after the custom of your clemency, bring them to effect.

VIII.12 KING ATHALARIC TO THE ILLUSTRIOUS ARATOR
(a.526, after Aug. 30th)

1. I judge necessary business to be perfect and completed if, even as I have provided for the military section of the state by selecting the magnificent Patrician [Tuluin], so I take thought to associate with him a man of the highest skill in letters. For it befits those to whom exalted power is entrusted to have learned counsellors, so that measures provided to benefit the state may be set forth unhindered by a lack of worthy men. Other posts may organise themselves with a commonplace provision; but he who cares for the general security must have such an associate as is unrivalled in his studies.

2. For you are not still regarded as untried, although you have come to honours as a young man. The field of advocacy trained you; the summit of my judgement selected you. For so great was the devotion to letters found in you that I could not allow your genius to grow old there. You are entering on state service, although you might be acting as an attorney; and, though eloquence may once have lured you to

declaim for the defence, equity was then persuading you to pronounce
as a judge. Eloquence armed with good character is of proven utility.
For, as it is fatal when the learned persuade men to crime, so it is a
healing benefit when fluent speech is incapable of passing the bounds
of truth.

3. But, that I may instead proclaim your merits by laudable
examples, it is a pleasure to recount that solemn embassy, which you
transacted not in commonplace words, but by a torrential river of
eloquence. For, when sent from the region of Dalmatia to the lord my
grandfather [Theoderic], you so expounded the needs of the provincials
and the good of the state that you spoke at length without wearying a
conscientious and highly cautious man. Indeed, the abundance of your
words gave sweet pleasure as it flowed, and, when you were drawing
to an end, you were asked to go on speaking. By moving and delighting
the audience, you best fulfilled the endeavour of a true orator, although
you had now abandoned the work of a barrister. 4. Indeed, you were
also helped by the eloquence and character of your father, whose
rhetorical skill was able to instruct you, although you did not lack the
books of the ancients.[3] For he was, as I know, a man outstandingly
learned in letters.

And - to discourse to a scholar on the recherché - these letters, as
common opinion has it, were first assembled by Mercury, the inventor
of many arts, from the flight of the birds of the river Strymon. 5. For,
even today, the cranes, which gather in flocks, are taught by nature to
represent the shapes of the alphabet.[4] Reducing these to a seemly
order, with an appropriate mixture of vowels and consonants, he
invented a road for the senses by which meaning[5] can make for the
heights, and reach at its swiftest the inner shrine of understanding. Of

---

[3] Arator is usually identified with Ennodius' friend, the poet Magnus Arator; I am
uncertain, since the latter was orphaned at an early age, brought up by bishop Laurentius
of Milan, and trained in rhetoric by Ennodius and Deuterius.

[4] Strymon: a river in Thrace, famous in ancient literature for its cranes.

[5] *Mens* here, I think, untranslatably denotes both the mind of a writer, and the
significance of his words.

this, the Greek author Helenus[6] has said much and well, describing the nature and form of letters in a most exact account, so that the wealth of noble literature can be understood in its very origin.

6. But, to return to my theme, you may therefore be supposed to have improved your talent by paternal example, and without nourishing your eloquence in the forum of Rome. O happy master! O fortunate pupil, who learnt by love what terror has forced from other educated men![7] 7. Indeed, you discovered Roman eloquence in regions not its own; and where the Gallic tongue once sounded, the reading of Tully [Cicero] made you an orator. Where are those who claim that Latin literature can be learnt at Rome, and nowhere else? Had earlier ages produced this advance, Caecilius would have escaped the weight of shame. Indeed, that verdict has lost its force: Liguria, too, has sent out its Tullys.[8]

8. You ·must realise my opinion of your merits, when you see yourself linked to the counsels of one who handles the secrets of my empire. Hence it is that you hold the illustrious rank of Count of the Bodyguards, and that I adorn you with that honour.[9] Thus, you may rightly hope for greater rewards from my judgement, since I expect to find in you still better qualities. You see that great affairs are entrusted to you: whatever you do affects the public. For he who has the opportunity to sin against all men wins great glory if he is incapable of transgression.

---

[6] A grammarian attested only in Cassiodorus; his existence has been doubted.

[7] Teaching methods were commonly brutal; cf. Augustine, *Confessions* I.14, 23.

[8] Caecilius Statius, fl.179 B.C., was a comic poet from Milan, then in Celtic speaking Cisalpine Gaul; Cicero (*Brutus* 258) condemned his Latin style.

[9] Is the honour that of Count of the Bodyguards or merely *consiliarius* to Tuluin, the Patrician-in-Waiting commanding the Gothic army? Arator may already hold the former. Against Martindale (*PLRE* II, s.v.) and Sundwall (92f.), he is not being promoted to Count of the Private Estates.

VIII.15 KING ATHALARIC TO THE SENATE OF THE CITY OF
ROME (a.526, after Aug.30th)

1. Your response to the decision of the glorious lord my grandfather
over the episcopal election gives, I declare, great satisfaction to my
mind. For it was right to obey the judgement of a good prince: taking
thought with prudent deliberation, although about an alien faith, he
evidently chose such a pontiff [Pope Felix IV] as should displease no
worthy man. You may thus appreciate that he specially desired that
religion in all churches should flourish with good priests. You have,
therefore, accepted a man who has been worthily formed by divine
grace, and praised by royal scrutiny.

2. No one should still be engaged in the old rivalry. He whose
hopes the prince has overcome should not feel the shame of defeat.
Indeed, if he loves the new pontiff without guile, he makes him his
own. For why grieve, when the rival's partisan finds in this man the
same qualities he hoped for? These contests are civil ones, wars
without weapons, quarrels without hatred; this affair is carried on by
acclamations, not lamentations. For although one person has been
debarred, still the faithful have lost nothing, seeing that the longed-for
bishopric is occupied.

3. Therefore, with the return of your envoy, the illustrious
Publianus, I have thought it proper to send letters of greeting to your
assembly. For it gives me great joy to converse with the chief men of
my realm. And I am very sure that this too will give you much
pleasure: your knowledge that obedience to Theoderic's command has
gratified me likewise.

[Felix's rival cannot be identified; according to the *Liber Pontificalis* (Davis, 50f., 105),
there was an interregnum of 58 days before his peaceful ordination by command of
Theoderic on July 12th, 526. As Theoderic died on August 30th, the controversy lasted
well over three months.]

VIII.28 KING ATHALARIC TO THE ILLUSTRIOUS CUNIGASTUS[10] (a.526-7)

1. The lamentable grievance of Constantius and Venerius has moved my serenity: they complain that they have been deprived by Tanca[11] of their legal property, a piece of land called Fabricula, together with its livestock. They add that, lest they should try an action to reclaim their own, he is imposing on them, who are free, the status of meanest slavery.

2. And therefore, your mightiness, in obedience to this decree, is to command the afore-mentioned person to attend your court. There the whole truth of the case between the parties is to be examined, and you are to dispense a justice that accords with law, and corresponds to your character. For, as it is a serious thing for a master to lose his rights, so it is opposed to my times to press free necks with the yoke of slavery. 3. If they request it, the invaded property is initially to be restored to them by the right of interim possession, but in such a way that a party to the action shall not withdraw from the case. This violent anticipation of the laws must cease, so that the case may be heard and judged by a magistrate, and the defendant either possess his proven slaves with the associated goods, or leave them free men, unharmed in person and estate. For it is enough that I am forgoing the penalty due from him who has dared this injury.

VIII.31 KING ATHALARIC TO THE DISTINGUISHED SEVERUS[12] (a.526-7)

1. Since, as I believe, you learned all that belongs to the organisation of the state when playing a praiseworthy part in the counsels of the Praetorian Prefecture, you have fully realised, with

---

[10] On Cunigastus, cf. Boethius, *C.Phil.* I, prose iv; for his judicial position, cf. III.13.
[11] His name suggests that he was a Goth.
[12] Severus was probably governor of Lucania-and-Bruttium.

your literary education, that a city which is a populous community presents a beautiful appearance. For thus the glory of freedom shines out in it, while my ordinances find their necessary execution.

It is the way of animals to seek out the woods and fields, but of men to love their hearths and homelands above all things. 2. The very birds, those of a gentle and harmless character, fly in flocks: the tuneful thrushes love a throng of their own kind; so too, the chattering starlings always gather in armies; the murmuring wood-pigeons delight in their own regiments; and nothing that lives an honest life disdains the pleasures of unity. 3. By contrast, the fierce hawks and hunting eagles, more keen sighted than all other birds, wish to fly alone, since, intent on their hunting, they have no interest in harmless assemblies. For, not wishing to come on their prey in another's company, they take care to act in solitude. So with mortal men, the purpose that shuns human sight is usually detestable, and nothing good can be truly believed about him whose life goes unwitnessed.

4. Let the land-owners and town-councillors [*possessores* and *curiales*] of Bruttium return to their cities: those who ceaselessly till the fields are the peasants [*coloni*]. Those to whom I have granted honours, whom I have approved and entrusted with public affairs, should accept that they are cut off from the life of a yokel. Especially they should do so in that region where good things come in abundance and without toil. 5. There the corn grows rich and full; the olive too rejoices in its fruitfulness; the valleys smile with fertile pastures, the hillsides with vineyards. It abounds in flocks of many kinds of cattle, but especially it glories in its herds of horses: deservedly so, since so spring-like are those woods in the heat of summer that the animals are unharassed by the stings of flies, and are fed to satiety on grass that is always green. You may see streams of the purest water flowing among the mountain heights; they run downwards through the high hills as if springing from the tallest peak. Furthermore, on either side, the province has much trade and sea-borne traffic, so that it both abounds in a wealth of its own produce, and, through its neighbouring coasts, is supplied with a store of foreign goods. There the yokels feast like townsmen; men of modest rank also enjoy the superfluity of the great, so that even the

smallest fortune is not without provisions.

6. Men declare their great delight even in the countryside of this province; do they then have no desire to inhabit its cities? What is the use of men lying hidden, when they have been so refined by education? Boys seek out the assemblies of humane schooling, and, just when they might be worthy of the forum, promptly bury themselves in their country dwellings. They make progress only to unlearn; they become learned to forget; and, while they love the countryside, they do not know how to love themselves. A man of learning should ask where he can live and be famous. No wise man despises an assembly of people in which he knows that he will be praised. Moreover, virtues lack good report, if their merits are unknown among men. 7. For how can men long to abandon the assembly of their fellow citizens, when they see that certain kinds of bird also mingle with human society? For the swallow trustingly hangs its nest in the homes of mortal men, and feeds its chicks without fear among the throngs of inmates. Hence, it is a vile act for a nobleman to bring up his sons in the wilderness, when he sees how the birds entrust their offspring to a human concourse.

Let the cities return, then, to their original glory; let no-one prefer the delights of the countryside to the public buildings of the ancients. 8. How can you shun in time of peace a place for which wars should be fought to prevent its destruction? Who does not welcome a gathering of noblemen? Who does not enjoy conversing with his peers, visiting the forum, looking on at honest crafts, advancing his own cases by the laws, or sometimes playing at draughts, going to the baths with his fellows, exchanging splendid dinner parties? He who wishes to lead his life in the constant company of his slaves will assuredly lack all these things.

9. But, in case a mind otherwise instructed should slip back again into the same habit, both land-owners and town-councillors are to provide guarantors, and, under a penalty externally assessed, to promise that they will spend the greater part of the year in the cities that they have chosen as their official residence. So it is decreed, that they may neither lack the splendours of the city, nor be denied the delights of the countryside.

VIII.33 KING ATHALARIC TO THE DISTINGUISHED SEVERUS
(a.527, before Sept.1st)

1. As it is the wish of a wise man to know the unknown, so it is folly to conceal proven facts, especially in a time when abuses can be very rapidly corrected. Now, by frequent proofs, I have learnt of events at the Lucanian assembly to which ancient superstition gave the name of Leucothea,[13] from the clarity and great whiteness of the water in that place. There the merchants' wealth has often been damaged by the lawless seizures and hostile plundering of the country people, so that those who had come in all devotion to honour the anniversary of St Cyprian [Sept.14th], and to adorn with their merchandise the form of civilised life [*civilitas*], have departed poor, shamed, and empty-handed.

2. I have judged that this can be corrected by a straight-forward and easy remedy. At the afore-mentioned time, your distinction, together with the owners and tenants of the various great estates, must obtain peace for those who meet there, by sureties given in advance; thus you need not detect and punish guilty men for their shocking crimes. But, if any of the country people, or a man from any place, should give cause for a wicked quarrel, he must be arrested at the very outset, and immediately punished by cudgelling. Thus, he who was previously attempting to stir up secret crime will correct his evil purpose in a public display.

3. Now that same gathering is both a festival of great fame, and highly profitable to the surrounding provinces. For all the notable exports of industrious Campania, or wealthy Bruttium, or Calabria rich in cattle, or prosperous Apulia, with the products of Lucania itself, are displayed to the glory of that most admirable commerce. Hence, you would be right to suppose that such a mass of goods had been assembled from many regions. For there you may see wide meadows gleaming with the loveliest of market-stalls, temporary homes quickly woven from leafy and beautiful branches, and a coming and going of

---

[13] The White Goddess : a sea goddess.

people who sing and rejoice. 4. Though you will see no public
buildings there, you may still behold the glory of a famous city. Boys
and girls are on display,marked out by their differences in sex and age,
brought on the market not as captives, but by freedom: their parents
are right to sell them, since they benefit by slavery itself. Indeed, there
is no doubt that slaves can be improved by transference from field
work to service in the town.[14] Why should I mention the clothes,
interwoven with a countless variety of threads? Why the sleek and
well-fed animals of various kinds? Everything is for sale there at such
a price that even the most reluctant purchaser may be tempted. So, if
praiseworthy discipline sets all in order, no-one will leave that fair in
discontent.

    5. Now the site itself spreads over delightful meadows, a kind of
suburb of the ancient city of Consilinum, which has taken the name of
Marcellianum from the founder of the sacred springs. An abundance of
sweet, translucent water bursts out here, where the hollow of an apse
shaped like a natural cave pours forth a fluid of such clarity that you
would suppose to be empty a pool which you know is brimful. It is
transparent to the very bottom, so that it seems more air than liquid to
your gaze. The pure water rivals the light of day, for whatever is
thrown into it is visible with undiminished clarity. 6. A school of fishes
plays happily in it. They come boldly to the hands of those who feed
them, as if they know they are not to be caught: for whoever dares to
do such a deed is swiftly seen to feel the vengeance of the Deity.[15] It
is a long task to recount the wonders of that spring. I will move on to
that extraordinary gift and holy miracle. 7. For when, on the occasion

---

[14] Parents might sell their children for a limited period (perhaps 25 years) without
ultimate prejudice to their freedom; cf. *C.Th.* III.3, Valentinian III, *Novel* 33, H.
Chadwick, *Journal of Theological Studies*, n.s. 34 (1983), 432,n.8. Despite Cassiodorus'
rosy picture of southern Italy (given small support by current archaeology), this usually
resulted from great hardship; cf. *Edict of Theoderic* 94: 'Parents who, compelled by
necessity, sell their sons for the sake of food, do not prejudice their free status; for no
price can be put on a free man.'

[15] These sacred fish probably dated back to the pagan shrine; to Christians they would
symbolise both Christ, and those baptised into his Church.

of the sacred night, the priest begins to pour forth the prayer of baptism, and the springs of speech flow from his holy mouth, a wave immediately leaps on high, and sends out the waters not by their usual channels, but in a lofty mass. The mindless element rises up of its own will, and miraculously prepares itself in a kind of solemn devotion, that the consecration of the divine majesty may be made manifest. For, although the spring itself covers five steps, and submerges only them in its untroubled state, it is seen to swell to the other two, which it is never known to cover save at that time. It is a great and wondrous miracle that the flowing waters should so stand or swell at human speech that you would think they took pains to listen.

8. May this heavenly spring be venerated in the speech of all men. May Lucania have its own Jordan. The one gave us the model of baptism; the other guards the sacred mystery with annual devotion. Hence both profit, and the reverence due to the place, should confer holy peace on the people; for all will judge him the wickedest of men who dares to violate the joys of such a time. Let my decree be read and displayed to the people, so that they will not think themselves licensed to crime in the belief that it will go unpunished.

IX.15 KING ATHALARIC TO POPE JOHN [II] (a.533)[1]

1. If it was the task of the princes of old to seek out laws by which the peoples they ruled might enjoy the pleasures of tranquillity, it is much more glorious to make such decrees as will agree with the rules of the Church. Thus, damnable gains should be alien to my age. That alone can truly be called profit which we know that the divine judgement does not punish. 2. Now, a law-officer [*defensor*] of the Roman Church has recently come to me with the lamentable allegation that, when a bishop was being sought for the Apostolic See, certain men exploited the needs of the times by nefarious scheming, and so burdened the wealth of the poor[2] with extorted promises that - merely to mention it is impious - even the sacred vessels were openly put on sale to the public.[3] The savagery of committing this act measures the glory of eradicating it by recourse to piety.

3. And therefore, your holiness must know that I have decreed in this regulation - which I also wish to extend to all patriarchs[4] and metropolitan churches - that, from the time of the holy Pope Boniface [II], when the fathers of the Senate, mindful of their nobility, passed

---

[1] John II was ordained on Jan.2nd, 533; Cassiodorus became Praetorian Prefect on Sept.1st, 533; Salventius, addressee of the linked IX.16, succeeded his dead brother as Urban Prefect some time after April 22nd. Krautschick (90), assumes that Salventius did not continue in office after Sept.1st, the start of the new indiction, since the office normally changed hands annually. Therefore, Cassiodorus must have been engaged in official drafting before becoming Prefect. Possible, but his assumption seems to me uncertain.

[2] I.e. the Church estates from which the poor were supported.

[3] The long hiatus of two and a half months between the death of Boniface II and election of John II, suggests the intensity of intrigue. In 531, Boniface had tried to designate his successor, and been defeated.

[4] Patriarch usually means the bishop of an apostolically founded see; Cassiodorus seems to apply it to any metropolitan bishop.

a measure for the prohibition of such fees,[5] if any man, whether in his own person or through another, is shown to have promised anything to procure a bishopric, that accursed contract is to have no force. 4. Moreover, if anyone is convicted of involvement in this crime, I leave him no plea; also if he thinks to reclaim a debt, or to retain what he has received, he will necessarily be held guilty of sacrilege, and will restore what he has received by compulsion of the competent judge. For, even as just laws open up legal actions for the good, so they close them for men of evil character. 5. Furthermore, whatever that measure of the Senate decreed, I order to be upheld in every way against those who have in any way involved themselves or any intermediaries in criminal contracts.

6. And, because all things must be moderated by reason, and excessive dealing cannot be called just, I decree that, whenever a contest about the consecration of the apostolic pontiff happens to arise, and the people's dispute is brought to my palace, those who make me the recommendation will receive no more than 3000 *solidi* with the assemblage of documents.[6] However, out of respect for the nature of the business, I exclude from their number all the rich, since it is rather the poor who should be looked after by an ecclesiastical gift. 7. But I decree that the other patriarchs shall spend no more than 2000 *solidi* on the terms and persons mentioned above, when their ordination is considered at my court. They must know, however, that, in their own cities, they are not to distribute more than 500 *solidi* to the poorest of

---

[5] *ut a tempore....Bonifatii, cum....patres conscripti senatus consulta....condiderunt* - I have translated *cum* as temporal, but it may be causal. The *consultum* mentioned has been identified with a *contestatio senatus* of 530 (in the pontificate of Felix IV) prohibiting intrigue within a Pope's life-time for his successor; I disagree - the *consultum* probably dated under Boniface (530-2), and concerned financial malpractices in elections; cf. Harnack, 38f.

[6] Against Traube (index, s.v. *collectio*), I do not think this a reference to fees (*sportulae*) paid by petitioners to palatine officials for the production of documents. Rather, this is a reward paid by the candidate to the successful delegation of his supporters.

the people.[7] Other recipients will be restrained by the penalty both of this edict and of the Senate's recent decree; but the severity of canon law will pursue the givers too.

8. But, as for those of you who with patriarchal honour supervise the remaining churches, since my decree has freed you from illicit promises, it remains that you should follow good examples, and, without any cost to the churches, provide bishops worthy of [God's] majesty. For it is very wrong that bribery should find a place with you which I have barred to laymen through respect for the divine. 9. Therefore, if any ruler of the Apostolic Church, or any patriarch should see fit to promote a bishop through some corrupt favour [*suffragium*], whether he does so in person, or through his relatives, or any of those serving him, he is to return what he has received, and is to suffer in every way what canon law prescribes. But if anyone fears to reveal what he gave or promised in that man's lifetime, the Church shall reclaim it from the heirs (or their representatives) of him by whose favour the bishop is found to have been ordained, and those survivors shall likewise be branded with the mark of infamy. Moreover, the other [ecclesiastical] orders, I decree, will be subject to the same sanction. 10. But if, through the devising of a cunning plot, anyone should be so bound and hindered by oaths that, for his soul's salvation, he cannot prove, and does not dare to denounce the committed crime, I license any persons of standing in any of the individual cities to bring this charge before the competent judges.

As to anything that can be recovered through that evidence - so that I may encourage the prosecutors to produce evidence - he who has been willing to prove such a deed shall receive a third of the property informed on; the remainder, which has evidently been plundered,[8] will go to those churches, and will be applied either to their buildings, or similarly to their services. For it is right to turn to a good use what

---

[7] The wording is vague, but it seems that two classes of poor might be involved in elections: real paupers, and those respectable enough to share in delegations to the court. The latter got more money - did they belong to the plebeian *ordo* of citizens?

[8] Fridh, followed here, reads *proficiant quae*, Mommsen *proficiat quod*.

VIII.15 KING ATHALARIC TO THE SENATE OF THE CITY OF ROME (a.526, after Aug.30th)

1. Your response to the decision of the glorious lord my grandfather over the episcopal election gives, I declare, great satisfaction to my mind. For it was right to obey the judgement of a good prince: taking thought with prudent deliberation, although about an alien faith, he evidently chose such a pontiff [Pope Felix IV] as should displease no worthy man. You may thus appreciate that he specially desired that religion in all churches should flourish with good priests. You have, therefore, accepted a man who has been worthily formed by divine grace, and praised by royal scrutiny.

2. No one should still be engaged in the old rivalry. He whose hopes the prince has overcome should not feel the shame of defeat. Indeed, if he loves the new pontiff without guile, he makes him his own. For why grieve, when the rival's partisan finds in this man the same qualities he hoped for? These contests are civil ones, wars without weapons, quarrels without hatred; this affair is carried on by acclamations, not lamentations. For although one person has been debarred, still the faithful have lost nothing, seeing that the longed-for bishopric is occupied.

3. Therefore, with the return of your envoy, the illustrious Publianus, I have thought it proper to send letters of greeting to your assembly. For it gives me great joy to converse with the chief men of my realm. And I am very sure that this too will give you much pleasure: your knowledge that obedience to Theoderic's command has gratified me likewise.

[Felix's rival cannot be identified; according to the *Liber Pontificalis* (Davis, 50f., 105), there was an interregnum of 58 days before his peaceful ordination by command of Theoderic on July 12th, 526. As Theoderic died on August 30th, the controversy lasted well over three months.]

worldly and corrupt ambition may be removed from the honour of Holy Church. I wish you to bring this without any delay to the notice of the Senate and Roman people, so that a measure which I desire to be carefully observed by everyone may be fixed in the hearts of all. 3. Indeed, to impress this princely benefit on both present and future ages, I order my command and the Senate's resolution alike to be fittingly engraved on marble tablets, and placed in the atrium of the church of the blessed Apostle Peter as a public testimony. For the place is worthy to hold both my glorious gift, and the praiseworthy decree of the noble Senate. For this purpose, I have sent X, on whose return I may know that my commands have been carried out. For a man is uncertain that his orders have been obeyed if he is belatedly informed of their fulfillment.

IX.18 AN EDICT OF KING ATHALARIC (a.533-4)

The ancients wisely resolved that the public should be admonished with general edicts, by which every crime is corrected, and the transgressor is not burdened with shame. For all men think themselves referred to where it is clear that no individual is named, and he who is reformed as one of a group resembles an innocent man. Hence, too, my pity is maintained, when fear is born from an unused sword, and correction comes without bloodshed. For I am both angry and merciful, I threaten without action, and I unite wrath and clemency, by condemning vices only.

For a long time, the complaints of various persons have sounded in my ears with frequent whisperings that certain men have despised civil order [*civilitas*], and have chosen to live with the savagery of beasts, since, returning to primitive rusticity, they have formed a feral hatred for human law. I now rightly judge that these men must be repressed; thus I will harass the crimes that are hostile to good morals at the same time that, by the divine power, I am resisting the enemies of the state. Both, indeed, are deadly; both must be repelled; but vices ravage the more seriously the more internal they are. The one is supported by the other. Indeed, if we subdue our own crimes, the armies of our enemies will fall more easily.[10]

1. By the severity of the laws and my own anger, I condemn that chief poison of the human race, the seizure of property [*pervasio*], under which civil order [*civilitas*] can be neither claimed nor maintained.[11] I decree that the law of the divine Valentinian, long seriously neglected, shall rouse itself against those who despise legal process, and, in person or by their servants, dare to expel the owner and violently occupy estates in town or country.[12] Nor do I intend any of its severity to be abated by abhorrent relaxation. In addition, if any free man is too poor to satisfy the law confirmed above, he is immediately to submit to the punishment of exile, since he who knows himself unable to undergo the penalty in another manner should pay the more heed to the public laws.

As for the competent governors to whose jurisdiction the admitted crime may belong, if they allow the invader to hold what he has seized when they could eject him, they are both to be deprived of the honour of the belt of office they have assumed, and be liable to my treasury to the extent of the sum due from the seizer. However, the decrees shall remain valid against the authors of the crime. But, if anyone is carried away to such madness that, in a spirit of tyranny, he fails to obey the public law, and, in his outstanding power, despises the small numbers of the [governor's] staff concerned, he will be brought to my ears and marked out by a report from the governor; an execution by *saiones* will be granted; and he who has refused to obey the judge will feel the vengeance of the royal might.

2. And, because even high princes must live under the common

---

[10] This may refer to an Ostrogothic campaign against the Gepids about this date, mentioned by Procopius (*Wars* V.iii.15), or to the growing threats from Franks and Byzantines.

[11] About this time Amalasuintha checked Theodahad's *pervasio*, denounced by the provincials of Tuscia.

[12] The eighth *Novel* of Valentinian III, dated 440 is probably meant; not, as Mommsen suggested, Valentinian II's law, *C.Th.* IV.22.3, of 389. The former fined *pervasores* by the value of the estate seized.

law, if anyone, omitting legal process, shall presume, or has presumed to post up titles of ownership in the public name, he is to be liable to the owner to the extent proclaimed by the aforementioned decree. For he who has dared to burden the majesty of the royal name with the evil weight of illicit seizure is also and rightly smitten by the punishment for sacrilege. Moreover, he who is beaten in court is to pay the expenses of the case, since it applies stimulants to hateful disputes when scoundrels are defeated without injury, and false claimants do not grieve for lost honour if they have escaped without cost to their estates. 3. But should a member of my secretariats suppose that anything is to be claimed, he shall think to conceal none of the following series of ordinances from his adversary, so far as concerns his case. He will lose what he petitioned for, should he disobey. Or, should he try to deprive him of anything, it will similarly be held invalid, since I wish only those to enjoy my benefits whom I do not find practising trickery.[13]

4. If a man, by punishable seduction, labours to break up another's marriage, his own union will be held illicit, so that he may instead experience himself the fortune which he, in his malignity, tried to inflict on another. But should he lack married love, I deny him the right of future matrimony, since he who has dared to behave without restraint in dividing the marriage bed, does not deserve to obtain the benefit of conjugal reverence. But, lest my vengeance should pass by any of those guilty of this crime, should those without hope of present or future marriage attempt anything by cunning devices against another's bedchamber, they are to be deprived of half their property, which is immediately to be applied to the benefit of the treasury. But, if poverty prevents the taking of vengeance against the possessions of some, they are to be punished by exile, lest - and to mention it is a sin - they should be seen to escape the threat of public law because they are known to be of the meanest fortune. But my piety has decreed this for the seducers of another's love. 5. For the rest, in cases of adultery,

---

[13] Prosecutions brought, or informations laid are envisaged; these would result in confiscation of property held by criminals and those deprived of the right of testacy. The informer, or his sponsor, would usually petition for at least part of the property.

I wish everything that was decreed by imperial rebuke to be most strictly upheld.

6. No one shall be married to two wives at one time, for he will know that he is to be punished by loss of his possessions. For this is either lust, whose enjoyment is not morally allowed; or it is covetousness, and is legally punished by poverty. 7. But if anyone, in wanton and shameful desire, despises married decency, and prefers to go to the embraces of a concubine, if she is a free woman, she and her children will, in all cases, be made over to the wife, under the yoke of slavery. Thus, by a moral sentence, she will experience subjection to one above whom she expected to be placed in her illicit lust. But if it is a slave woman that attains to such debauchery, she is to be subject to the vengeance of the wife, excepting the penalty of blood, so that she may experience as a judge her whom she should have feared in her absence.

8. No one is to extort deeds of gift by fear; no one should desire acquisitions by fraud or accursed immorality: honesty alone has the right to seek profit from the laws. When lawful generosity is alleged, I wish that investigation to be observed which the laws of the past decreed through concern for truth. For thus, as they bear witness, no opportunity will be given to fraud, and truth will grow in authority. In general, I decree that no one is to regard as valid a deed which the author made unsure by not fulfilling what justice and the laws command.

9. Magicians, moreover, and those who have thought to gain anything by their nefarious arts, are to be pursued with the rigour of the law, since it is impious for us to be negligent towards those whom the pity of heaven does not allow to go unpunished. For what stupidity it is to desert the creator of life [God], and follow instead the originator of death [Satan]! Disgraceful actions should be wholly shunned by the magistrates. No one should do what the laws condemn, since those who have shared in forbidden transgressions must be punished by the decreed penalty. For what can they condemn in other men, if they themselves are stained by shameful pollution?

10. A man of modest fortune must also be safe from the rich. All must refrain from the madness of slaughter. For to dare a physical

assault is plainly to commit an act of war, especially against those defended by the authority of my protection [*tuitio*]. But if anyone, with wicked daring, should attempt to oppose this, he will be held a violator of my command.

11. I do not allow a suspect to appeal from the provincial governors for a second time in one case, lest what was devised to assist the innocent should appear a kind of refuge for the criminal. But should anyone attempt this forbidden repetition, he will depart having lost his case.

12. But lest, by touching on a few laws, I should be supposed not to desire the maintenance of the rest, I decree that all edicts, both my own, and the lord my grandfather's [Theoderic's], that were drafted with honoured deliberation, as also the ordinary public laws, are to be kept with full force and rigour. Such are the defences with which they shield themselves that they are also walled round by the addition of my sworn word. Why should I continue indefinitely? The ordinary rule of the laws and the integrity of my commands are everywhere to be upheld.

IX.19 KING ATHALARIC TO THE SENATE OF THE CITY OF ROME (date as IX.18)

1. The censurable transgressions of others often give rise to laudable decrees, and impulses to justice are wonderfully born from a criminal circumstance. For equity is silent, if an admitted crime is not proclaimed, and the spirit of a prince rests idle, if it is not aroused by some grievance.

2. Now, impelled by the voices of plaintiffs, and warned by appeals from many of the people about certain matters, I have set down certain things as necessary for the Roman peace and to be maintained for ever, by an edictal proclamation of twelve chapters, in the manner that the civil law, as we read, was instituted.[14] The keeping of these should

---

[14] The allusion is to the *Twelve Tables*, the earliest Roman law code.

not be supposed to weaken the remaining laws, but rather to reinforce them. 3. They are to be read out in the splendour of your assembly, and the Urban Prefect shall have them solemnly published for thirty days in the most frequented places, so that my good order [*civilitas*] may be recognised, and men of aggressive character deprived of hope. For how can the violent confidently undertake what they know the prince's mercy has condemned? Let all men recover the love of discipline, by which small things grow strong, and great are preserved.

4. For with this aim, I mobilise my army for frequent expeditions by God's help: that I may know the public to be living at peace under the laws. May I be granted this exchange of benefits, so that he whom you know to be busy in the service of the state shall seldom be assailed by the approach of petitioners. The judges should maintain their legal severity; they should reject the prayers of vile corruption. If the defendant finds no crime in his judge, fear will set all things in order.

IX.20 KING ATHALARIC TO ALL PROVINCIAL GOVERNORS
(date as IX.18)

1. Although, by God's help, I provide for my provinces by the annual renewal [of governors], and courts are distributed through every corner of Italy, I have learnt that a wealth of cases are arising from the shortage of justice. It is clearly the fault of your negligence, when men are forced to request from me the help of the laws. For who would choose to seek so far afield what he sees arriving in his own territory? 2. But, to deprive you of your cunning excuses, and the provincials of their harsh necessities, I have decided to regulate with an edictal decree certain cases heretofore neglected by scandalous torpor. Thus your confidence in correctly judging may grow, and malign daring be gradually diminished. This edict you are solemnly to publish by posting it for thirty days in the public assemblies, so that he who, after this remedy, dares to continue in wickedness may justly be condemned.

IX.21 KING ATHALARIC TO THE SENATE OF THE CITY OF
ROME (a.533)

1. As you know, I have referred disputes involving sons to the
Fathers [the senators], that they may take thought for the careers of
those affected by the advancement of education at Rome. For it is
incredible that you should lack concern for something which brings
honours to your offspring, and gives your assembly the counsel that
comes from constant reading. Now recently - for I am always careful
and anxious for your sake - I came to know by discreet report from
various people, that the teachers of eloquence at Rome are not
receiving the constituted rewards for their labours, and that the
trafficking of certain men has caused the sums assigned to the masters
of the schools to be diminished.
    2. Therefore, since it is clear that rewards feed the arts, I have
judged it abominable that anything should be stolen from the teachers
of youth; they should instead be incited to their noble studies by an
increase in their fees. 3. For the school of grammar has primacy: it is
the fairest foundation of learning, the glorious mother of eloquence,
which has learnt to aim at praise, to speak without a fault. As good
morals view an alien crime, so it views a dissonant error in the course
of declamation. For, as the musician creates the sweetest song from a
choir in harmony, so, by well ordered modulations of sound, the
grammarian can recite in metre. 4. Grammar is the mistress of words,
the embellisher of the human race; through the practice of the noble
reading of ancient authors, she helps us, we know, by her counsels.
The barbarian kings do not use her; as is well known, she remains
unique to lawful rulers. For the tribes possess arms and the rest;
rhetoric is found in sole obedience to the lords of the Romans. Thence
the battle of the orators sounds the war-call of civil law; thence noble
eloquence recommends all leading men; and thence, to say no more,

my present words derive.[15]

5. Therefore, fathers of the Senate, with God's approval, I enjoin on you this duty, this authority: a succeeding professor in the school of liberal studies, whether the grammarian, the rhetorician, or the teacher of law, shall receive from those responsible, without any diminution, the income of his predecessor. And, once confirmed by the authority of your chief order and the rest of the most noble Senate, so long as he is found fit for the work he has undertaken, he must suffer no man's improper challenge involving either the transfer or the reduction of his salary; but, under your ordinance and protection, he is to enjoy his emoluments in security. The Urban Prefect, too, is to maintain these lawful rights. 6. And, lest there should be any loophole left to the whim of those who dispense the income, immediately six months have passed, the aforementioned masters are to receive half the decreed sum; the remainder of the year shall be concluded with the due payment of the salary outstanding: those for whom it is a sin to be idle for an hour must not be forced to wait on another's pride. 7. For I want the laws to be upheld with such firmness that, if anyone concerned should think to delay this tax - so to speak - that is owing, he shall be charged interest as expiation, since, with criminal greed, he has deprived of their revenues those engaged in valuable labours. 8. For, if I bestow my wealth on actors for the pleasure of the people, and men who are not thought so essential are meticulously paid, how much more should payment be made without delay to those through whom good morals are advanced, and the talent of eloquence is nurtured to serve my palace!

9. Furthermore, I command your venerable assembly to explain this to the present masters of letters: as they recognise my concern for their revenues, so they should know that I require their more zealous attention to the education of young men. That disposition adopted by

---

[15] 3-4 may have echoes of Ennodius, 452. 11-12, 14, 16 (*Opusc*.6), an exhortation to learning and sound morals, addressed to students at Rome. Cf., also, Ennodius, 80.90 (*Life of Epiphanius*), where the warlike Visigothic king Euric admits himself defeated by Roman eloquence.

the whingeing dons of satire must now cease, since talent should not be dominated by 'two interests'. It is clear that they already have 'an adequate lodging':[16] hence it is right that they should now cling steadily to a single concern, and be turned with all their mental energy to the study of the noble arts.

IX.24 KING ATHALARIC TO [CASSIODORUS] SENATOR, PRAETORIAN PREFECT (a.533, Sept.1st)

1. If my approval had chanced to find you still obscure and unhonoured, I would indeed be rejoicing at my discovery, but in much doubt as to the result, since there is more hope than fruit in novelty. But since you glory in the countless promotions and mighty approval of the lord my grandfather [Theoderic], it is unfitting to scrutinise one for whom I can scarcely express my admiration. Indeed, the verdicts of such a prince should not be examined, but revered - his actions cannot be questioned, since I am aware that I too was his selection. Ever assiduous in prayer, he deservedly obtained for his doings the protection of Heaven's grace. 2. For when did he give a man charge of an army, and not receive him with victory, or appoint a magistrate, and not prove him to be upright? You would think he had some converse with the future; for what his mind conceived was always accomplished, and, by a marvellous operation of wisdom, he never doubted in events which he truly foresaw.

3. Again, I can demonstrate in your person this outstanding characteristic of the king. He took you up in your youth, and soon found you endowed with probity, mature in legal learning, and ready for the office of Quaestor. No wonder you were the chief glory of those times, since your unoffending service gave him tranquillity in his care for all things, while the power of your eloquence upheld that great

---

[16] Cassiodorus quotes Juvenal, *Satire* vii.63-70. (Ennodius, 452.4, quotes vii.209f.) For the taste of late 4th century senators for Juvenal, see Ammianus Marcellinus, XXVIII.4.14.

mass of the royal mind. He held you elegant in official composition, strict in justice, and free from cupidity. 4. Indeed, you never sold his favours at a scandalous valuation, so that your position brought you the riches of respect, since it never submitted to a bribe. Hence, being cut off from crime by an obvious gulf, you were clearly linked in glorious affection to a most upright prince. That wisest of judges burdened you with a weight of appeals, and trusted so much in your well known legal judgement that, as a favour, he unhesitatingly gave your verdict to disputing parties. 5. How many times did he use you to shame aged courtiers, when those whom long life had instructed could not rival your youthful efforts? Clearly, he had an outstanding quality to proclaim in you: a soul accessible to men's claims for favour, and shut fast against the vice of avarice. (Closed hands and open justice are mysteriously rare among men.)

6. Let me move on to the post of Master, which we know that you obtained not through lavish gifts of money, but the advocacy of your character. Once in that office, you constantly assisted the Quaestors; for, when refined eloquence was needed, the case was straightway entrusted to your genius. A kindly prince required from you what he knew he had never committed to you; by an unfair favour, he freed others from toil that he might fill you with the generous praise of his good opinion. 7. For with you no office kept to its proper limits, since what was in reality the business of many courtiers was openly entrusted to your honour. Nobody could whisper a word of opposition to you, although you were enduring the envy that arises from royal favour. The integrity of your actions defeated your would-be slanderers; your enemies were often forced to admit what they did not feel in their hearts. For all malice fears to expose itself to general hatred by maligning manifest good. 8. To the master of the state, you acted as a household judge, and a private courtier. For, when free from public business, he asked you to recount the opinions of the wise, so that he might compare his own deeds with those of antiquity. The courses of the stars, the gulfs of the sea, the marvels of springs were investigated by this shrewd enquirer, so that, by diligent scrutiny of the natural

world, he might seem a kind of purple-clad philosopher.[17] It would be a long task to tell all. No, I will turn instead to my own favour, so that you may feel that his evident debt to you is duly paid by the heir to his rule.

9. Therefore, by God's help, under whose inspiration all things prosper, I appoint you, from the twelfth indiction [533-4], to the Praetorian Prefecture, with its tribunal and insignia. Thus, the provinces, which, I realise, have heretofore been harassed by the activity of scoundrels, may fearlessly receive a well-tried magistrate. But, although you have your father's Prefecture, praised throughout the realm of Italy, as a model, I still do not present you with other men's examples. Show your own character, and you will fulfil the prayers of all. 10. With God's help, traverse that field of glory which, I know, you have always sought. For if, as I believe, this honour too will demonstrate your integrity, you will have conquered the vain ambitions of the world. It is not, indeed, your practice to sell justice; but now you must help zealously those harmed by deliberate injury. Your incorruptible judgement must guard against hands accustomed to evil. Let the efforts of the deceitful be everywhere warded off, for this is a worthy achievement for an honest magistrate. Moreover, by long postponing your promotion, I have worn out everyone's petitions on your behalf, thus proving the public's goodwill for you, and making your arrival more desired by all. For it is human nature to despise what is quickly procured, since every precious thing is cheapened when offered, and, by contrast, a gift is more welcome when received after some delay.

11. But I am not content only to praise your period of office. Vindicate all the revenues to which the Praetorian Prefecture is entitled, and which other men's greed is plainly embezzling. Let no one glory

---

[17] On historical examples and the moral training of rulers, cf. Ammianus Marcellinus, XXX.8.4-9; contrast IX.25.11. Theoderic's taste for natural marvels is confirmed by the 300 ton monolith which he 'sought out' (*Anonymus Valesianus* 96), as a cupola for his tomb. The phrase 'purple-clad philosopher' evokes the Platonic ideal of the philosopher king, and may echo Themistius, *Or.* 34.viii.34.

in his thefts or privileges. I have sent you as a light into hidden things, since no man can deceive your intelligence, or bend your loyalty with any bribe. 12. In previous posts, you gave examples of wonderful integrity: establish a rule for this office also.[18] For, although you have discharged almost all high appointments with consistency, you still retain the good resolves of honour, in which there should be no measure. For here it is proper to fix no boundary; here honourable ambition is demonstrated, even the excess of which is pleasing. Indeed, with any praiseworthy thing, the more eager the search for it, the more glorious its attainment.

IX.25 KING ATHALARIC TO THE SENATE OF THE CITY OF ROME (date as IX.24)

1. Fathers of the Senate, I have truly loaded with my favours a man well endowed with the virtues, rich in character, filled with high honours - [Cassiodorus] Senator. If you consider his merits, all that I have paid him is a debt. For what reward should distinguish one who has often filled the ears of his masters with shining oratory, who has managed the offices entrusted to him with outstanding authority, and has striven to shape an epoch for which the prince would deservedly be praised?

The truth and eloquence of his speeches have swayed the mind of the king, whose every deed he so recounted that the doer himself might wonder at them. 2. His unaided arguments delighted all men; and, by investing purple praises with his hearer, he made you welcome my rule. He who softens and appeases the heights of royal power by his orations commends his race, for another of your number will be supposed a man of similar character, from whom like services may be requested. 3. Furthermore, with what loyal eloquence did he proclaim

---

[18] Avienus, son of Faustus Niger, succeeding a corrupt Praetorian Prefect in 527, was similarly urged to clean up the administration, and (perhaps ironically) to imitate his father (VIII.20).

the father of my clemency [Eutharic] in the very Senate-house of
Liberty! You remember how that noble orator extolled his deeds,
showing his virtues to be more wonderful than his honours. I can prove
my words to the hilt. Consider, fathers of the Senate, the favour with
which you were viewed by one who saw himself so exalted by your
body. Indeed, to glorious rulers, eulogies are more welcome than taxes,
since dues are paid even to a tyrant, but only a virtuous prince deserves
oratory.[19]

Why, honourable sirs, should you suppose that Cassiodorus was
content merely to essay the praise of living lords, a task of inevitable
tedium, although they may be expected to reward it? 4. He extended
his labours even to the ancient cradle of our house, learning from his
reading what the hoary recollections of our elders scarcely preserved.
From the lurking place of antiquity he led out the kings of the Goths,
long hidden in oblivion. He restored the Amals, along with the honour
of their family, clearly proving me to be of royal stock to the
seventeenth generation.[20] 5. From Gothic origins he made a Roman
history, gathering, as it were, into one garland, flower-buds that had
previously been scattered throughout the fields of literature. 6. Think
how much he loved you in praising me, when he showed the nation of
your prince to be a wonder from ancient days. In consequence, as you
have ever been thought noble because of your ancestors, so you shall
be ruled by an ancient line of kings. I can say no more, fathers of the
Senate; and, should I persevere in recounting his benefits, those
collected here would be surpassed.

7. With what toil, too, he devoted himself to the first days of my
reign, when the newness of the regime required that much be set in
order. Alone, he sufficed for all things: the composition of state
documents demanded him; so too did my counsels; and his labour
meant that my rule did not labour. 8. I found him, admittedly, Master
of the Offices, but he filled the post of Quaestor for me; and, carrying
out my acts of beneficence with justice and loyalty, he willingly showed

---

[19] For the fragments of this panegyric, see *MGH AA* XII, 465-72.

[20] On Cassiodorus as Amal genealogist, see Heather.

the careful diligence which he had learnt from my grandfather [Theoderic] to the benefit of his heir.

But to all this he added something greater, and aided the first days of my reign with arms, as well as letters. 9. For, while the royal mind was obsessed by defence of the coasts, he was suddenly expelled from his literary sanctuary, equalled his ancestors, and fearlessly took up a general's command [*ducatum*].[21] In this, since the enemy did not appear, he triumphed by his outstanding character. For he fed the Goths assigned to him at his own expense, so that he neither injured the provincials, nor loaded my treasury with the burden of expense. His arms brought no loss to the land-owners. No wonder that he was the truest guardian of the province, for he who protects without damage rightly earns the name of defender. 10. But soon, when the season checked the movement of ships, and the fear of war was dissolved, he employed his talent instead as a champion of the laws, healing, without loss to the litigants, wounds which, it was well known, were formerly inflicted for bribes. Such, you may read, were the general's commands of Metellus in Asia,[22] of Cato in Spain, men praised more for their discipline than their battles; for the result of an engagement is always unpredictable, but to keep the measure of good conduct is an undisputed glory.

11. What then? It is usual for men to be puffed up when they know themselves well thought of; but surely he did not presume on such an achievement, and boast himself vaingloriously? Did he not behave with such courtesy that you would suppose the royal favour had been bestowed on him as an act of kindness, not a reward? He showed goodwill to all, was moderate in prosperity, and knew no anger, unless when gravely wronged. Although he is a man of strict justice, he does not refuse, in his severity, to forgo his wrath. He is remarkably

---

[21] Theoderic's last years had been marked by a quarrel with the Vandals, chief naval power in the western Mediterranean, who were then coming under imperial influence; they may have been responsible for this threat to the coasts.

[22] This may be Q.Caecilius Metellus Numidicus, Consul in 109 B.C.; if so, 'Asia' is an error for Africa.

generous with his goods, and, while incapable of pursuing others' property, he knows well how to be a lavish giver of his own. Now this disposition his studies in divinity have confirmed, since affairs are always well conducted if the fear of heaven is opposed to human impulses. For thence is derived the clear understanding of every virtue; thence wisdom is seasoned with the flavour of truth. Thus, the man imbued with the discipline of heaven is rendered lowly in all things.

12. To this man, then, fathers of the Senate, with God's approval, I have assigned the office of Praetorian Prefect, for him to govern from the twelfth indiction [533-4]. Thus, by God's help and his own integrity, he may allay all the disputes which have accumulated through the trafficking of the untrustworthy, and, too long awaited, so act that he may serve all men. May heaven assist his plans, so that he, whose wisdom I have proved by long acquaintance, may be found successful in his own case, loyal to me, and useful to the state. May he leave to posterity a reputation by which he will make his family famous for ever.

X.3   QUEEN AMALASUINTHA TO THE SENATE OF THE CITY OF ROME (a.534, after Oct.2nd.)

1. Following the lamentable death of my son of divine memory, love of the common good overcame the soul of his devoted mother, so that she considered not her reasons for grief, but rather your profit. I looked to a ruler's cares as a source of strength and comfort. But that unique author of purity and pity [God], while depriving me of a youthful son, preserved for me the love of an adult cousin. 2. With God's favour, I have chosen as partner in my realm the most fortunate Theodahad. Thus I, who previously bore the burden of the state in solitary cogitation, may now pursue the good of all with united counsels, so that we who are two in our processes of thought may seem one person in our conclusions. The very stars of heaven are governed by mutual help, and order the world with their light by sharing and exchanging toil. Furthermore, Providence has given man himself two hands, a pair of ears, twin eyes, that the work accomplished by two partners may be done more effectively. 3. Rejoice, fathers of the Senate, and commend my deed in your prayers to the powers above. I who have chosen to order all things with another's counsel, have willed nothing blameworthy. In fact, a shared rule is a guarantee of good character, since the ruler who has a partner in power is rightly credited with a mild disposition.

Therefore, by God's help, I have kept my palace for a noble and distinguished man of my family: one who, sprung of Amal stock, will display royal stature in his actions. He is patient in adversity, moderate in prosperity, and - the hardest power to wield - has long been governor of himself. 4. To these good qualities is added enviable literary learning, which confers splendour on a nature deserving praise. There the wise man finds what will make him wiser; the warrior discovers what will strengthen him with courage; the prince learns how to administer his people with equity; and there can be no station in life which is not improved by the glorious knowledge of letters.

5. Receive something greater that the common prayers have earned: your prince is also learned in ecclesiastical letters. They

constantly remind us of what benefits mankind: to judge justly, to know the good, to venerate the divine, to think on the coming judgement. For he who believes that he must stand trial for his verdicts will inevitably follow the path of justice. I may be acquainted with the reading that whets the intellect; but divine reading strives ever to make a man devout.

6. I will move on to that most lavish sobriety he showed in private life: it won him so much wealth through his gifts, such a store of things through his banquets that, when his former efforts are considered, there seems nothing new in his kingship. He has been most ready in hospitality, most pitiful in charity: thus, while he spent so much of his own, his estates increased by heavenly recompense. All the world should wish for such a man as I have chosen, one who orders his property by the light of reason, and does not desire another's. For princes are not driven to extortion when they are used to administering and restraining their private affairs.[1] 7. No wonder that precept has been praised which counsels moderation, since even the good displeases us in excess.

Rejoice, now, fathers of the Senate, and make your prayers for us to the heavenly grace, since I have appointed as my fellow prince a man who will both execute the good deeds that spring from my justice, and display what belongs to his own devotion. For he is both admonished by the virtue of his ancestors, and effectively stimulated by his uncle Theoderic.

X.5 KING THEODAHAD TO HIS SERVANT THEODOSIUS (date as X.3)

1. It is my will that restraint should be the arbiter of affairs in my state of power, so that, the more I receive divine blessings, the more I may love equity. Indeed, private interests are clearly excluded from

---

[1] Amalasuintha had recently checked Theodahad's notorious land-grabbing; the irony is probably deliberate.

my heart, because, as common lord, I am made, by God's help, the guardian of all.

And therefore, by this order, I command that no one who is known to belong to my household, and is entrusted to your supervision, is to become overbearing in his arrogance; for only he who is at peace with the laws shall be called my own. Increase my reputation by your patience. 2. If anyone should happen to have a dispute with another, they must resort to the common laws: let the courts protect you, not wicked arrogance. I intend discipline to begin with my household, so that others may be ashamed to go wrong, when they see that I give my own men no license to transgress. I have changed my conduct with my station; and if, before, I keenly defended my just rights, I now temper all things with mercy. For a prince has no personal household; but I declare that whatever, by God's help, I rule, that thing is peculiarly my own. Take great care, then, about those who were formerly under my legal control: allow no one to transgress the laws in anything. Praise of you should reach my ears, rather than some complaint, since a good conscience is truly in command only when it hastens to excel in every way.

X.11   KING THEODAHAD TO THE ILLUSTRIOUS MAXIMUS,
         MEMBER OF THE CORPS OF BODYGUARDS[2]
         (a.535, Sept.1st)

If it is the glory of worthy princes to distinguish unknown persons by honours, since rulers win praise for the advancement of their subjects, how much more important it is for me to render to a most noble family what I know it has deserved even by the fortune of birth! For it is thus that I follow justice, by not denying to worthy heirs the

---

[2] Anicius Maximus, Consul in 523 (V.42), was a kinsman of Boethius, and probable descendant of the emperor Petronius Maximus (455). He was driven from Rome in 537 on suspicion of pro-Gothic treachery, but was killed by the Goths in 552; the name of his Amal bride is unknown.

rewards due to their forebears. For those who have deserved to live in my reign should surpass even their ancestors. 2. Assuredly, ancient times begot the Anicii, a house almost equal to princes; the dignity of their name, channelled down to you from the fountain of blood, gathering its powers, has shone out renewed and with greater joy. Who, then, would bequeath to posterity with lessened honour those who have so long been outstanding? My age would be condemned if such a family could lie hidden. But if only a greater span of life had preserved the Marii and Corvini for me![3] Had it befallen me to rule over men of such merits, a prince's hopes would be fulfilled - if only just. Yes, how could I, who long for things past, now neglect what I have discovered?

3. And therefore - may the decision be fortunate - I confer on you from the fourteenth indiction [535-6] the rank of senior membership [*primicerius*], which is also called the *domesticatus*.[4] You will enjoy all the rights that pertain to its functions. Although this honour may seem inferior to your origins, it still seems more fortunate than all your magistracies: for, in my time you have earned a bride of royal blood whom you did not dare to hope for in your Consulship.

4. Now so act as to make the honour you prayed for acceptable to me. Think on what you have earned, and you will behave as a man worthy of my kinship. For he who is united to a ruler's family is placed in the very bosom of fame. Gentleness is now given a greater

---

[3] Gennadius Avienus (Consul, 450), father of Faustus Niger, claimed descent from the Valerii Corvini of the republic (Sidonius, *Ep.* 1.9.4); apparently he united his line with the Anicii. The Anician link with the republican general Marius (c.157-86 B.C.) is otherwise unattested.

[4] This rank was originally reached by seniority in the bodyguards (*domestici*); like their Countship (II.16), it is probably now honorary. Theodahad's apologetic gift of a non-*illustris* rank to a former Consul may be diplomatic: early in 536, he was to undertake not to confer Patriciates and *illustris* offices without imperial consent (Procopius, *Wars* V.vi.3). However, Maximus' title may have been that of *primiceriatus cubiculi* given with the office of Count of the Sacred Largesses (cf. VI.7.4,9, Mommsen, 1889, 463f., *PLRE* II, 748). If so, Theodahad may be conferring *illustris* rank without offending Justinian!

task: beneficence and courtesy must now be dedicated to all, thus proving me to have chosen a man whom no prosperity can change. Enjoy your glory in humility, since fame is earned by modesty, hatred aroused by arrogance. Indeed, envy is the sure companion of promotion; pugnacity always increases it, but it is best overcome by forbearance. 5. Above all other virtues, cherish patience, which is dear to the wise. Elevated by me, you will be praised more for enduring than avenging wrongs. Overcome anger; love kindness. Take care that your good fortune does not seem superior to your character; instead, being bound to my family, prove yourself close kin by your glorious actions. Heretofore, your family has indeed been praised, but it has not been adorned by such a bond. There is no further way for your nobility to increase. Whatever you achieve with distinction will make you seem worthy of your own marriage.

[Maximus' unprecedented marriage, and the honour here conferred may mark an alliance between Theodahad and associates of Boethius (Barnish, 1990, 28ff.); they certainly show royal anxiety to reconcile the Senate on the eve of war.]

X.13   KING THEODAHAD TO THE SENATE OF THE CITY OF ROME (a.535, late/536)

1. I acknowledged the embassy of the venerable bishops and sent them back; nor did I oppose your requests, although I disapproved of them. Afterwards, certain men came to me, and reported that the city of Rome was still troubled by foolish anxiety, and was so behaving as to create from doubtful suspicions a certain peril for itself, unless it should concern my kindness to intervene.

Consider, from this, who should be blamed for the senseless fickleness of the people except the Senate, by which all things should be controlled and calmed. 2. All the provinces should, in fact, be so admonished by your wisdom that they adopt an attitude to do credit to the new reign of their prince. Indeed, if Rome offends, what city cannot be pardoned? The lesser hastens to model itself on the greater, and those who give a model to the erring rightly bear the blame for another's deed. 3. But I give thanks to God, who has instead enhanced His gifts by your transgressions. Behold, I have pardoned your faults before experiencing any acts of loyalty. I am no debtor, but I still pay; I am your benefactor in advance, so that later I may find you grateful. But, although, in this case, the strictness of my restraint is affirmed, I still wish myself to be honoured only if the goodwill of Roman loyalty can also be demonstrated. For I profit more from your reputation than from praise for my constant composure. 4. Discard suspicions that are for ever alien to your order. The Senate, which ought to govern others by its paternal exhortation, should not require correction. For whence will good conduct derive its inspiration, should the fathers of the state be found unequal to their task? It is enough for noblemen, it is enough for men of honour, that I am encouraging in the aim of perfect loyalty those whom I have blamed a little for their perverse suspicion.

For, in requesting your presence [at court], I have taken deep thought to benefit, not to injure and harass you; hence, you should carry out all the more what I know will be to your advantage. 5. To see the prince is a sure favour. Men usually seek it as a reward; through you, I intend it to benefit the state. But, lest this very medicine should seem, in any way, a bitter one, I have ordered individuals to be summoned to me as affairs require, so that Rome is not stripped of its citizens, while my counsels are assisted by men of wisdom.[5]

6. Return, then, to your original loyalty, and let my cares, which I sustain for the common good, be instead assisted by your talents. For this has always been grafted on you, to offer resolute integrity to your princes, and to obey not from the compulsion of fear, but rather from love of the ruler. I have charged X, the bearer of this letter, with the remainder to be delivered orally, so that you may trust in my admonitions, with all doubtful thoughts removed.

[Roman fears seem to have been aroused by Theodahad's proposal to install a Gothic garrison; cf. X.14, 18. (Officially, this was to provide external, not internal security, an

---

[5] Cf. III.28.

excuse which helps to date the letters.) He is politely threatening to hold senators hostage
at the court. However, when Witigis replaced him, both intentions apparently had still
to be fulfilled (Procopius, *Wars* V.xi.26). Theodahad's position was very weak, and, at
some stage, he reassured the Senate and people by an oath of goodwill (XI.16-17).]

X.20   KING THEODAHAD TO THE EMPRESS THEODORA
(a.535, perhaps in May)

1. I have received your piety's letters with the gratitude always
due to things we long for, and have gained, with most reverent joy,
your verbal message, more exalted than any gift. I promise myself
everything from so serene a soul, since, in such kindly discourse, I
have received whatever I could hope for. 2. For you exhort me to bring
first to your attention anything I decide to ask from the triumphal
prince, your husband. Who can now doubt that what so great a power
deigns to advocate will attain its object? Previously, indeed, I relied on
the justice of my cause, but now I have more happiness in your
promise. For my pleas cannot be adjourned when they involve her who
has a right to an audience. Now fulfill your promises, that you may
cause the man to whom you gave a sure hope to hold his own.

3. It also adds to my joy that your serenity has despatched such
a man as so much glory shou'd send, and your service should retain.[6]
For inevitably, she in whom it is constantly observed chooses a man of
good character, since a mind formed by worthy precepts is clearly
purified.

Hence it is that, advised by your reverence, I ordained that both
the most blessed Pope [probably Agapitus] and the most noble Senate
should reply without any delay to what you saw fit to request from
them: thus, your glory will lose no reverence because a spirit of delay
opposed it; but rather, speed of action will increase your favour that we

---

[6] This is Peter, later Justinian's Master of Offices, and a learned and eloquent historian
praised by John Lydus. Cassiodorus is here praising an ex-prostitute for her moral
upbringing!

pray for. 4. For, in the case of that person[7] too, about whom a delicate hint has reached me, know that I have ordered what I trust will agree with your intention. For it is my desire that you should command no less in my realm than in your empire, through the medium of your influence. Now, I inform you that I made the venerable Pope issue the afore-mentioned reply before your envoy, the bearer of this letter, could leave the city of Rome, lest anything might happen to oppose your intention.

5. Therefore, saluting you with the reverence that should be shown to such merits, I have taken special care to send the venerable [bishop] X, a man of weight, both for character and doctrine, and to be revered for the honour of his holiness, with the office of envoy to your clemency;[8] for I believe that you will welcome those persons whom I judge acceptable in the divine mysteries.

X.21   QUEEN GUDELIVA TO THE EMPRESS THEODORA
(date as X.20)

1. You should consider, wisest of empresses, how urgently I desire to win your favour, which the lord my husband also wishes very zealously to obtain. For, although this is dear to him in every way, to me, though, it is clearly of special importance, since the love of such a queen can so exalt me that I evidently find something superior to a kingdom.[9] For what can be more welcome than to appear a sharer in the glory of your love? Since you shine out so profusely, make a willing loan to me from your own splendour, for light loses nothing when its radiance is lavished on another. Encourage my desires, which you know to be altogether sincere. Your favour should commend me

---

[7] Is this Amalasuintha?

[8] This is probably not the Rusticus of Procopius, *Wars* V.vi.13, who was probably identical with a deacon of Rome.

[9] Theodahad and Gudeliva hoped to find 'something superior to a kingdom' in a title, estates, and the emperor's friendship at Constantinople (Procopius, *Wars* V.vi.12, 15-26).

in every realm. For you should make me bright, since I wish to shine from your lustre.

2. Therefore, giving your serenity a reverent greeting, with affectionate daring I commend myself to your heart. I hope that your marvellous wisdom may so order all things that the trust which your heart grants me will grow ever fuller. For, although there should be no discord between the Roman realms, nonetheless, an affair[10] has arisen of a kind which should make me still dearer to your justice.

X.22   KING THEODAHAD TO THE EMPEROR JUSTINIAN
(date probably as X.20)

1. You remember, wisest of princes, thanks both to my envoys, and to the most eloquent Peter, whom your piety recently despatched to me, the zeal with which I am seeking peace with your imperial serenity. And now I must again make the same requests, through the most holy [bishop] X, so that pleas which you know have been frequent, you may judge to be true and affectionate. Indeed, since I have no reasons for conflict, I ask for peace in all sincerity. May such a peace come to me, so well settled, so glorious, that I may seem to have done right in seeking it by such prayers. But the task I have undertaken should not be a burden; instead, consider what is right for me. 2. For he whose cause is supposed to be ordered by reason is drawn to acts of kindness; nor can he who wins more glory by helping one who trusts him prefer his own profit.

Consider, also, learned prince, the historical records of your ancestors.[11] Remember how much your predecessors took care to

---

[10] Is this the murder of Amalasuintha? Cf. Bury, II, 167.

[11] For *et abavi vestri historica monimenta*, Mommsen (also Fridh) read *et Ablabi vestri...*, seeing a reference to the lost history of Ablavius, 'describer of the Goths', cited in Jordanes' *Getica*, and so probably known to Cassiodorus. In favour of the MSS, see Goffart, 1988, 62, n.208, followed here. Justinian was the second emperor of his house; 'ancestors' is merely an elegant variation on 'predecessors'. The *Getica* is interested in treaty relations between emperors and Goths.

concede from their legal rights, that they might procure alliances [*foedera*] with my forebears. Weigh up the gratitude with which things repeatedly demanded should be received when freely offered. I am stating the truth, not speaking in arrogance. What I am trying to prove is really to the advantage of your glory, since those who know themselves to be better than their forebears are now seeking an increase of your favour. Let those whom you once joined to you by zealous generosity be linked to your heart in gratuitous friendship; otherwise, good things may be thought to belong only to those times which you are surpassing with a wealth of kindness and a flow of gifts.

3. And therefore, addressing you in advance with an honourable greeting, I have caused the venerable X, distinguished by his priesthood and famous for the praise of his doctrine, to convey to your love the prayers of my embassy. For I trust in the divine power, that he will both please you amply by his merits, and achieve the aims of a sincere request; I hope to receive him quickly, with the business carried out. But, because a letter cannot include everything, I have entrusted some material to be brought verbally to your sacred notice, lest the lengthy reading of documents should weary you.

[Much of Justinian's propaganda from this period asserts his superiority to previous emperors, but affirms historical interests, and respect for Roman tradition (see Maas). Cassiodorus seems alive to this in his diplomatic drafting.]

X.26   KING THEODAHAD TO THE EMPEROR JUSTINIAN (a.535)

1. I appreciate that the favour of your serenity is richer than any gift, since what you urge me to do would profit me in every way. Such, indeed, is the constant prayer of one who loves you: that you should request me to take up cases of pity which may commend me to the divine power.

2. And therefore, I bring to the notice of your glory the monastery of God's servants, which was reported to you to be labouring under heavy taxation, since its land has been covered by a great flood, and has become barren through hostile waters. What is more, I have given instructions to the most eminent Praetorian Prefect [Cassiodorus] Senator that, by his provident ordinance, a careful inspector should go to the estate complained of; and, when an orderly enquiry has taken place, and things have been weighed up, whatever burden the holding may suffer from shall be reasonably removed. Thus, its owners will be left with a proper and sufficient benefit, since I judge concessions made in accordance with the wish of your kindness to be truly my most precious gain.

3. Furthermore, about the case of Ranilda, of which your serenity deigned to remind me, it happened a long time ago, under the rule of my kin. However, it is my duty to settle the matter from my own generosity, that, by such a deed, her change of religion may cause her no regret.[12] 4. Indeed, I do not presume to exercise judgement in those cases where I have no special mandate. For, since the Deity allows various religions to exist, I do not dare to impose one alone. For I remember reading that we should sacrifice to the Lord of our own will, not at the command of anyone who compels us [Psalm 53.8 / 54.6]. He who tries to do otherwise clearly opposes the heavenly decree. Rightly, then, your piety requests me to do what is enjoined on me by the divine ordinances.

[This letter shows Justinian's interference in Italian affairs before the outbreak of war. Catholic-Arian relations may have been a pretext for invasion which Procopius ignored. Despite its servility, the letter - as published - implies a criticism of the intolerant emperor; cf. II.27.]

---

[12] Ranilda had presumably converted from Arian to Catholic Christianity.

X.31   KING WITIGIS TO ALL THE GOTHS (a.536, about Dec.1st)

1. Although every promotion must be ascribed to the gift of God, nor is anything a blessing unless we know that He bestowed it, nonetheless, the case of royal office must be especially ascribed to the judgement of Heaven. For God Himself has certainly ordained the man to whom He assigns the obedience of His people.

Hence I thank my originator most humbly, and announce that my kinsmen the Goths, placing me on a shield among the swords of battle, in the ancestral way, have conferred on me the kingly office by God's gift. Thus arms bestow an honour based on a reputation won in war. 2. For you must know that I was chosen not in privy chambers, but in the wide and open fields; I was not sought among the subtle debates of sycophants, but as the trumpets blared, so that the Gothic race of Mars, roused by such a din, and longing for their native courage, might find themselves a martial king.[13] For could brave men, nourished among the turmoils of war, long endure a prince so untried that they were anxious for his fame, although they trusted in their own courage? For inevitably, the reputation of a whole people corresponds to the ruler which that race has earned. 3. Now as you may have heard, I was summoned by the perils of my kindred, and came prepared to endure the common fortune with you all; but those who were looking for an experienced king did not suffer me to be their general [*dux*]. Therefore, give your assent first to the judgement of divine favour, then to the judgement of the Goths, since, by voting for me unanimously, all of you make me king.

Put aside now your fear of punishment, discard suspicions that you will suffer loss: you need fear no harsh treatment under my rule. I who have waged war many times know how to love the brave. Moreover, I am the witness to each of your warriors. There is no need for another to recount your deeds to me: I am a partner in your toils, and know them all. Gothic arms will never be broken by any change

---

[13] Like others, Cassiodorus falsely identified the Goths with the warlike Thracian Getae, who worshipped the war-god Mars.

in my promises to you: all that I do will look to the benefit of our race; I will not have private attachments; I promise to pursue what will honour the royal name.[14] 5. Finally, I promise that my rule will, in all things, be such as the Goths should possess following the glorious Theoderic. He was a man peculiarly and nobly formed for the cares of kingship, so that every prince is rightly considered excellent only in so far as he is known to love his policies. Hence, he who can imitate his deeds should be thought of as his kinsman. And therefore you should take thought for the general good of our realm, with, by God's help, an easy mind as to its internal affairs.

[Exasperated by Theodahad's military lethargy, the Gothic army elevated Witigis while it was on campaign; it had apparently played no part in the accessions of Theodahad or Athalaric. In his panegyric on Witigis, Cassiodorus stressed his warlike qualities, and contrasted Athalaric (*MGH AA* XII, 473-9).]

X.32   KING WITIGIS TO THE EMPEROR JUSTINIAN
   (a.537, Dec.)

1. What the prayed-for sweetness of your favour means to me, most merciful emperor, may be understood from this fact: after so many terrible injuries, and the infliction of so much bloodshed, I am to be seen asking you for peace, as though none of your servants had previously injured me. I have endured such wrongs as might trouble even the perpetrators: persecutions with no charge brought, hatred unaroused by offence, losses where no debt was incurred. And this cannot be passed over as trivial: it was inflicted not in the provinces only, but in the capital itself. Think what grievances I am setting aside to obtain your justice. A deed has been done for the world to talk of, and it should be so settled by you that all may wonder at your equity. 2. For if vengeance on king Theodahad is sought, I deserve your love. If you have before your eyes respect for Queen Amalasuintha of divine

---

[14] The Goths had suspected Theodahad of treason, and had resented his favouritism.

memory, you should think on her daughter [Matasuentha], whom the efforts of all your men should have brought to her kingdom, so that every race might appreciate the return of favour you rendered to such a daughter.

3. This fact, moreover, should influence you: by a marvellous design, God made us acquainted with each other before reaching the summit of rule, thus giving a motive for love to those on whom He had bestowed the pleasure of that sight. For with what reverence can I honour the prince whom I admired while still placed in a private station? But, even now, you can heal all that has been done, since it is easy to keep the affection of one who is evidently and sincerely seeking your favour.

4. And therefore, greeting your clemency with due honour, I inform you that I have sent X and Y as envoys to the wisdom of your serenity. Thus, after your habit, you may give thought to all things, so that either commonwealth may endure in harmony restored. Thus, too, what was established and praised under previous princes may, by God's help, be increased all the more in your reign. But the rest I have entrusted to the aforementioned envoys to be delivered by word of mouth, so that the brevity of a letter may touch on some matters, while those who report to you will advise you more fully of my case.

[Krautschick (95) connects this letter with the embassy sent to Justinian when it became clear that the siege of Belisarius in Rome was failing (Procopius, *Wars* VI.vi-vii.15). Was Cassiodorus was the 'Roman distinguished among the Goths' (VI.vi.3) who negotiated an armistice before the embassy departed?]

XI.1 [CASSIODORUS] SENATOR, PRAETORIAN PREFECT, TO THE SENATE OF THE CITY OF ROME (date as IX.24)

1. You commend my promotion to me, fathers of the Senate, by my knowledge that you prayed for it: for I believe that an event assuredly desired by so many men of good fortune must have been highly propitious. Indeed, your wishes clearly inaugurate all good things, since no one can be honoured by such as you unless Providence has ordained his advancement. Receive my thanks, then, in return, even as you require my dutiful obedience. It is natural to love a colleague. In fact, it is your own glory that you extoll, if you exalt the honour given to a Senator [Cassiodorus]. 2. Anxiety for the senators drives me urgently into public service: thus, when I have earned approval by such assistance, it may be ascribed instead to your glory. Next to the princes [Athalaric and Amalasuintha], it is my concern to commend myself to you, for I trust that you love what I know the lords of the state also command. The first command is that I should think honesty the best policy; that justice should always accompany and wait on my acts; and that I should not disgrace and prostitute a post which I obtained unpurchased from an upright prince.

3. You have heard my praise, princely gentlemen, and the weight of the affairs which I have taken on.[1] An eulogised entry on high office makes demands beyond one's strength. I do not dare to give these words the lie, but I admit their too powerful influence: for such judgements have not discovered my merits, but created them. Neither do I boast myself of them, understanding that our lords wished to exalt the lowly: they must not seem to have conferred such powers on the unworthy. The blessings of a famous reign are whirling me away, and inviting a man thirsty, as it were, with long drought to take a drink of sweetest savour.

4. O blessed fortune of the age! The king is on holiday, and his mother's affection holds rule; thereby, she so acts in everything that we may feel the protection of a universal love. He to whom all things are

---

[1] This alludes to IX.25.

subject accords this lady a glorious obedience. With wonderful restraint and harmony, he now begins to command his own character before he can rule the people. This is truly the hardest kind of rule, for a young man to bear sway over his own senses. It is the rarest of blessings when a king triumphs in character, and reaches in the prime of life what grey-haired restraint can hardly attain.[2] 5. Let us rejoice, fathers of the Senate, and give thanks to the majesty of heaven with prayerful devotion; for, as time moves on, no act of clemency will be difficult for our king, who has learned as a boy to be the servant of piety.

But we must ascribe this wonder to the characters of them both; for such is his mother's genius, whom even a foreign prince should rightfully obey. 6. For every realm most properly reveres her. To behold her inspires awe; to hear her discourse, wonder. In what tongue is not her learning proven? She is fluent in the splendour of Greek oratory; she shines in the glory of Roman eloquence; the flow of her ancestral speech brings her glory; she surpasses all in their own languages, and is equally wonderful in each. For if it is the part of a man of sense to be well acquainted with his native tongue, how should we value the wisdom which retains and faultlessly practises so many kinds of eloquence? 7. Hence, the different races have a great and necessary safeguard, since no one needs an interpreter when addressing the ears of our wise mistress. For the envoy suffers no delay, and the appellant no damage from the slowness of his translator, since each is heard in his own words, and is answered in the speech of his nation. To this is added, as it were a glorious diadem, the priceless knowledge of literature, through which she learns the wisdom of the ancients, and the royal dignity is constantly increased. 8. But, although she rejoices in such linguistic perfection, she is so silent in public business that you would think her indolent. She unties the knots of litigation by a few words; she quietly calms heated conflicts; she acts in silence for the public good. You do not hear proclaimed the measures which are

---

[2] Procopius (*Wars* V.ii) shows Athalaric as a drunken lecher, resisting his mother's discipline. Cassiodorus probably draws deliberate attention to this by describing the opposing qualities.

openly adopted; and, with wonderful restraint, she transacts by stealth
what she knows must be done in haste.

9. Has revered antiquity achieved the like? There is Placidia, with
a famous reputation in the world: we have learnt that she was glorious
for her descent from various emperors, and cared for her imperial son.
But we know that the empire she slackly ruled for him was shamefully
diminished. Eventually, she purchased a daughter-in-law by the loss of
Illyricum: rulers were united, but the provinces lamentably divided.[3]
Moreover, she weakened the soldiery by too much peace. Protected by
his mother, he endured what he · could scarcely have suffered if
abandoned. 10. But under this queen, all whose kindred is royal, with
God's help our army will terrify foreign powers. By prudent and nicely
calculated policy, it is neither worn down by continual fighting, nor,
again, is it enervated by prolonged peace.

Moreover, at the very outset of the reign, when a new regime
always attracts danger, she made the Danube a Roman river against the
will of the eastern prince [the emperor]. 11. The sufferings of the
invaders are well known: in my judgement, they should be passed over,
lest the spirit of an allied prince should bear a loser's shame.[4] For his
opinion of our lands may be understood from the fact that, despite his
injury, he granted us a peace which he refused to the prayers of others.
Then, too, he has honoured us with many embassies, although we
seldom approached him; and that outstanding power has bowed down
the awe-inspiring glory of the East that it might elevate the lords of
Italy.[5]

12. Again, there are the Franks, of great power from so many

---

[3] Galla Placidia, daughter of Theodosius I, ruled the western empire for her son
Valentinian III, from 425 to 437; he married Licinia Eudoxia, daughter of the eastern
emperor Theodosius II in 437. The marriage was purchased with part of the Diocese of
Illyricum, including areas later controlled by Theoderic and Athalaric.

[4] This otherwise unattested incident probably occurred under Justin, but Justinian will
have been responsible; barbarian tribes, rather than imperial troops, may have been used.

[5] This suggests that Justinian angled diplomatically for control of the Gothic kingdom
during much of Athalaric's reign; the lack of response may have been due less to
Amalasuintha than to her enemies among the tribal nobility; cf. Procopius, *Wars* V.ii.

victories over barbarians: how vast was the expedition that dismayed them! When attacked, they feared to join battle with our troops, although they constantly carry war to other tribes in sudden assault. But, though this proud nation declined the conflict, they could not avoid the death of their own king. For their Theoderic, who had long gloried in a mighty name, was conquered by sickness, rather than battle, and died to the triumph of our princes. This, I believe, was ordained by God, lest war with our kindred should defile us, or a justly mobilised army should not enjoy some vengeance. Hail to you, army of the Goths, of happiest fortune! You have slain a royal enemy without costing us the death of the meanest soldier.[6]

13. Indeed, the Burgundian also, to regain his own, has become a loyal subject; he has surrendered himself wholly, to recover a small territory. In fact, he has chosen to obey us uninjured, rather than to resist with his land diminished; when he laid down his arms, then he defended his realm more securely. For what he lost in battle, he has regained by petition. Blessed are you, mistress, rich in praise; one from whom God's favour removes all need for war, since you either subdue the enemies of the state by heavenly fortune, or join them to your sway by spontaneous generosity. 14. Rejoice, Goths and Romans alike: this marvel is worthy of all men's praise. Behold, by God's favour, our fortunate mistress has achieved the glory of either sex: for she has both borne us a glorious king, and has secured a spreading empire by the courage of her soul.

15. At all events, her praises have been recounted, so far as they relate to war; for, should I wish to enter the halls of her devotion, 'a hundred tongues and a hundred mouths' [Vergil, *Aeneid* VI.625] would hardly suffice me: her justice and goodwill are equal, but her kindness is a greater thing than her power. Let me then say small things about great matters, a few words about many. You know how many blessings, with her heavenly kindness, she has bestowed on our order:

---

[6] Theoderic I, son of Clovis, was king of the eastern Franks from 511 to 533; in 531 he had defeated the Thuringi, whose queen Amalaberga was a cousin of Amalasuintha (IV.1); his wife was Amalasuintha's niece.

there can be no doubt, where the Senate bears witness. She has restored the afflicted to a better state;[7] and she has exalted with honours the uninjured of whom she is the general protector, and bestowed goods on each of them.

16. Already the benefits I proclaim have increased. For consider the Patrician Liberius, also Prefect of Gaul, a man of military experience, charming for his courtesy, distinguished by his merits, good to look on, but made still more handsome by his scars. He has obtained the reward of his labours, so that he does not lose the Prefecture he wielded so well, but, as a great man, is adorned by a twofold honour. One honour only does not suffice for his reward, but the pair proclaim his deserts. For he also receives the office of Patrician-in-Waiting [*patricius praesentalis*], lest one who has deserved well of the state should be thought unwelcome through his long absence. 17. O wonderful kindness of our lords, which has so far exalted the aforementioned man that, after conferring high office, it also sees fit to extend his patrimony. This has been as gratefully received by the public as if all men thought themselves enriched, in fact, by the gift made to him; for whatever is bestowed on one worthy man is felt unquestionably to be conferred on many.[8]

Why, then, should I mention her firmness of mind, which surpasses even the most famous philosophers? From the queen's mouth issue words of goodwill, and promises that can be trusted. 18. The things I speak of, fathers of the Senate, have not been untested by me; the praise of the experienced is a truthful witness. For you know what wishes fought against me: neither gold, nor powerful pleas could prevail. All things were tried, that the glorious constancy of our wise queen might be tested.

19. The form of the declamation demands that I should compare the

---

[7] This may refer to her restoration of confiscated property to the family of Boethius and Symmachus (Procopius, *Wars* V.ii.5).

[8] On Liberius, see II.16; he was later to enter the service of Justinian in anger at Amalasuintha's murder; from this passage, it is tempting to give him some share in her purge of her Gothic enemies, and to link him politically with Cassiodorus.

parade of past empresses with her recent case. But how could these feminine examples suffice for one who surpasses all the praise given to men? If the royal band of her ancestors were to look on this woman, they would soon see their glory reflected, as in a clear mirror. For Amalus was distinguished for his good fortune, Ostrogotha for his patience, Athala for mercy, Winitarius for justice, Unimundus for beauty, Thorismuth for chastity, Walamer for good faith, Theudimer for his sense of duty, her glorious father, as you have seen, for his wisdom.[9] Assuredly, all these would here individually recognise their own qualities; but they would happily admit that these were surpassed, since one man's glory cannot rightly equate itself with a throng of virtues. 20. Think what their joy would be in such an heir, one who can transcend the merits of them all.

Perhaps you request separate treatment for the good qualities of the king; but he who praises the parent extols the child abundantly. Then, you should recall the remarkable words of the eloquent Symmachus:[10] 'Expecting cheerfully his growth in virtue, I put off praising his beginnings.' Assist me, fathers of the Senate; and, by giving thanks for me to our common lords, discharge my debt with your repayment: for, as one man is powerless to satisfy the wishes of all, so many can fulfill the requirements of one.

XI.2   [CASSIODORUS] SENATOR, PRAETORIAN PREFECT, TO POPE JOHN [II] (date as IX.24)

1. I must beseech you, most blessed Father, that the joy which, by God's generosity, I have obtained through you, I may know to be preserved for me by your prayers. For who could doubt that my good fortune must be ascribed to your merits, since I, who do not deserve God's love, have attained to honour, and, by a reversal of obligation,

---

[9] On these ancestors, see Jordanes, *Getica*, 79-81, 199f., probably deriving from Cassiodorus' *Gothic History*.

[10] Probably the elder Symmachus, Consul 391.

have received good things, although I did not perform the like? For by the fasting of churchmen, famine is banished from the people; by their seemly tears, ugly grief departs; and holy men hurry away troubles that might otherwise be prolonged.

2. And therefore, greeting you with proper dutifulness, I beg you to pray earnestly for the welfare of our rulers, so that the Prince of Heaven may give them long life, diminish the enemies of the Roman state, and grant us quiet times. May He also adorn our peace by bestowing on us from the granaries of His abundance the food we need. And for me, your son, may He open up the spirit of understanding, that I may pursue those things that are truly profitable, and avoid those that should be shunned. 3. May that rational force of the soul give me counsel; may the face of truth grow bright, lest the body's darkness overcloud my mind; may I follow what is within me, lest I become a stranger to myself; may that which is wise with the true wisdom instruct me; may that which shines with the light of heaven illumine me. In short, may public affairs find me such a magistrate as the Catholic Church should send out as her son. May holy virtue guard me even among her gifts, since when I receive her favours, I then endure the deadlier wiles of the ancient adversary [Satan].

4. Do not hand over to me alone the care of that city which, in fact, is safe by your excellence. For you preside as a sentinel over the Christian people; with a father's name, you love all men. The safety of the people, therefore, redounds to your fame, to whom God has entrusted their protection. Hence, I must think on some things, but you on all. For you give spiritual food to the flock entrusted to you, but you cannot neglect what supports the substance of the body. For, as man consists of two natures, so it is the part of a good father to cherish them both. First, by your holy prayers, avert the bad seasons that our sins deserve. But if any such should occur - and may they never - dearth is effectively banished when planned against in time of plenty. 5. Advise me of the duties I should perform with care. Even under your rebuke, I wish to do right, since it is harder for the sheep to stray which hopes to hear the shepherd's voice; nor is a man easily corrupted when under pressure from a constant censor. I am indeed a palatine judge, but I will not cease to be your disciple; for my actions will then

be correct if I keep closely to your principles. But, since I wish to be both advised by your counsels and assisted by your prayers, it must now be ascribed to you if anything undesirable is found in me.

6. May that see, a marvel throughout the globe, cover its own congregation with a love which, although it is bestowed universally on the whole world, is also locally allotted to us. We possess something special of the holy Apostles [Peter and Paul], if it is not estranged and severed from us by our sins. For happy Rome has attained to holding in her breast those burial places that all Christians long to see. 7. Therefore, with such patrons we fear nothing, if the bishop's prayers are not lacking. It is, indeed, a hard task to satisfy the wants of so many; but the Deity knows how to give great gifts. May he subdue the envious, form for us citizens of loveable character in their hopes of Heaven, and bestow on your prayers such times as proclaim the indulgence of divine favour.

XI.13 THE SENATE OF THE CITY OF ROME TO THE EMPEROR JUSTINIAN (date as X.20)

1. It seems a most honourable and necessary undertaking to appeal to a dutiful prince for the safety of the Roman state, since it is proper to request from you what may assist our freedom. For, to the other blessings that Providence has especially bestowed on you, nothing more glorious is added than your knowledge that you can confer benefits in every place.

We beseech you therefore, most merciful emperor, stretching out both hands from the lap of the Senate, to bestow on our king [Theodahad] your most enduring peace. Do not let us, who have always seemed welcome to your friendship, become your enemies. 2. If you grant your kindness to our lords, you are, in fact, commending the Roman name. Your favour raises and protects us, and we know your feelings are deserved. Let your treaty, therefore, establish the peace of Italy, for if the bond of love we prayed for is tied by you, then we will be cherished.

Should our pleas still seem insufficient in this matter, imagine that
our country breaks out into these pleadings: 3. 'If I was ever esteemed
by you, most devoted of princes, love my defenders. Those who rule
me should be at one with you, lest they begin to do such deeds against
me as they know to differ from your wishes. Do not be the cause of
my cruel death, you who have always bestowed on me the joys of life.
Look how my children have increased under your peace, how I shine
in the glory of my citizens. If you allow me to be injured, where will
you now display your name for devotion? My religion, which is your
own, is known to be flourishing; why then do you try to do more for
me? My Senate grows in honours; its wealth is constantly increased. 4.
Do not waste through enmity what you should defend in war. I have
had many kings, but none of such education; I have had many wise
men, but none of such might in learning and piety. I love the Amal
who has sucked at my breasts, the brave man formed by my society,
dear to the Romans for his wisdom, revered for his courage by the
tribes. No, no: join your wishes to his, share counsels with him, that
any increase in my prosperity may redound to your glory. Do not seek
me in such a way that you will not find me. I am no less yours in love,
if you cause no-one to tear my limbs. 5. For, if Africa deserved to
receive her freedom through you, it is cruel for me to lose a freedom
which I have always been seen to possess. Greatest of victors, control
the impulses of your anger. The general petition carries more weight
than the conquest of your soul by the assault of some ill will.'[11]

6. These are the words of Rome, as she supplicates you through her
senators. But, if this is of small force, you should think on the most
holy petition of the blessed Apostles Peter and Paul. For your princely
power should grant anything to the merits of those who have often
defended Rome against her enemies. But, that all things may seem
fitting to your reverence, we have decided to submit our pleas through
the venerable bishop X, sent to your clemency as the envoy of our

---

[11] This first person appeal has precedents in Cicero (*Against Catiline* I.18, 27-9), but may
be modelled on Ennodius, 80.157-63 (*Life of Epiphanius*). Imperial forces had
reconquered parts of Africa from the Vandals in 533-4.

most pious king: thus, those who might win single favours from pious souls, should now achieve many aims.

[The Senate may have sent this appeal under threat of massacre; cf. Bury, II, 168.]

XI.14 [CASSIODORUS] SENATOR, PRAETORIAN PREFECT, TO GAUDIOSUS, *CANCELLARIUS* IN THE PROVINCE OF LIGURIA (a.533-7)

1. Since many roads make for the city of Como, its land-owners report that they are so exhausted from the constant provision of extra post-horses, that they are in fact trampled down by the passage of too many steeds. By royal indulgence, I command that favour shall always be maintained towards them, lest that city, attractively habitable from its location, should grow depopulated through the frequency of the damage.[12]

For, behind the distant mountains and the vast expanse of the clear lake, it is a kind of wall for the Ligurian plain. Although it is evidently a key defence of the province, such is its beauty that it seems to be formed for pleasure alone. 2. To its rear, it supplies cultivated levels, both suited for the amenity of riding, and fit for a generous supply of food. To its front, it enjoys the amenity of sixty miles of sweet water, so that the spirit is gratified with refreshment and delight, while no storms drive away the supply of fish. Rightly, therefore, it has received the name of Como, rejoicing in the gifts that make it comely.

Here the lake is indeed enfolded in the depth of a very great valley; exquisitely imitating the shape of a shell, it is picked out with white on its foamy shores. 3. Around it the beautiful peaks of lofty mountains are gathered like a crown; its coasts are exquisitely adorned by great and gleaming villas, and are enclosed as though by a belt with the perennial greenery of a forest of olives. Above this, leafy vines climb

---

[12] Cassiodorus failed to show how the postal burdens were to be relieved! Were *breves* attached to give the detail? It may have been specified in the petition from Como.

the mountain sides. But the summit itself, curled, so to speak, with thick hair of chestnut-trees, is painted by adorning nature. Thence torrents that shine with snowy whiteness are hurled downwards by the height, and fall to the levels of the lake. 4. Into its bays, the river Addua flows from the south, and is received with open jaws. It is so named for this reason: because, fed from a double source, it flows down as though into a sea of its own. Such is the speed with which it enters the waves of the vast expanse that, keeping its name and colour, it is poured northward in a swollen bellied stream.[13] You would think that a darker line had been drawn across the pale waters; and the discoloured character of the influx, which is supposed to mingle with a liquid like itself, is strangely visible. 5. This also happens even to the waves of the sea, when rivers flood in. But the reason is very obvious, since headlong torrents, polluted with mud and filth, differ in colour from the glass-clear sea. But this will be rightly thought a natural wonder, when you see a sluggish lake traversed with great speed by an element like it in so many qualities. You would suppose the river was flowing over solid ground when you see it unable to mix in colour with the alien waters.[14]

6. And so, the inhabitants of these places should rightly be spared, since everything beautiful is too tender for toil, and those who habitually enjoy sweet delights easily feel the burden of affliction. Let them therefore enjoy a royal and perpetual gift, that, as they are happy in their native luxuries, so the prince's generosity may give them joy.

[With this letter, compare XII.15. Ennodius, 10 (Ep.I.6), shows that an earlier Quaestor

---

[13] Cassiodorus etymologises the name as a duobus, 'from two,' - the two rivers Mera and Addua enter the lake very close together. The Addua in fact flows through the lake from north to south!

[14] This account of the Addua seems to use and echo Ammianus Marcellinus' description (XV.4.3-6) of the Rhine flowing through Lake Constance - important evidence for sixth century knowledge of the greatest historian of the late empire among the senatorial class which had snubbed him in his own life-time. (On possible use of Ammianus by Cassiodorus in the Gothic History, see Heather, 110-18.)

and Praetorian Prefect, Faustus Niger, wrote an eulogy of the Como region; certain themes - fish, olive groves, great villas, the flow of the rivers through the lake - reappear in XI.14. Was Cassiodorus consciously rivalling his predecessor? He may also be replying to Ennodius' humorous claims that the amenities of Como were disastrous: while struggling to maintain their ancestral stately homes, its landowners attracted the attentions of the tax-assessor.]

XI.16 [CASSIODORUS] SENATOR, PRAETORIAN PREFECT, TO THE LIGURIANS (a.533-7)

1. It is my duty to support with zeal those whom the royal pity has decided to assist, for those on whom the clemency of our rulers has descended should also use their own magistracies to provide for the subjects. You have recently thanked me for giving you a hope of good things, rather than any fruition. By receiving my promises with great joy, you have encouraged me to confer benefits. I have discharged the vow of a magistrate under an obligation. Former promises are now demonstrably fulfilled.

2. Let me, then, make a start with the scales, since the discourse of a magistrate should begin at that point where it is right to apply one's conscience. Hence it is that you report yourselves to be oppressed in the matter of weights and measures. And therefore, my care will provide that no man's evil doing shall trouble you further from that quarter, since I think it a heavy crime either for measures to exceed the mode, or for scales to lack the justice of an equitable weight.[15] 3. Moreover, as to the civil servants of my office and the civic tax collectors [*exactores* and *susceptores*], who have, you complain, inflicted heavy losses on you, I have commanded them to be summoned, that they may clarify their accounts, and pay off without delay any fraud that may be found in them. For this, I declare, is at odds with my time of office, that one man should rejoice in another's loss.

---

[15] Official scales and weights were used by collectors to weigh coins and produce; for abuses, cf., e.g., *C.Th.* XII.16.19,21, Majorian, *Novel* 7.14-15.

4. Now turn your purpose to the supply of the most flourishing army, and procure everything without any complaint or delay. For you effectively constrain me to every act of kindness if you readily carry out your orders. He on whom the common cause enjoins action should obey with joy. Only those losses should cause pain which have clearly been inflicted by greed. For that which is commanded by necessity gives no trouble to the spirit of the wise.

[The Prefect sees just and efficient administration under the old Roman convention of exchange of services (*beneficium* and *officium*) between patron and client.]

XI.36 [CASSIODORUS] SENATOR, PRAETORIAN PREFECT, TO ANATOLICUS, *CANCELLARIUS* IN THE PROVINCE OF SAMNIUM (a.534, late)

1. He who invented laborious services and duties demanding great pains, also, and with reason, appointed time limits, so that the reward established for old age should have no uncertainty. Otherwise, who could be for ever watchful[16] and capable when the very light is withdrawing itself from mortal men? Hence, in this uncertain life, state service is certain, and he who has deservedly reached the appointed time without transgression has nothing to fear.

2. The stars themselves, as the astronomers will have it, although they circle and return without cease, keep the set times of their courses. Bodies kept within their own bounds cannot be unpredictable. Saturn travels his appointed space of the heavens in thirty years. The planet of Jove illuminates the region given him in twelve years. The star of Mars, swept onwards by fiery haste, races through its assigned course in eighteen months. The sun flies through the signs of the zodiacal belt in the space of a year. The star of Venus crosses its allotted space in fifteen months. Mercury, girt with speed, courses the distance fixed for him in thirteen months. The moon, closer to us, and peculiarly our

---

[16] I prefer the MSS' *spectare*, retained by Fridh, to Mommsen's *expectare*.

neighbour, travels in thirty days what the orbiting and golden sun completes in the space of a year. 3. It is right, then, that mortals should find an end to toil, since, as the philosophers tell us, even those bodies that can perish only with the world have received, and with reason, limits to their course. There is, though, this difference: they finish their task to return to the beginning, but the human race so serves that, once its labours are completed, it may find rest.

4. And therefore, to X, who has blamelessly discharged the office of *cornicularius*, you are to hand over without question the 700 *solidi* assigned to him by ancient custom, drawing them from the third tax installment of the province of Samnium in the nth indiction: he who has been honestly vindicated and commended by his minister can suffer no doubt over his reward. For he managed the judicial bench [*cornua*] of the praetorian bureau, whence his title is derived;[17] he was approved, and his actions were praised. With his assistance, I used without corruption the official inkstand, which men hoped to fill with vast bribes:[18] I obliged those whom the law favoured; I denied those to whom justice made no promise. 5. No one owed sorrow to legal victory; for he procured it with his property intact, since he did not purchase his superiority. You[19] know all that I am saying, for your secretarial work was not transacted in my privy chambers; what I did the staff knew. No wonder I showed myself a private person in doing harm, but a minister in doing good. My rigour was confined to words; my kindness was felt in my deeds. I became angry in mercy, I threatened without injury, and was seen to cause terror that I might

---

[17] In fact, the *cornicularius* was originally a military clerk, owing his name to the soldier's decoration *corniculum*; John Lydus, *De Mag.* III.3, is better informed. The title was now given to the senior official on the judicial staff of a provincial governor, and of the Urban and Praetorian Prefects.

[18] Stands for pens and ink are sometimes depicted on consular diptychs, and in the *Notitia Dignitatum* among official insignia, including the Praetorian Prefect's; made from gold and silver, they clearly had symbolic value; cf. *De Mag.* II.14.

[19] Cassiodorus abruptly shifts from an address to the *cancellarius* to one to the retiring *cornicularius*, showing his hasty compilation. Similarly, he has not consistently eliminated personal and temporal details.

inflict no hurt. As you used to say, you have a minister of great integrity; I will leave you as my most upright witness.

XI.38 [CASSIODORUS] SENATOR, PRAETORIAN PREFECT, TO JOHN, *CANONICARIUS* OF TUSCIA (a.534-5)

1. Antiquity, which ordered all things, took careful thought that there should be no deficiency in the supply of paper, since great numbers have to consult our secretariat [*scrinia*]. Thus, when judges give rulings that will be of use to many, their sweet services will suffer no hateful delays. This benefit is granted to petitioners: that they shall not be forced from avarice to pay a fee for things which are known to be supplied by the liberality of the state. The opportunity for a most impudent piece of extortion is removed: those for whom the prince's humanity has made a grant, it has especially exempted from loss.[20]

2. The ingenuity of Memphis conceived a product of evident beauty: what the work of one place has elegantly woven has clothed every secretariat. On the Nile there rises a forest without branches, a grove without leaves, a reed-bed in the waters, a beautiful head of hair for the marshes. It is more flexible than saplings, stiffer than grass, filled with a kind of hollowness, and hollow by its fullness, an absorbent softness, a spongy wood, whose strength, like an apple's, is in its rind. Its pith is soft, it is tall and slender, but it stands of itself, the lovely fruit of a filthy flood.

3. For does a crop grow in any field to equal this, on which the thoughts of the wise are preserved? For previously, the sayings of the wise and the ideas of our ancestors were in danger. For how could you quickly record words which the resistant hardness of bark made it almost impossible to set down? No wonder that the heat of the mind

---

[20] This practice had recently ceased in the Praetorian Prefecture of the East, according to John Lydus (III.14). The state no longer financed the purchase of high quality papyrus; instead, successful litigants had to pay a small fee to be issued with documents badly written on the worst material.

suffered pointless delays, and genius was forced to cool as its words were retarded. 4. Hence, antiquity gave the name of *liber* to the books of the ancients; for even today we call the bark of green wood *liber*. It was, I admit, unfitting to entrust learned discourse to these unsmoothed tablets, and to imprint the achievements of elegant feeling on bits of sluggish wood. When hands were checked, few men were impelled to write; and no one to whom such a page was offered was induced to say much. But this was appropriate to early times, when it was right for a crude beginning to use such a device, to encourage the ingenuity of posterity. The tempting beauty of paper is amply adorned by compositions[21] where there is no fear that the writing material may be withheld. 5. For it opens a field for the elegant with its white surface; its help is always plentiful; and it is so pliant that it can be rolled together, although it is unfolded to a great length. Its joints are seamless, its parts united; it is the snowy pith of a green plant, a writing surface which takes black ink for its ornament; on it, with letters exalted, the flourishing corn-field of words yields the sweetest of harvests to the mind, as often as it meets the reader's wish. It keeps a faithful witness of human deeds; it speaks of the past, and is the enemy of oblivion. 6. For, even if our memory retains the content, it alters the words; but there discourse is stored in safety, to be heard for ever with consistency.

Therefore, I command you to pay to X the deputy assistant [*subadiuva*][22] the assigned sum of y *solidi* from the third instalment of the tax revenue of the province of Tuscia, to be entered on the accounts of the thirteenth indiction [534-5]. Thus, the public secretariat may maintain its faithful integrity in laudable perpetuity. The secretariat does not know the weakness of mortality; it grows by annual accumulation, constantly receiving the new and preserving the old.

---

[21] The MSS read *invitatrix pulchritudo chartarum affluenter dicitur...* Mommsen conjectures *affluenter exhibitarum iure dicitur*; Fridh (1968, 89f.) *affluenter describitur*, or *affluenter dictione describitur*; I follow the last.

[22] *illi subadiuvae*: Fridh, with most MSS, omits *subadiuvae*; but cf. XI.37.4, *illi primiscrinio*.

XI.39 [CASSIODORUS] SENATOR, PRAETORIAN PREFECT, TO THE RIGHT HONOURABLE VITALIANUS, *CANCELLARIUS* IN LUCANIA-AND-BRUTTIUM (a.533-5)

1. It is evident how great was the population of the city of Rome, seeing that it was fed by supplies furnished even from far off regions, and that this imported abundance was reserved for it, while the surrounding provinces sufficed to feed only the resident strangers. Never[23] could a people that ruled the world be small in number. 2. For the vast extent of the walls bears witness to the throngs of citizens, as do the swollen capacity of the buildings of entertainment, the wonderful size of the baths, and that great number of water-mills which was clearly provided especially for the food supply. For, if this last equipment had not been of practical use, it would not have been thought necessary, as it serves neither the beauty of Rome, nor anything else. In short, these things are tokens of their cities, as precious clothing is of bodies, since no-one rests in devising the luxuries whose great cost he can display.

3. Hence, then, it came about that mountainous Lucania provided pigs, hence that Bruttium furnished herds of beef cattle from its native abundance. Surely both these facts are marvellous, that such provinces should suffice for such a city, and that so large a city should have no shortage of victuals through their services. It was, indeed, their glory to feed Rome; but the cost of their ability to persevere in supplying levies by weight through so many journeys was evident, since no-one could calculate the obvious decrease! 4. The weight was converted to its monetary value, in which they could suffer no loss, since it is neither diminished by journeys, nor injured by fatigue. The provinces should appreciate their blessings. For if their ancestors loyally payed out to their own loss, why should they not be generous in paying out

---

[23] Fridh conjecturally emends *nam quam* to *numquam*.

their profits?[24]

And therefore, your diligence will procure both levies, now converted into public taxes, by the statutory instalments, so that those who have obeyed ministers of alien origin with commendable honesty may not appear neglectful in my period of office. 5. For, although I have taken care to revive other provinces too, still, nothing has been done in them that I would wish to claim as my own. The people [of Lucania-and-Bruttium] have known me as their governor, and those whom, by the custom of my ancestors, I helped when a private person, I strove vigorously to benefit when in office. Thus, those whose great and ready joy at my promotion I experienced, saw that I kept my affection for my own country. They should obey, therefore, not from any compulsion, but from love, since I have reduced for them this sum that was usually paid. For, although 1200 *solidi* were previously delivered annually, through the royal generosity I have reduced them to 1000, so that men may rejoice, their happiness increased by the decrease of their burdens.

---

[24] Pigs (presumably beef cattle too) lost weight in the journey to Rome, becoming the sort 'that climbs Matterhorns and wins the annual Stock Exchange walk from London to Brighton' (P.G. Wodehouse). The drovers' and butchers' guild was compensated by the land-owners on whom the pigs were levied, to make good this short-fall in meat; land-owners also suffered from general transportation costs. Cash commutation (*adaeratio*) apparently improved the situation – pigs were now purchased from the taxes of the province concerned; it may have stimulated the market in pork, and the provincial economy; hence, perhaps, Cassiodorus' allusion to profits now made. Cf. *C.Th.* XIV.4.4., Valentinian III, *Novel* 36; Jones, 1964, 702ff., Barnish, 1987. esp. 166ff.

XII.5 [CASSIODORUS] SENATOR, PRAETORIAN PREFECT, TO THE DISTINGUISHED VALERIANUS[1] (a.535-6, probably 536, before July)

1. Certainly, a magistrate of highest rank should spread his favours widely, since he who is known as everyone's governor is expected to distribute his benefits to all. But, by nature's gift, we owe the more to those who are joined to us by some relationship, it seems a kind of right principle to depart from the practice of equality. 2. For we show modesty to our companions, to our fathers we give reverence, to our fellow citizens we owe a general liking, but a special love to our children; and such is the force of family ties that no-one will think himself insulted if he realises that another's offspring have been preferred to him. And therefore, there is nothing unjust in being specially concerned for one's native land, above all at that time when we may be seen to assist it in its peril. For those whom we hurry to rescue, we are supposed to love especially.

3. Now, a large army has arrived, known to be assigned to the defence of the state, and is reported to have ravaged the fields of Lucania and Bruttium, and to have lessened the wealth of those regions by enthusiastic robbery. But since some must give and others take according to the need of the times, know that, by royal order, the prices established long ago have been modified: supplies will be credited to the public tax-accounts at a much higher price than you were wont to sell at, so that the landowner will bear no loss, and the army, in its labours, will feel no shortage. 4. So, do not be troubled. You have escaped the hands of the collectors, as this provision has removed your taxes.[2] But, for your easier information, I have seen fit to give figures for the credits in the schedules [*breves*] recorded below, so that no-one may sell you a benefit that you know has been bestowed on you by the state's generosity.

---

[1] Probably the governor of Lucania-and-Bruttium.

[2] Supplies seized by the army would be valued in cash (above the market rate), and regarded as tax already paid.

Restrain, therefore, the reckless tumult of the landowners. Let them love tranquillity, since no one is driving them into danger. While the Gothic army wages war, let the Roman be at peace. What is enjoined on you is the aim of the fortunate: it is to prevent the savage race of countrymen from being carried away by lawless ventures when they escape the routine of their work, and those whom you can barely control in peacetime from starting to rebel against you. 5. Therefore, by royal command, you are to admonish the individual tenants of the great estates, and the powerful landowners, that they are to arouse no savagery in this conflict, lest they should be hastening less to help in the war than to disturb the peace. Let them draw the steel, but steel to till the fields; let the spears they use be ox-goads, not the goads of warlike rage. It will be the greatest glory of the defenders if, while they guard the regions mentioned, the civilians continue to cultivate the lands of their own country.

6. Let the magistrates gain strength from the laws; the judicial bench must not cease to thunder out the laws against the wicked. The robber must fear the judgement which has always terrified him; the adulterer must shudder at the judge's heart; the forger must tremble at the voice of the court-usher; the thief must not laugh at the forum. For freedom rejoices only when such things give them no pleasure. Thus, then, if you are taking common council about social order [*civilitas*], you will not feel the war that is being successfully waged. Let no-one oppress the poor: seize those who seize men's land, hunt down other men's hunters. A citizens' war is your duty. If you restrain the leaders of crime, you will create a general peace. Take care, too, in crediting the military supplies, lest anyone should be defrauded by some man's cunning.

7. You must know, moreover, that our rulers have charged the commanders of the army, through my authority, that, when, of necessity, they take instructions from you, it is to come to the help of those who have suffered injury. Likewise, they should preserve discipline, always the strongest weapon of an army. Moreover, by a kind of generosity, the royal commands have added that not even the estates of the divine house shall be excepted from the present levies,

but, instead, everything decreed for the general good shall be borne in common.

8. Now, therefore, take energetic action with your brethren, and, with all care, provide what is needed, so that the production of this lengthy document may prove of real benefit to our most noble homeland. For even men of modest ability can govern what is at peace, and administer their provinces according to custom; but 'this is the task, this the toil' [Vergil, *Aeneid* VI.129], to rule, instead, a province that cannot control itself on its own. For the sailors' skill is idle in calm weather, and does not give the expert his reputation without the help of great danger. 9. You, then, have an opportunity to acquire the name of a wise man, and, by God's aid, to act with care, and earn praise in every case.

However, I am certainly not commending my own people to you beyond others, since what I hope will befall to my home, I wish to happen to all. For, since I began to give thought to guarding the whole public, my personal concern has slipped away. I do indeed desire what is good for my people, but a common good, since it is highly unjust for a magistrate to wish for himself something which the public cannot experience.

[Cassiodorus' values are interesting: he proudly declares, while eventually rejecting, the special obligation owed by a minister to his home province.

Procopius (*Wars* V.viii.1-4) gives us a Byzantine view of events in the south: no mention of civil disorder, merely a ready surrender (in July to September, 536) by misgoverned Romans and a Gothic general to the 'liberating' army; as it took three months to reach Naples, resistance may have been ignored. For his part, Cassiodorus does not mention outright treachery to the Goths.]

XII.8 [CASSIODORUS] SENATOR, PRAETORIAN PREFECT, TO THE GOVERNOR OF THE PROVINCE OF LIGURIA (a.533-7)

1. It seems a new kind of profit when petitioners gain, and their benefactors feel no loss. For one man receives in such a way that the other is not deprived; it is a donation without expense, a concession

without loss; and a sum that cannot leave the ruler's control is called his generosity.

2. Hence, X reports that the finances of his properties located in province Y, as described in the schedule [*brevis*] attached below, are troubled by the unjust demands of the civic tax-collectors [*exactores*]. He asks that he should pay the dues straight to my treasurers, without any detriment to the public purse. I, who am known to have no interest in causing loss to anyone, willingly grant this, so long as the dues of the fisc are properly satisfied, since unlawful actions block good intentions.

3. Your distinction is to advise the town-councillors and collectors of arrears [*compulsores*] of this, as also those whom you know to be involved; and, from indiction y, to have the exaction removed from the properties referred to under this condition: that if, before the first day of month z, the sum owing is not paid to the treasurer, the official exaction shall be carried out within the province. But not if he proves by the treasurers' receipts that his promise was fulfilled: then the designated estates are to be freed from all harassment by the collectors of arrears, since what a willing spirit offers without suspicion of causing loss should be given special preference. For I welcome tax collection without pressure from the collector of arrears, and a loyal subject who does what a man under coercion could scarcely discharge. But if only a willing land-owner would free me from inevitable delay, and himself from loss by proper payments! For he who puts off paying his dues makes a tax-enforcer necessary.

[This letter has been adapted to a *formula*, but the title still shows that it was written to deal with a specific request. For the privilege granted, cf. II.24.4.]

XII.12 CASSIODORUS SENATOR, PRAETORIAN PREFECT, TO ANASTASIUS, GOVERNOR OF LUCANIA-AND-BRUTTIUM (a.534-5)

1. When, by his favour, I was officially banqueting with the lord of the state [probably Theodahad], the various provinces were being

praised for their delicacies. The conversation running on as usual, we came to the wines of Bruttium and the sweet cheese of Sila. Thanks to the grass, the latter is made there with such natural flavour that you would think its taste was of honey, though you can see it is unmixed with any substance. There, under slight pressure, milk flows through the teats from the udders; and when collected, by the gift of nature, into other stomachs, so to speak, it does not drip and dribble, but pours in by swift streams. A sweet and subtle odour of grass arises; the nose recognises the cattle's pasture, which, with its many scents, is felt to breathe a fragrance like incense into the milk. 2. To this such creaminess is added that you would think olive oil was mingled with its flow - save that its snowy whiteness distinguishes it from the grass green of the other. Then the over-joyed shepherd receives that marvellous liquid in wide-mouthed jars. Mixed with rennet, it begins to harden into something soft but solid. Shaped into a beautiful sphere, it is placed, for a time, in an underground store, and yields the long-lasting substance of cheese. You are to load this onto ships and despatch it with all speed, that I may gratify the royal wish by this small offering.[3]

3. Furthermore, seek out the wine which the ancients, in their wish to praise it, called the wine that takes the palm [*Palmatianum*], not over-rough in its acidity, but of a welcome fullness.[4] For, although it may be the most remote of Bruttian wines, by almost universal consent it has the chief place. For there they find it equal to Gazan, resembling Sabine, and remarkable for its fine bouquet. 4. But because it has won itself this noble reputation, you must procure the most refined of the variety, lest the wisdom of our ancestors should seem to have bestowed the name in vain. For it is sweet and full-bodied, soft and well-rounded, very well-structured, with a pungent nose, white and

---

[3] Cassiodorus was perhaps making a present of goods from his province, but XII.4 shows smilar supplies from Venetia procured by compulsory purchase.

[4] I have followed Traube's reading (index, s.v. *stipsis*) of *non stipsi nimis asperum* for the MSS' *nos stipsim (sc. nominavimus), asperum*... XII.4.4 shows *stipsis* a property, not a name of wine, perhaps related to the binding medicinal qualities referred to below.

clear too, and has such a bouquet when rolled in the mouth[5] that it deserves to be named from the palm. 5. It binds loosened bowels, dries up suppurating wounds, and strengthens a weak chest. What an artfully compounded medicine can hardly achieve, this wine bestows in its natural and unblended state. Take care, though, to send the precise type described above, since I, who remember it with patriotic accuracy, cannot be deceived; for, at the moment, I have produced what was wanted from my own cellars. But you will send at your peril wine unlike that of which, as you know, I already have a sample.

XII.13 AN EDICT [OF CASSIODORUS SENATOR, PRAETORIAN PREFECT] (a.533-6)

1. The largesse bestowed by our lords should be secured by a common effort, since what they clearly accomplished through divine prompting must needs benefit all men. Indeed, the piety of princes guards the whole empire; and, while they enjoy a fitting reward, the limbs of the state are preserved in safety.

Now, long ago imperial decrees aided the holy churches in Bruttium and Lucania with a certain tribute of gifts. But, since it is the way of sacrilegious minds to sin even against the divine reverence, the *canonicarii* have been subtracting a considerable part in the name of the accountants [*numerarii*], turning clerical property into laymen's gain. 2. The accountants of my bureau have spurned, cursed, and hated this deed, reporting that nothing which impious hands have embezzled by such a crime has been paid in to them. What will you yet attempt, utterly inhuman audacity, if you extend your thefts even where you know you cannot possibly escape notice? To think that you may elude mortal eyes, although it is a criminal, is not a baseless assumption. But as for the man who expects to carry out what God will not observe, how great is the blindness that condemns him! 3. But, lest similar presumption should happen to commit further ravages, or repeated

---

[5] Conjecturally, I read *iactatum* for *ructatum*.

transgressions provoke the divine patience, I decree by this edict that he who is involved any further in this fraud shall be deprived of his official position, and shall lose the benefit of his own property. For he who has extended his audacity even to the injury of God, should be smitten by a heavy penalty.

Let the poor possess the gifts of their rulers; let those who have no property own something. 4. Why should another's wealth, founded on royal generosity, be usurped? Its possession is the prince's gift. How can a subject dare to appropriate what he sees his lord's humility is offering to God? Moreover, not to give to such men is to take from them; and rightly so, since he who can help the hungry kills them if he does not feed them. We should be ashamed to steal from those to whom we are commanded to give. The will to gain riches from a beggar's poverty surpasses all cruelty. We should love honest profits, shudder at damnable gains. Hence, let no man dare to steal what might lose him his acquisitions. He who acquires by withholding loses by his increase; and, if he does not reject the moneys of the poor, he in fact brings poverty on himself.

XII.15 [CASSIODORUS] SENATOR, PRAETORIAN PREFECT,
        TO THE RIGHT HONOURABLE MAXIMUS,
        CANCELLARIUS IN LUCANIA-AND-BRUTTIUM
        (a.533-6)

1. It is reported that Squillace, the chief city of Bruttium, whose founder, we read, was Ulysses, the bane of Troy, is being afflicted beyond reason by the arrogant. Their exactions should not have been made during my ministry, since injuries to the place force me to grieve more deeply, as they obviously affect me with patriotic feeling.

That city is sited on the Adriatic gulf, and hangs from the hillside like a bunch of grapes, not that it may swell with pride in the difficulty of its ascent, but that it may gaze with delight on green meadows, and the blue back of the sea. 2. It watches the sun's birth in its very cradle, where the coming day sends no light of dawn before it, but straightway, as it begins to rise, the flashing rays reveal its torch. It gazes on the joys of Phoebus, and so shines there with his own pure radiance that you would think it his true country, and the fame of Rhodes surpassed.[6] It enjoys transparent light, and is blessed, too, with temperate air, experiencing warm winters and cool summers; and life is lived without gloom, where no bad weather is feared. Hence, men are more large minded, since the temperate climate governs all things. 3. For indeed, a hot country makes men cunning and fickle; a cold makes them sly and sluggish; it is only the temperate that sets human nature in good order by its own quality. Thus it is that the ancients called Athens the country of the wise; one which, pervaded by the purity of its air, through a happy generosity predisposed the clearest minds to the role of philosophy. For is it really the same thing for a body to gulp down swamp-water as to drink at a sweet and translucent spring? So, the burden of a heavy atmosphere weighs down the vigour of the soul. For we are necessarily subjected to such a state when clouds depress us; and, again, since it is the essence of the heavenly soul to enjoy all that is pure and untainted, we naturally rejoice in bright weather.[7]

4. Squillace also enjoys plentiful and delicious sea-food, since it has nearby the enclosed pools that I created. For at the foot of Mount Moscius, I allowed an orderly inflow of the waves of Nereus [the sea] to caves excavated in the rocks, where a shoal of fishes, playing freely in captivity, both refreshes the delighted spirit, and pleases the wondering eye. They rush greedily to the hand, and ask for titbits before they become food themselves. A man feeds his own delicacies;[8] and, while he has their capture in his power, it often happens that he

---

[6] The island of Rhodes was famous for its cult of the Sun-god, identified with Phoebus Apollo.

[7] *quia caelestis animae substantia ad infecta et purissima quaeque laetatur* - see Fridh, 1968, 93ff., on the translation of *infecta*, rejecting the lacuna supposed by Mommsen. Cassiodorus might have praised Vivarium as 'a college situated in a purer air' (Clarendon)!

[8] There is an untranslatable pun in the word *delicias*, meaning pets, or table-delicacies.

is contented, and relinquishes them all.

5. Furthermore, residents in the city are not deprived of the fine sight of workers in the fields. They look out to their satisfaction on abundant grape harvests; on the threshing-floors, productive work is in their view; the olives too display their greenery. No-one lacks the pleasures of the countryside who can see all this from the city. Just because this place has no walls, you would think it a rural city; you could likewise judge it to be an urban villa; and, as half one, half the other, it is clearly rich in praise.

6. Since travellers often long to admire it, and wish to escape the fatigues of their journey, the citizens are worn out by their own expenses,[9] thanks to the city's charm, and the provision of rations and extra post-horses. Therefore, lest its charm should injure the city, or a thing of fame become a cause of loss, I have decided that the provision of rations and extra post-horses, according to the allotted travel-warrants, shall be entered on the state tax-account. 7. Furthermore, I abolish altogether the judge's travel-fees [*pulveratica*], and decree that, in accordance with the regulations of former times, governors shall receive three days' rations only; if they prolong their stay, they shall live at their own expense.[10] For those who administer the laws meant them to be a help, and not a burden.

Therefore, my city, comfort yourself with the sight of equity:[11] what I am granting you is no special indulgence, but your lawful due.[12] By God's help, live in enjoyment of the justice of the times, and of a special and joyful safety. Others may talk of the Fortunate

---

[9] Mommsen reads *proprii cives fatigantur expensis*; Fridh follows the main MSS reading *propriis...expensis*.

[10] *suis expensis facta tarditate victuri* - Fridh's reading; Mommsen conjectures *...vecturis*. Judge and governor are identical.

[11] *Qua de re aequitatis intuitu, civitas nostra, relevare*: Mommsen supposes a lacuna after *nostra*, rejected by Fridh.

[12] On the reading and translation of this sentence, see Traube, index, s.v. *iudicarius*, followed by Fridh, against Mommsen.

Islands;[13] I would rather give the name to your dwelling.

[With XII.15, compare XI.14.]

XII.16 INSTRUCTIONS ON TAX COLLECTION
[*CANONICARIA*][14] (a.537, Sept.1st)

1. Time, which is always adapted to human affairs, since it constantly takes the opportunity of reconciling us even to our troubles, warns me to revive my care for the tax revenues by the annual celebration, since the fabric of the state is clearly based on that institution. And it is rightly to be prayed for, being provided for the good of all. We must love those things from which the state is seen to derive its solidity; so long as it is revived by returning revenue, its constitution is held together in solid strength. 2. Therefore, while a display of loyalty is a great thing at any time, the more necessary it is, the more acceptably it is rendered. Let the landowners, then, pay the dues that will win them favour. Indeed, a debt that cannot be evaded should always be cheerfully produced, so that a payment clearly made without compulsion may thereby become a gift.

And therefore - may the command be blessed - I order you to advise the land-owner in your province, for the first indiction [537-8], that he must loyally pay his tax money, keeping to the three instalments. Thus, no one shall grumble that he has been forced to pay too soon; nor, again, shall anyone claim that he has been passed over by prolonged[15] leniency. Let no man exceed the amount of the just weight, and let the scales be altogether just: there will be no end to

---

[13] The mythical paradise of dead heroes, somewhere in the Atlantic.

[14] This is an annual letter of exhortation and instruction distributed among the provincial governors; XI.7 and XII.2 are other examples; cf. III.8.2.

[15] The MSS read *letata*; Accursius conjectured *lentata*; Mommsen *protelata*; Traube *largata*; Fridh *plectenda*; cf. Fridh, 1968, 97ff. I prefer the first two emendations; delays in collection were common, and could mean a disastrous accumulation of arrears; cf. III.8.

plundering, should it be permissible to exceed the weight.[16] 4. Furthermore, you are to send my secretariat, in regular form, an accurate four monthly record of the expenses of collection, so that truth may shine out from the public accounts, with all error and obscurity wiped away.

But so that, by God's help, you may fulfill the statutes, I have directed X and Y, civil servants of my office, to oversee you and your staff, remembering their own risk. Thus, the command you know of may achieve its purpose without blame. Beware, then, lest the blame either of dishonest bribery, or of sluggish idleness, should attach to you, and the business you have failed to advance should bring loss to your own fortune.

XII.20 [CASSIODORUS] SENATOR, PRAETORIAN PREFECT, TO THE RIGHT HONOURABLE THOMAS AND PETER, TREASURERS (a.536, later than February)

1. Your fidelity will remember, as I do, the case of the holy Agapitus, Pope of the city of Rome, when, by royal command [Theodahad's], he was sent on an embassy to the prince of the East [Justinian]. He gave pledges, and received from you y pounds of gold, with a receipt made out in due form, so that our provident lord might also speed the departure of one whom he had suddenly ordered away.[17] By lending him money in necessity, the king initially made a generous provision; but how much more gloriously has he acted by giving away what might have been returned to him with thanks. 2. Need was overcome without loss: the hands of the Pope bestowed money which his estate did not possess, and that journey which was certainly crammed with giving has been rendered free of cost. What a sight it was when the bishop gave largesse to those who asked it, yet the Church felt no loss! He was more a deputy than a donor, for he

---

[16] See n.15 to XI.16.
[17] On the punctuation, see Traube, index s.v. *iubere*.

whose property is seen to bear the cost must get the credit. What may not be the influence on a pious prince of such an embassy, assuredly despatched in so remarkable a manner?

3. Therefore, advised by my instructions, and fortified by the royal command, you are to give back the vessels of the saints and the signed obligation, without delay, to the holy Apostle Peter's men of business, so that objects returned to our advantage may soon fulfill their wish. Let the church utensils that are famous throughout the world be restored to the hands of the deacons. Let them be given what was once their own, since what the Pope legally pawned, he justly receives as a gift.

4. This surpasses the example I related so carefully in my history. For, when king Alaric [I], glutted with the booty of Rome, received vessels of the Apostle Peter from those who brought them in, he soon made an enquiry, realised the situation, and ordered them to be returned to the sacred threshold by the hands of the plunderers. Thus, greed, which had permitted a crime in its urge for booty, wiped out the transgression by an act of most generous devotion. But is it surprising that he who had enriched himself by the plunder of such a city should be unwilling to pillage the reverend property of the saints?[18]

5. Our king, however, by a religious resolve, has returned vessels that were made his own under the law of pledges. And therefore, after such an action, many prayers should be made for us, since we trust that joy will be conferred when we ask a reward for righteous deeds.

[Agapitus' mission to Constantinople, where he died on April 22nd, took place in the early months of 536. His secular diplomacy was ineffectual; for the ecclesiastical side, see *Liber Pontificalis* (Davis, 52f.). Theodahad appointed his successor Silverius against the wishes of the clergy, perhaps helped by the debts to the crown described in this letter. Agapitus' inability to finance his journey illustrates the effect of electioneering on Church property (IX.15-16).]

---

[18] The Visigoth Alaric I sacked Rome in 410. This story derives largely from Orosius, *History against the Pagans*, VII.39.7-11; Jordanes, *Getica*, 156, although using Cassiodorus' *Gothic History*, mentions only that Alaric spared the holy places.

XII.22 [CASSIODORUS] SENATOR, PRAETORIAN PREFECT, TO THE PROVINCIALS OF ISTRIA (a.537, autumn)

1. The public budget, fluctuating with seasonal conditions, can be kept in bounds by this method: if the wholesome commands of the state match the local production. For, where the crops are richer, there procurement is easy. For, if something which hungry barrenness has denied is levied, then both the province is injured, and the desired result is not obtained.

Now, by travellers' report, I have learnt that the province of Istria, which owes its glorious name to the triad of noble crops, and, by divine gift, teems with wine, oil and corn, is enjoying fertility in the present year. And therefore, the aforementioned foodstuffs, paid as tax to the value of y *solidi*, shall be credited to you for this, the first indiction [537-8]; but the surplus I leave for official expenses to the loyal province. 2. But, since I have to procure greater quantities of what I mentioned, I have also sent you z *solidi* from my treasury, that these necessities may be collected in great quantities without cost to you. For often, when you are under pressure to sell to outsiders, you suffer loss, especially at that season when you are deprived of foreign purchasers; and it is unusual to obtain gold when, as you know, the merchants are not there. But how much better it is to obey your rulers than to provide for distant regions, and to pay your dues in victuals, rather than to endure the arrogance of purchasers.[19]

3. Moreover, what I, from love of justice, am proclaiming, is something that you might propose to me, since, where I am not burdened by shipping costs, I should do no injury in the price. For yours is the nearest region to us across the Ionian [Adriatic] Sea, covered with olives, glorious for its corn, rich in vines, where all crops

---

[19] The commutation of taxes in kind for money (*adaeratio*) had grown greatly during the 5th century; procurement of the cash meant both economic problems and advantages for the tax-payer; cf. Barnish, 1987, 166f. This year, the Istrians are to pay at least part of their tax in kind. Cassiodorus is also operating a levy by compulsory purchase (*coemptio*); cf. II.38, *C.Th.* XI.15.2.

flow in desirable fertility, as though from three udders generous in their milk. Not undeservedly, it is called the Campania of Ravenna,[20] the store-room of the royal city, an only too pleasant and luxurious retreat. With its northward location, it enjoys a wonderfully mild climate. 4. It also has certain Baiaes of its own - I am not talking nonsense - where the rough sea enters the hollows of the coast, and is calmed to the smooth and lovely surface of a lake. These places also supply many *garum* factories,[21] and glory in their wealth of fish. Not one Lake Avernus is found there. Many salt-water fish-pools can be seen, in which oysters breed everywhere spontaneously, even without labour. Thus, there need evidently be no care in feeding, nor uncertainty in catching these delicacies. 5. Great villas shine out far and wide: you would think them sited like pearls to show the taste of your ancestors in this province, which is plainly adorned by such buildings. That coast also has a most beautiful chain of islands; arranged with charm and utility, it both shields ships from danger, and enriches the farmers by lavish harvests. Istria clearly refreshes our hard-working court; it feeds the nobles on its luxuries, lesser men on its output of foodstuffs, and almost its entire produce is enjoyed by the royal city.

Now let the loyal province more willingly furnish its supplies. It should comply fully when called on, since it used to perform most lavishly when there was no request. 6. But, lest any hesitation should arise over my commands, I have sent to you, by this authority, the most industrious Laurentius, tested by me in great labours for the state, so that, according to the appended directives [*breves*], he may expedite without delay what he knows has been entrusted to him for the state budget. Now procure what you are commanded to. For you will render yourselves loyal public servants by receiving your orders with pleasure.

7. But I shall declare the prices regulated for you on a subsequent

---

[20] Campania, long famous for its fertility, its bathing resort of Baiae, and its sulphurous and unwholesome Lake Avernus, was still a Riviera for the aristocracy, and important to the food-supply of Rome.

[21] *Garum*, a kind of fish-sauce, was one of the most traded products of the coasts of the Roman empire.

occasion, when the bearer of this letter has sent me a report on the state of the harvest. For it is impossible to assess anything with justice unless the resources can be clearly ascertained. Indeed, it is an unfair judge who promulgates an impossible decree, and he who would pronounce without consideration clearly has a bad conscience.

XII.24 [CASSIODORUS] SENATOR, PRAETORIAN PREFECT, TO THE TRIBUNES OF THE COASTS (date as XII.22)

1. I previously ordered that Istria should send to the court at Ravenna the commodities of wine, oil and corn, of which, this year, it enjoys a lavish quantity. But do you, who have many ships on its borders, provide with equally obliging loyalty, and take pains to transport speedily what that region is ready to supply. Indeed, the favour of accomplishment is alike for both parties, since the one without the other cannot complete the work. Be prepared, then, for a voyage to neighbouring parts, you who often cross vast distances. 2. You are, in a way, traversing your own guest-rooms, as you sail through your country.

Among your advantages, moreover, another route is available to you, forever safe and calm. For, when the sea is closed by the raging of the winds, a path through pleasant river country is opened to you. Your keels do not fear the storm blasts; in their great good fortune, they hug the land and often run aground but are never lost. From a distance, when their channel cannot be seen, it looks as if they are moving through the fields. They were kept still by ropes, but they move drawn by cables; the course of things is changed, and men help their ships on with their own feet. Without effort, they pull their carriers; and, instead of the risks of sailing, the ships employ the more fortunate footsteps of the crew.

3. It is a pleasure to mention how I have seen your dwellings to be sited. The Venetian districts, famous and filled with noblemen from

of old,[22] touch Ravenna and the Po on the south. On the east, they enjoy the pleasures of the Adriatic coasts, where alternate tides in their movement now cover, now expose the face of the land, by their ebb and flow. Here you have your homes like sea-birds. For a man is seen now as a mainlander, now as an islander, so that you might think that here, instead, are the Cyclades, where you suddenly see the shapes of places changed.[23] 4. Indeed, like those islands, houses can be seen stretching far away among the waters, not the work of nature, but built by human labour. For there, solid ground is heaped together by wattling flexible withies, and there is no hesitation in opposing so frail a bulwark to the sea's flood, since the shallows of that coast are unable to throw up a great weight of waters, and, unaided by depth, the waves have no force.

5. Now the inhabitants have one source of supply: they cram themselves with fish alone. There, rich and poor feed together on equal terms. One food keeps all alive; a similar dwelling houses everyone; they know no envy over their homes; and, living under this rule, they avoid a vice to which all the world is plainly subject. 6. All your rivalry, though, is in the salt-works. Instead of using ploughs and sickles, you roll grinding cylinders. Thence all your harvest is produced, since in them you have a resource you do not make. A food-stuff currency is coined there, so to speak. Every wave is the servant of your art. A man may have small interest in seeking gold, but there is no one who does not wish to acquire salt - rightly so, since all kinds of food owe to it the pleasure that they give.

7. So then, diligently refit the ships which you tie up to your walls like animals. Thus, when the most industrious Laurentius, who has been sent to obtain these victuals, shall remind you of your orders, you shall make all haste, and not delay the necessary supplies by any difficulty, since you have the advantage of being able to choose your

---

[22] *Venetiae praedicabiles quondam plenae nobilibus:* cf. Jordanes, *Getica* 148: *its* [Venetia's] *landowners, our forebears tell us, were formerly called* [in Greek] *'ainetoi', that is 'praiseworthy'.*

[23] Cyclades: a complex group of islands in the Aegean.

route to fit the weather.

[XII.24 is of interest as showing something of the settlements and commerce from which Venice later developed. In 552, the barges of these coast-dwellers helped a Byzantine army to march from Salona to Ravenna, outflanking Gothic defences.]

XII.25 CASSIODORUS SENATOR, PRAETORIAN PREFECT, TO THE ILLUSTRIOUS AMBROSIUS, HIS DEPUTY (date as XII.22[24])

1. Those who survey the changed order of things are often troubled men, since the clearly unusual is frequently a portent. For nothing is done without a reason, nor is the world involved in fortuitous happenings; but all that we see brought to a conclusion must be the plan of God. When kings have changed their decrees, men are in suspense, lest things should go in in a guise other than use has accustomed them to. But who will not be disturbed, and deeply curious about such events, if something mysterious and unusual seems to be coming on us from the stars? For, as there is a certain security in watching the seasons run on in their succession, so we are filled with deep curiosity, when we see that such things are changing.

2. How strange it is, I ask you, to see the principal star [the sun], and not its usual brightness; to gaze on the moon, glory of the night, at its full, but shorn of its natural splendour? All of us are still observing, as it were, a blue-coloured sun; we marvel at bodies which cast no mid-day shadow, and at that strength of intensest heat reaching extreme and dull tepidity. And this has not happened in the momentary loss of an eclipse, but has assuredly been going on equally through almost the entire year. 3. How fearful it is, then, to endure for so long what will terrify a people, even when it passes quickly! So, we have had a winter without storms, spring without mildness, summer without heat. Whence can we now hope for mild weather, when the months that

---

[24] Ruggini, 325, n.336, would date this to late spring, 534.

once ripened the crops have been deadly sick under the northern blasts? For what will give fertility, if the soil does not grow warm in summer? What will open the bud, if the parent tree does not absorb the rain? Out of all the elements, we find these two opposed to us: perpetual frost, and unnatural drought. The seasons have changed by failing to change; and what used to be achieved by mingled rains cannot be gained from dryness only.

4. And therefore, from the crops of the past, your prudence is to defeat the future dearth; for such was last year's fortunate abundance that provisions will also suffice for the coming months. Everything that is sought for as food must be put in store. The private person will easily find what he needs when the public supply system has filled itself.

5. But, lest the present situation should be tormenting you with deep doubts, return to pondering the order of nature: what seems mysterious to the marvelling crowd should be reasonable to you. For it has certainly been so arranged by divine ordinance, the stars of this year have so met in their houses by joint operations, that winter is rendered drier and colder than its wont. Hence, the air, condensed from snow by excessive cold, is not thinned by the sun's fire; but it endures in the density it has acquired, obstructs the heat of the sun, and cheats the gaze of human frailty. For things in mid space dominate our sight, and we can see through them only what the rarity of their substance allows. 6. For this vast inane, which is spread between earth and heaven as the most tenuous element, allows us to see clearly so long as it is pure, and splashed with the sun's light. But, if it is condensed by some sort of mixture, then, as if with a kind of tautened skin, it permits neither the natural colours, nor the heat of the heavenly bodies to penetrate. In other ages, too, this has often temporarily happened with a cloudy sky. Hence it is that, for so long, the rays of the stars have been darkened with an unusual colour; that the harvester dreads the novel cold; that the fruits have hardened with the passage of time; that the grapes are bitter in their old age.

7. But, if this is to be ascribed to divine providence, we should not be troubled, since, by God's own command, we are forbidden to

look for a sign [Matthew, xvi.1-4]. However, we understand that all this is plainly harming the fruits of the earth, when we fail to see our customary foods nourished by their own natural law. Therefore, your care must see to it that one year's dearth does not throw us into confusion, since the first administrator of our office [Joseph] took care that past plenty should suffice to mitigate succeeding scarcity.

[For possible influences on this letter by Boethius' *C.Phil.*, see Barnish, 1990, 28.]

XII.26 CASSIODORUS SENATOR, PRAETORIAN PREFECT, TO HIS ACTIVITY [*VIR STRENUUS*] PAUL (date as XII.22)

1. The good of the state is often maintained by a profitable act of pity, since a remission made at the plea of worthy men is in fact a gain. Now the venerable [bishop] Augustine, a man distinguished by both his name and his way of life, has come, and has made a lamentable report to me of the needs of the Veneti.[25] Neither wine, nor corn, nor millet has been produced among them; and he declares that the fortunes of the provincials have reached such a state of penury that they can hardly endure the risks of life unless the royal pity should take thought for them with its usual humanity. This seems cruelty to me, to make any demands on suppliants, and to request what the province clearly lacks. For he who levies the non-existent extracts only tears from such people.
2. And therefore, moved by the report of so good a man, by this authority I remit the wine and corn that I had made you collect for the supply of the army from the cities of Concordia, Aquileia, and Forum Iulii [Cividale del Friuli]; only the meat, as detailed in the schedule [*brevis*] given you, is to be provided thence. For I will send a sufficient quantity of corn from here, when it proves necessary. 3. And, since I have learnt that much wine has been produced in Istria, you are to demand from there an amount equal to what had been requested from

---

[25] Augustine's diocese was presumably in Venetia.

the above mentioned cities - at market rates, so that the Istrians themselves may suffer no injury, when just prices are preserved for their benefit. You must realise that no venality is to put a price on the present indulgence, for this reason: that, as the remedy has been disinterested, so its glory may remain untarnished. Know that you will be subjected to a heavy punishment, should you be seen to have accepted what it is unlawful to give.

XII.27 [CASSIODORUS] SENATOR, PRAETORIAN PREFECT, TO DATIUS, BISHOP OF MILAN (date as XII.22)

1. There is small use in a good command if I do not mean to carry it out through holy men. For the upright purpose of the just increases the benefit, and anything carried through without fraud is rightly ascribed to the merits of the donor. For it is fitting that priestly integrity should execute royal generosity. For he whose task it is to do good on his own account can laudably fulfill the wishes of others.

2. And therefore, I request your sanctity, whose aim it is to serve the divine commands, to cause the distribution to a famished people of a third of the millet in the granaries of Pavia and Dertona, as ordered by the king, at the price of 25 pecks [*modii*] for a *solidus*,[26] under your own regulation; thus no man's venality will supply it to those who can keep themselves from their own resources. He who has little should receive the royal kindness. The command is given to help the needy, not the rich.The man who puts his bounty into a full vessel in fact pours it away, for only what is collected in empty ones is in fact saved. 3. Hence, your holiness should not consider the offices of pity an insult, since all is worthy of you where charity is found - indeed, to carry out another's wishes faithfully is to accomplish good works of your own.

---

[26] This was above normal, but well below current famine prices, apparently 10 *modii* the *solidus*; 1 *modius* of wheat would yield 25 lb. of bread; cf. XII.28.8, *Anonymus Valesianus* 73, Jones, 1964, 445ff., Ruggini, 361, 365.

To manage this affair, with God's help, I have taken care to appoint X and Y, who, following the orders of your holiness, will do nothing of their own accord, but will strive only to obey you. But, as to the *solidi*, as many as can be collected by the sale of the above-mentioned quantity of millet, inform me by your own report. So they may be deposited in the treasury, and reserved for replacing the afore-mentioned foodstuff, by God's help, at some future time. This is like renewing a garment, which is unthreaded and taken apart, that it may be rewoven in a new form, and with greater magnificence.

[In 538, Datius was to take a leading part in the revolt of Milan and much of Liguria from the Gothic side; the result was the destruction of his city in 539. Visiting Rome in winter, 537, to prepare the revolt, he may have reported the ravages of famine in Liguria (Procopius, *Wars* VI.vii.35, *Liber Pontificalis*, Davis, p.55); this helps to date **XII.26-27**. If his report was reliable, Cassiodorus' efforts had proved rather ineffectual.]

GLOSSARY
OF ALLUSIONS AND TECHNICAL TERMS
IN THE TRANSLATION

Ammianus Marcellinus: soldier and historian. The surviving part of his history of the Roman empire runs from 353 to 378, and was published c.390.

Attila: king of the Huns c.435-453, he raided both the eastern and the western empire. He was defeated in 451 at the battle of the Catalaunian Plains in Gaul, by a Romano-Visigothic coalition led by Aetius.

Augustus: the first Roman emperor, 27 B.C. - A.D.14.

Cancellarius: the term may denote an usher for the Praetorian Prefect (q.v.), but, in the letters translated here, the Prefect's administrative deputy in a province. Despite high rank and major responsibilities, overlapping with the governor's, he was probably appointed by the Prefect, not the monarch.

Canonicarius: a clerk (*scriniarius*) of the Praetorian Prefecture, routinely despatched to supervise tax collection in the provinces.

Cato: M.Porcius Cato, 'the censor,' Roman general and statesman, 234-149 B.C.; commanded in Spain in 194; a type of stern, traditional morality.

Cicero: see **Tullius.**

Coemptio: levy of supplies by compulsory purchase.

Comitiacus: general-service agent of the Ostrogothic kings; Roman equivalent of the *saio* (q.v.), except in the provision of *tuitio* (q.v.).

Compulsor: a special tax-collector sent from the Praetorian Prefecture to enforce the payment of arrears.

Consul: two Consuls were nominally the chief magistrates of the Roman state, dating back to the foundation of the Republic. The Ordinary Consuls, who took up office on January the 1st, gave their names to the year. A former Consul was called a **Consular** (as also were governors of certain provinces).

Curiales (*decuriones*): see under town-councillors.

Diana: Italian goddess, identified with the Greek huntress Artemis, whose legendary cult in the Scythian Crimea involved human sacrifice. Both might also be identified with the moon goddess, and with goddesses of the underworld, such as Proserpine.

Diptychs: these double tablets of ivory for select recipients commemorated consular games or other senatorial functions. They were usually carved with portraits and appropriate scenes.

Distinction, Distinguished: used to translate *spectabilitas, spectabilis*; the title of the second grade in the senatorial class.

Edict: a legal measure, an order, a letter of advice or consolation, addressed directly to the people, or a group of them by the monarch or his Praetorian Prefect; the term is not always used correctly in the *Variae.*

Exactor: a local tax-collector, in the service of the town councillors (q.v.).

Indiction: strictly a late-Roman tax cycle of 15 years; but the term 'nth indiction' denotes a numbered year within the cycle. Starting on September the 1st, it timed official appointments as well as fiscal affairs.

Joseph: Jewish hero and patriarch; he became chief minister of an Egyptian Pharaoh, and his stores of grain relieved a famine (Genesis, xli).

Juvenal: Roman satirical poet, who wrote between A.D. 100 and 130, but was popular with late Roman senators.

Livy: historian of the Roman republic, who wrote under Augustus (q.v.), but was popular with late Roman senators.

Master of the Offices (*magister officiorum*): a minister with *illustris* rank, he controlled the bodyguards (*domestici*), the public post (*cursus publicus*), and the secretarial staffs of the palace (*sacra scrinia*), and regulated audiences with the monarch.

Mercury: Roman god, identified with the Greek Hermes, patron of commerce, music, literature, and oratory.

Muses: the nine goddesses of the arts and literature.

Notitia Dignitatum, Register of State Dignities: official list of civil posts and military commands in the Roman empire, illuminated with their insignia. The copy from which extant MSS derive probably dates c. 395/420.

Novels: imperial laws published after the *Theodosian Code* (q.v.) or *Code of Justinian,* and appended to them.

Patrician: the oldest Roman families had originally been called patrician, but, in the late Roman world, the title is bestowed by the monarch as a non-hereditary honour on leading senators, and habitually on the commander-in-chief (*magister utriusque militiae praesentalis,* or *General-in-Waiting*). The Ostrogothic rulers probably held the office of commander-in-chief, but a new title of *patricius praesentalis,* or *Patrician-in-Waiting* was apparently devised for the army commanders of the boy king Athalaric.

Patrimony, Count of the: an *illustris* minister, he seems to have had the land management of the crown properties in certain outlying provinces, whose taxes he also collected.

Praetorian Prefects: the highest ministers (numbering four in the undivided empire), they were responsible for financial budgeting and state supplies, collection of the staple land-tax, and general provincial administration; they had the right to issue edicts, and their jurisdiction was inappellable.

Prince: used to translate *princeps.* Usually (not exclusively) applied by Cassiodorus to Ostrogothic kings and Roman emperors, this word has overtones of good relations between monarch and subjects, and of traditional, legitimate and imperial authority. It is not, however, a fully imperial title. Cf. Reydellet, 214-31. (Also a civil service rank.)

Private Estates (*res privatae*)**, Count of the:** an *illustris* minister, he controlled rents from, and accessions to, the crown estates.

Quaestor (*quaestor palatii*): legal adviser, and drafter of state documents for kings or emperors; see introduction.

Right Honourable: used to translate *vir clarissimus;* the title of the third grade in the senatorial class.

Romulus: legendary founder and first king of Rome; at the games he gave on the site of the future Circus Maximus, the Romans abducted women of the Sabine tribe.

Sacred Largesses (*sacrae largitiones*), **Count of the:** an *illustris* minister, he controlled precious and semi-precious metals and similar materials, was responsible for the coinage, and military clothing, distributed pay and special donatives, and collected certain taxes, including customs dues.

Saio (plural *saiones*): a word of German origin for a personal retainer; in the *Variae* a general-service agent of the Ostrogothic kings, and barbarian equivalent of the *comitiacus* (q.v.). He was often used to give the royal protection (*tuitio*, q.v.) to those threatened by the lawless and powerful, and was assigned as enforcement officer to the *cancellarii* (q.v.).

Solidus: the standard gold coin of the late Roman world, weighing 1/72 of a pound; a year's food for the very poor might be less than 2 *solidi* in value.

Theodosian Code: a compilation of late Roman law, published by order of the emperor Theodosius II in 438.

Town councillors (*curiales, decuriones*): hereditary members of their councils (*curiae*), they were responsible for maintaining order, registering documents, collecting taxes, and furnishing supplies and services to the state in their cities and surrounding territories.

Tribune-and-Secretary (*tribunus et notarius*): originally associated with the secretariat of the emperor's consistory council, the title was awarded to retiring senior officials of the Praetorian Prefecture; it might also be held without specific duties by men of high social rank.

Tuitio: protection, especially that which the king, through his *saio*, or some leading man, might give against an aggressor.

Tullius (Tully): M.Tullius Cicero, statesman and philosopher, 106-43 B.C.; the most admired of all Roman orators.

Ulysses (Odysseus): Greek hero from Ithaca, famous for wisdom and cunning; after the fall of Troy, he spent ten years wandering the Mediterranean.

Urban Prefect (*praefectus urbi*): appointed by the monarch, usually from the high senatorial nobility, he governed Rome and Italy for one hundred miles around, for one year, with the rank of *illustris*. Answerable only to the monarch, he was his vital link with the Senate. The *Relationes* of Symmachus depict his duties in the late fourth century.

Vergil (Virgil): P. Vergilius Maro, poet, 70-19 B.C., born at Mantua; his epic the *Aeneid*, recounting the legendary origins of Rome, was almost a sacred text to the late Roman aristocracy.

Vicar (*vicarius*): the Praetorian Prefectures were divided into groups of provinces called dioceses, under Vicars with appellate jurisdiction and supervisory functions; the relation of their duties to the Prefects' is obscure. The *Vicarius Italiae* had authority in northern Italy (*Italia Annonaria*), the *Vicarius Romae* in the south and islands (*Italia Suburbicaria*). In Cassiodorus' time, the former may seldom have been appointed; the latter's judicial powers were apparently restricted to a forty mile radius from Rome.

TEXTS

Acta Synhodorum Habitarum Romae: ed. Th. Mommsen, *MGH AA* XII, Berlin, 1894.

Ammianus Marcellinus: *Res Gestae*, ed. with English transl. by J. Rolfe (Loeb); also transl. by W. Hamilton (Penguin Classics, abridged).

Anonymus Valesianus (chronicle): ed. Th. Mommsen, *MGH AA* IX, Berlin, 1892; with English transl. in Loeb Ammianus (above).

Boethius: *Consolation of Philosophy*, ed. with English transl. by H.F. Stewart, E.K. Rand and S.J. Tester (Loeb); also transl. by V.E. Watts (Penguin Classics); *De Arithmetica* and *De Musica*, ed. G. Friedlein (Teubner).

Cassiodorus: *Variae* - see the introduction, xxxiv-xxxv; *Chronicle*, ed. Th. Mommsen, *MGH AA* XI, Berlin, 1893-4; *De Anima*, ed. J. Halporn, *CCSL* 96, Turnhout, 1973; *Expositio Psalmorum*, ed. M. Adriaen, *CCSL* 97-8, Turnhout, 1958, English transl. by P.G. Walsh, *Ancient Christian Writers* series, 1991; *Institutiones*, ed. R.A.B. Mynors, Oxford, 1937, English transl. by L.W. Jones, *An Introduction to Divine and Human Readings*, New York, 1946; *Fragments of Panegyrics*, ed. L. Traube, *MGH AA* XII.

Edict of Theoderic: ed. J. Baviera in *Fontes Iuris Romani Anteiustiniani* II, Florence, 1968; also by F. Bluhme, *MGH Leges* (folio) V, Hanover, 1875.

Ennodius: *Works*, ed. G. Hartel, *CSEL* VI, Vienna, 1882; F. Vogel, *MGH AA* VII, Berlin, 1885; English transl. of *Life of Epiphanius* (80) by G.M. Cook, *Fathers of the Church* series, vol.15.

Epistulae Austrasicae, ed. W. Gundlach, *MGH, Epistulae* III, Berlin, 1892.

Epistulae Theodericianae Variae, ed. Th. Mommsen, *MGH AA* XII.

Isidore: *Etymologiae* or *Origines*, ed. W.M. Lindsay, Oxford, 1911.

John (Ioannes) Lydus: *De Magistratibus*: ed. with English transl. by

A.C. Bandy (*On Powers*, American Philosophical Society, 1983); also transl. by T.F. Carney (below).

Jordanes: *Getica*, ed. Th. Mommsen, *MGH AA* V.1, Berlin, 1882; English transl. by C. Mierow, *The Gothic History of Jordanes*, Princeton, 1915.

Liber Pontificalis: ed. L. Duchesne, Paris, 1886-92; English transl. in progress, vol.I, by R. Davis, *The Book of Pontiffs*, Liverpool, 1989, *TTH* series.

Procopius: *Wars, Anecdota*: ed. with English transl. by H.B. Dewing (Loeb); transl. of the *Anecdota* (*Secret History*) by G.A. Williamson (Penguin Classics).

Sidonius Apollinaris: *Poems and Letters*, ed. with English transl. by W.B. Anderson (Loeb).

Symmachus: *Letters*, ed. O. Seeck, *MGH AA* X, Berlin, 1883; ed. with French transl. of book I-V by J.P. Callu (Budé); book X (*Relationes*) ed. with English transl. by R.H. Barrow, *Prefect and Emperor*, Oxford, 1973.

Theodosian Code, with *Sirmondian Constitutions* and post-Theodosian *Novels*: ed. Th. Mommsen and P.M. Meyer, Berlin, 1905; English transl. by C. Pharr, Princeton, 1952.

MODERN WORKS CITED

G. Alföldy, *Noricum*, London & Boston, Mass., 1974.

P. Arthur, 'Some observations on the economy of Bruttium under the later Roman empire', *Journal of Roman Archaeology* 2, 1989, 133-42.

S.J.B. Barnish, 'The *Anonymus Valesianus II* as a Source for the Last Years of Theoderic', *Latomus* 42, 1983, 472-96; 'The Genesis and Completion of Cassiodorus' *Gothic History*', *Latomus* 43, 1984, 336-61; 'Taxation, Land and Barbarian Settlement in the Western Empire', *PBSR* 54 1986, 170-95; 'Pigs, Plebeians and *Potentes*: Rome's Economic Hinterland, c.A.D. 350-600', *PBSR* 55, 1987, 157-85; 'Transformation and Survival in the Western

Senatorial Aristocracy, c.A.D. 400-700', *PBSR* 65, 1988, 120-55;
'The Work of Cassiodorus after his Conversion', *Latomus* 48,
1989, 157-87; 'Maximian, Cassiodorus, Boethius, Theodahad:
Literature, Philosophy and Politics in Ostrogothic Italy',
Nottingham Mediaeval Studies 34, 1990, 16-31; 'Attila's Invasion
of Gaul in the Literary Sources', forthcoming in *Fifth Century
Gaul: a Crisis of Identity*, ed. J. Drinkwater.

M. Benner, *The Emperor Says. Studies in the Rhetorical Style in Edicts
of the Early Empire*, Göteborg, 1975.

J.B. Bury, *History of the Later Roman Empire, from the death of
Theodosius 1 to the death of Justinian*, London, 1923.

J. Caldwell, 'The *De Institutione Arithmetica* and the *De Institutione
Musica*', in Gibson.

Alan Cameron, *Porphyrius the Charioteer*, Oxford, 1973; *Circus
Factions*, Oxford, 1976.

Averil Cameron, *Procopius and the Sixth Century*, London, 1985.

T.F. Carney, *Bureaucracy in Traditional Society: Romano-Byzantine
Bureaucracies Viewed From Within*, Lawrence, Kansas, 1981.

L. Cuppo Csaki, 'Variarum I.X of Cassiodorus as a Program of
Monetary Policy', *Florilegium* 9, 1987, 53-63.

H. Chadwick, *Boethius: the Consolations of Music, Logic, Theology
and Philosophy*, Oxford, 1981.

Tim Cornell and John Matthews, *Atlas of the Roman World*, Oxford,
1982.

P. Courcelle, *Late Latin Writers and their Greek Sources*, Cambridge,
Mass., 1969.

G. Dagron, *Naissance d'une Capitale: Constantinople et ses Institutions
de 330 à 451*, Paris, 1974.

O.A.W. Dilke, *The Roman Land Surveyors: an Introduction to the
'Agrimensores'*, Newton Abbott, 1971.

D.R. Dudley, *Urbs Roma, a Source Book of Classical Texts on the
City and its Monuments*, Aberdeen, 1967.

H.R. Ellis Davidson, *The Sword in Anglo-Saxon England*, Oxford,
1962.

À. Fridh, *Études Critiques et Syntaxiques sur les 'Variae' de*

Cassiodore, Göteborg, 1950; *Terminologie et Formules dans les 'Variae' de Cassiodore*, Stockholm, 1956; *Contributions à la Critique et à l'Interpretation des 'Variae' de Cassiodore*, Göteborg, 1968.

M.T. Gibson, ed., *Boethius: his Life, Thought and Influence*, Oxford, 1981.

G. Gissing, *By The Ionian Sea*, London, 1901.

W. Goffart, *Barbarians and Romans, A.D. 418-584: the Techniques of Accomodation*, Princeton, 1980; *The Narrators of Barbarian History (A.D. 550-800)*, Princeton, 1988.

A. von Harnack, 'Der erste deutsche Papst (Bonifatius I) und die beiden letzten Dekrete des römischen Senats', *Sitzungsberichte der Preussischen Akademie*, 5, 1924, 24-39.

J.D. Harries, 'The Roman Imperial Quaestor from Constantine to Theodosius II', *JRS* 78, 1988, 148-72.

P. Heather, 'Cassiodorus and the Rise of the Amals: Genealogy and the Goths under Hun Domination', *JRS* 79, 1989, 102-28.

T. Honoré, *Tribonian*, London, 1978.

J.H. Humphrey, *Roman Circuses: Arenas for Chariot Racing*, London, 1986.

E. James, *The Franks*, Oxford, 1988.

A.H.M. Jones, *The Later Roman Empire, 284-602*, Oxford, 1964; 'The Constitutional Position of Odoacer and Theoderic', *JRS* 52, 1962, 126-30, reprinted in his *The Ancient Economy*, Oxford, 1974.

H. Kirkby, 'The Scholar and his Public', in Gibson.

S. Krautschick, *Cassiodor und die Politik seiner Zeit*, Bonn, 1983.

J.W. Leopold, '*Consolanda per edicta*: Cassiodorus, *Variae* IV.50, and Imperial Consolations for Natural Catastrophe', *Latomus* 45, 1986, 816-36.

M. Maas, 'Roman History and Christian Idealism in Justinian's Reform Legislation', *Dumbarton Oaks Papers* 40, 1986, 17-31.

S.G. MacCormack, 'Latin Prose Panegyrics', in *Empire and Aftermath*, ed. T.A. Dorey, London, 1975; *Art and Ceremony in Late Antiquity*, Berkeley, 1981.

R. Macpherson, *Rome in Involution: Cassiodorus' 'Variae' in their Literary and Historical Setting*, Poznan, 1989.

R.A. Markus, *The End of Ancient Christianity*, Cambridge, 1991.

J.R. Martindale, *Prosopography of the Later Roman Empire*, II, Cambridge, 1980.

G. Mathew, *Byzantine Aesthetics*, London, 1963.

J.F. Matthews, 'The Letters of Symmachus', in *Latin Literature of the Fourth Century*, ed. J.W. Binns, London, 1974; *Western Aristocracies and Imperial Court, A.D. 364-425*, Oxford, 1978; 'Anicius Manlius Severinus Boethius', in Gibson.

A. Momigliano, 'Cassiodorus and Italian Culture of his Time', in his *Studies in Historiography*, New York, 1966, reprinted from *Proceedings of the British Academy* 41, 1955.

Th. Mommsen, 'Ostgotische Studien', *Neues Archiv für Gesellschaft* 14-15, 1889-90, 225-49, 443-544, 181-6, reprinted in his *Gesammelte Schriften* VI, Berlin, 1910.

J. Moorhead, 'Boethius and Romans in Ostrogothic Service', *Historia* 27, 1978, 604-12; 'The Decii under Theoderic', *Historia* 33, 1984, 107-15.

J.J. O'Donnell, *Cassiodorus*, Berkeley, etc., 1979.

Ch. Pietri, 'Le sénat, le peuple chrétien et les partis du cirque sous le pape Symmaque', *Mélanges d'Archéologie et d'Histoire de l'École Française de Rome*, 78, 1966, 123-39.

U. Pizzani, 'Boezio "consulente tecnico" al servizio dei rei barbarici', *Romanobarbarica* 3, 1978, 189-242.

M. Reydellet, *La Royauté dans la Littérature Latine de Sidoine Apollinaire à Isidore de Séville*, Rome, 1981.

J. Richards, *The Popes and the Papacy in the Early Middle Ages, 476-752*, London, etc., 1979.

M. Roberts, *The Jeweled Style: Poetry and Poetics in Late Antiquity*, Ithaca, NY, and London, 1989.

L. (Cracco) Ruggini, *Economia e Società nell'Italia Annonaria*, Milan, 1961.

W. Sinnigen, 'Administrative Shifts of Competence under Theoderic', *Traditio* 21, 1965, 456-67.

E. Stein, *Histoire du Bas-Empire*, II, Paris, etc., 1949.

M. Steinby, 'L'industria laterizia di Roma nel tardo impero', in *Società Romana e Impero Tardoantico* II, ed. A.Giardina, Rome, 1986.

J. Sundwall, *Abhandlungen zur Geschichte des ausgehenden Römertums*, Helsinki, 1919.

G. Tabacco, *The Struggle for Power in Medieval Italy: Structures of Political Rule*, Cambridge, 1989.

S. Teillet, *Des Goths à la Nation Gothique*, Paris, 1984.

E.A. Thompson, *Romans and Barbarians: the Decline of the Western Empire*, Madison, Wis., 1982.

L. Traube, *Index Rerum et Verborum*, MGH AA XII.

A. Van de Vyver, 'La Victoire contre les Alamans et la Conversion de Clovis', *RBPh* 15-17, 1936-8, 859-914, 35-94, 793-813.

G. Vidén, *The Roman Chancery Tradition: Studies in the Language of 'Codex Theodosianus' and Cassiodorus' 'Variae'*, Göteborg, 1984.

W.F. Volbach, *Elfenbeinarbeiten der Spätantike und des frühen Mittelalters* (3rd ed.), Mainz, 1976.

J.M. Wallace-Hadrill, *The Barbarian West, 400-1000* (3rd ed.), London, 1967.

B. Ward-Perkins, *From Classical Antiquity to the Middle Ages: Urban Public Building in Northern and Central Italy, A.D. 300-850*, Oxford, 1984.

C.J. Wickham, *Early Medieval Italy: Central Power and Local Society, 400-1000*, London, 1981.

H. Wolfram, *History of the Goths*, Berkeley, etc., 1978.

I.N. Wood, 'Gregory of Tours and Clovis', *RBPh* 63, 1985, 249-72.

P. Wormald §1, 'Literacy in Anglo-Saxon England and its Neighbours', *Transactions of the Royal Historical Society* 27, 1977, 95-114; §2, '*Lex Scripta* and *Verbum Regis*: Legislation and Germanic Kingship from Euric to Cnut', in *Early Medieval Kingship*, ed P. Sawyer & I.N. Wood, Leeds, 1977.

O.J. Zimmermann, *The Late Latin Vocabulary of the 'Variae' of Cassiodorus, with special advertence to the technical terminology of administration*, Washington, D.C., 1944.

Aetius   xxxvii, xlii-xliii, I.4.11
Agapitus (Patrician)   I.23, I.27.3
Agapitus I (Pope)   lii, X.20.3-4 (?), XII.20
Alamanni   II.41
Alaric II   xii, III.1-4
Amalaberga   xxviii, IV.1, XI.1, n.6
Amalasuintha   xii-xiv, xvi, xxviii, xlviii, l-li, IV.1, endnote, IX.18,
   n.11 X.3, X.20.4 (?), X.21, n.10, X.32.2, XI.1, XI.2.2; in
   general, see VIII-IX, drafted in her regency.
Amals   xi-xiii, xxxii, IV.1.1, IX.24.4-6, X.11.3, XI.1.19-20, XI.13.4
Ammianus Marcellinus   II.16, n.5, II.32, n.18, II.40, n.25, III.51,
   endnote, VI.5, n.3, IX.21, n.16, IX.24, n.17, XI.14, n.14
Anastasius   xi, xlv, II.1, II.38, n.20, III.4, n.5, V.42, endnote,
   VIII.1.5 (?), X.22.2 (?)
Anicii   x, xxxvii-xxxviii, xliv-xlv, X.11.2; cf. Boethius, Faustus,
   Maximus
Arator   xxxix, VIII.12
Arigern   xlii, III.36, IV.22.4
Arles   III.32, III.44
Athalaric   xii-xiv, xvi, xxiii, xxxii, xxxviii, xlviii, l, VIII.1, X.3.1,
   X.31, endnote, XI.1, XI.2.2; in general, see VIII-IX drafted mostly
   in his name.
Attila   xliii, I.4.11-12, III.1.1
Anicius Manlius Severinus Boethius   xiii, xvi-xvii, xxi, xxv, xxviii,
   xxxvi-xxxviii, xl, xlii, xliv, xlvii-xlix, li (n.109), liii, I.10, I.45,
   II.40, III.52, n.39, IV.22, n.5, V.4, endnote, V.41, n.6, VIII.28,
   n.10, X.11, n.2, endnote, XI.1, n.7, XII.25, endnote
Boniface II (Pope)   IX.15.3
Bruttium   xxxvii-xxxviii, xlvi, xlix, lii, I.3.5, I.4.14, III.8,
   III.46.2-3, VIII.31, VIII.33.3, XI.39, XII.5, XII.12, XII.13,
   XII.15
Burgundians   I.45.2, I.46, III.2, III.32,n.23, III.41,n.26, XI.1.13

Caelianus I.23, I.27.3, IV.22.3
Calabria VIII.33.3
Campania   II.32, endnote, III.27, IV.5.2, IV.10, VIII.33.3,
XII.22.3-4
Cassiodorus (1) I.4.14
Cassiodorus (2) xxxvii, I.4.10-13
Cassiodorus (3) xxxvi-xxxix, xliv, xlvi, li, I.3-4, III.28, IX.24.9
Magnus Aurelius Cassiodorus **Senator**   introduction, passim, I.45,
n.24, endnote, II.40, n.24, III.1, n.1, III.51, endnote, IV.1,
endnote, V.1, endnote, V.40, n.5, V.42, nn.8,10, VI.3, n.2,
VIII.33, n.14, IX.15, n.1, endnote, IX.24-5, X.20, n.6, X.22,
n.11, endnote, X.26.2, X.31, n.13, endnote, X.32, endnote, XI.14,
nn.12-14, endnote; otherwise, see XI-XII sent mostly by him, and
notes.
Circus Maximus III.51
Clovis xii, xxxix-xl, II.20, n.8, II.38, n.20, II.40.1, II.41, III.1-4
Colosseum V.42.5
Como XI.14
Consilinum/Marcellianum VIII.33
Cunigastus xlix, VIII.28
Cyprian xlviii-xlix, V.40-1
Datius XII.27
Decii x, xxxviii, II.32, endnote, III.6, IV.22, n.4; cf. Decius,
Inportunus
Caecina Mavortius Basilius Decius   II.21, endnote, II.32, III.6, n.6,
IV.22.3
Decoratus xlviii, V.4
Dertona (Tortona) I.17, XII.27.2
Magnus Felix Ennodius   Introduction, nn. 40, 46, 54, 86-7, 109, xx,
xxiv, xxvi, xl, xliv, III.18, endnote, IV.6, endnote, IV.51, n.12,
VIII.12, n.3, IX.21, nn.15-16, XI.13, n.11, XI.14, endnote
Eutharic xii, xlvii-xlviii, VIII.1.3, IX.25.3
Anicius Probus Faustus **Niger**   xliv, II.38 III.20, III.21 (?), III.27.3
(?), III.28.2 (?), III.51, IX.24, n.18, X.11, n.3, XI.14, endnote
Felix (Consul) xlv, II.1, III.39

Felix IV (Pope) xlix, VIII.15, IX.15, n.5
Franks xii-xiii, xv, xviii, xxxix-xl, xliii, II.40.1, II.41, III.1.3, III.2.3, III.3.2, III.4, III.32, n.23, IX.18, n.10, XI.1.12
Gaul xii-xiii, xvi-xviii, xxvii, xliii, xlv, II.1.2, III.17, IV.5, XI.1.16; cf. III.18, III.32, III.41, III.44
Gemellus III.17, III.18, III.32, III.41; cf. xliii
Gudeliva X.21
Gundobad xl, xli (n.86) I.45.2, I.46, III.1.4, III.2, III.3.2, III.4, n.5
Herminafrid IV.1; cf. Thoringi
Heruls III.3
Honoratus xlviii, V.4
Inportunus xlv, xlviii, I.27.2, III.6, III.36, n.25; cf. xliii
Istria XII.22, XII.24.1, XII.26.3
John (governor) III.27, IV.10
John II (Pope) lii, IX.15, XI.2
John Lydus xiv-xv, xxiii, xxvi, xxxi, li-lii, X.20, n.6, XI.36, nn.17-18, XI.38, n.20
Jordanes xxvi (n.44), xxxi, xliii (n.89), III.1, n.1, IV.1, endnote, X.22, n.11, XI.1, n.9, XII.20, n.18, XII.24, n.22
Justin I xii, xli, xlvii, VIII.1, XI.1, n.4
Justinian I xiii, xv-xvi, xxvii-xxix, xliv, li, X.11, n.4, X.20.2, X.22, X.26, X.32, XI.1, nn.4-5, 8, XI.13
Petrus Marcellinus Felix Liberius xvi-xvii, xxxviii-xxxix, xlvi (n.97) II.16, XI.1.16-17; cf. xliii
Licinus, brick depot of I.25.2
Liguria xxxviii, I.17, n.13, II.20, VIII.12.7, XI.14, XI.16, XII.8, XII.27, endnote
Lucania xxxii, xxxvii-xxxviii, xlvi, xlix, lii, I.3.5, I.4.14, III.8, III.46.2, IV.5.2, VIII.31, n.12, VIII.33, XI.39, XII.5, XII.12, XII.13, XII.15
Majorian xlii, II.24, n.10, III.31, n.22, XI.16, n.15
Marseilles (Massilia) III.17, endnote, III.41.2
Maximus xlv, V.42, X.11
Milan (Mediolanum) xxxviii, xlv, III.39.2, VIII.12, nn.3,8, X.13, endnote, XII.27

Odoacer   xi, xxxiii, xxxvii-xxxix, I.3, n.1, I.4.6, n.5, I.18, n.16, II.16.2-3, V.41.5

Ostrogoths   xi-xvii, xxv-xxviii, xxxi-xxxii, xxxviii-xliii, xlvii-l, liii, I.4.17, I.17, I.18.2, II.1, endnote, II.16.5, II.40, n.31, III.13, III.23.2-3, III.36, n.24, V.29, endnote, IX.25.4-6,9, X.31, XI.1.12, 14, XII.5.3-4, endnote

Pannonia   xvii, xxvii, III.23; cf.xii

Pavia (Ticinum)   xx, II.20, n.2, XII.27.2

Peter (the Patrician)   li, X.20.3, X.22.1

Procopius   Introduction, nn. 12, 52, 62, 64, 81, 84, 98, 107, 111, 112, 114, li, II.1, endnote, VI.6, n.4, VIII.1, n.1, IX.18, n.10, X.3, n.1, X.5, endnote, X.11, n.4, X.13, endnote, X.20, n.8, , X.21, n.9, X.26, endnote, X.32, endnote, XI.1, nn.2, 5, 7, XII.5, endnote, XII.27, endnote

Ravenna   xi-xiii, xv, xx, xxv-xxvi, xxviii-xxix, xxxvii-xxxviii, xlii, xlvii, xlix, liii, II.20, II.21, endnote, VI.6.6, XII.22.3, XII.24.1, 3, endnote

Rome (city)   ix-x, xiii-xv, xxviii, xxxvii-xl, xlii-xliii, xlv-xlvii, xlix-l, lii-liii, I.25, II.21, endnote, III.20, n.12, III.21, III.30-1, III.51, IV.6, IV.51, V.42, VIII.12.6, IX.15-16, IX.21, X.13, X.32.1, XI.2, XI.13.6, XI.39.1-3, XII.27, endnote

Salona   III.7, XII.24, endnote

Samnium   xlii, III.13, IV.10, XI.36

Sicily   xxxvii, I.3.3, I.4.14; cf. IV.6

Sipontum   II.38

Spoleto   II.21, V.4.6, endnote

Squillace (Scillacium)   xxxvii, xlvii, XII.15; cf. Vivarium

Q.Aurelius Memmius Symmachus iunior   xiii, xxxvi-xxxvii, xl (n.83), xlv, xlvii-xlviii, li (n.109), liii, I.10, endnote, I.23.2, II.14, IV.6, IV.22.3, IV.51, XI.1, n.7

Theatre of Pompey   IV.51

Theodahad   xiii-xiv, xvi, xxviii, xliii, l-li, IV.1, endnote, IX.18, n.11, X.3, X.21.1, X.31, n.14, endnote, X.32.2, XI.13, XII.12 (?), XII.20; X is drafted mostly in his name.

Theoderic (the Ostrogoth)   xi-xiv, xviii, xx, xxii, xxv-xxix, xxxiv, xxxvi-xlix, VIII.1.3,5, VIII.12.3, VIII.15, VIII.33, n.14, IX.18.12, IX.24.1-8, X.3.7, X.31.5, XI.1, n.3; in general, see I-V drafted mostly in his name.
Theodora   li, X.20-1
Thoringi   III.3, IV.1, XI.1, n.6
Tuluin   xxxix, VIII.12.1   *Placidia's reputation*
Tuscia   IV.5.2, IX.18, n.11, XI.38
Valentinian III   I.4.10, VIII.33, n.14, IX.18.1, XI.1.9, XI.39, n.24
Vandals   x, xii-xiii, I.4.14, IV.1, endnote, IX.25.9-10, XI.13, n.11
Venantius (governor)   xlvi, III.8, III.46
Venantius (son of Liberius)   xxxix, II.16
Venetia   XII.24, XII.26.1
Visigoths   xii, xxviii (n.50), xliii, III.1, III.3.2, IX.21, n.15, XII.20, n.18
Vivarium   xxix, xlvii, I.45, endnote, XII.15, n.7
Warni   III.3, V.1
Witigis   xiii-xiv, l, liii, II.1, endnote, X.13, endnote, X.31-2

INDEX 2: SUBJECTS, DIGRESSIONS AND ALLUSIONS

Accessions of Ostrogothic Rulers   xi-xiii, xvi, xlviii, l, I.18.2, VIII.1, IX.25.7, X.3, X.31
Agriculture and Fisheries   xxxviii, xlvi, II.21, II.32, II.41, n.32, III.52, VIII.31.4-5, VIII.33.3-4, X.26.2, XI.14.2-3, XI.39.3-4, XII.5.5, XII.12, XII.15.4-5, XII.22, XII.24, XII.25, XII.26, XII.27
Allusions, Digressions: the Bible   xix, xxi, xxix, lii, II.40.11, VI.3.1-2, 9, IX.15.11, IX.25.11, X.3.5, X.26.4, XII.25.7

Allusions, Digressions: Classical Literature, Myth and Legend
(select)   xxi, Preface, 2,4,9, I.3.4, I.45.4,10, II.40.6-10, 14, 17,
III.4.4, III.6.3-4, III.31.4, III.51.3, 11-13, IV.51.7-9, endnote,
V.1.2, V.4.6, V.42.2-3, 11, VI.5.3, VIII.12.4, 7, VIII.33.1,
IX.21.9, X.3.4, X.31.2, XI.1.7, 15, 20, XI.14.4-5, XII.15.1-3, 7
Allusions, Digressions: Cultural History, Cultural Themes   xix,
xxii, xxiv-xxvi, xxxix-xl, I.10 (mathematics, coinage), I.45
(mechanics), II.40 (music), III.31.4, III.51 (chariot racing), III.52
(mathematics,   surveying),   IV.51   (theatre),   V.1,   V.42
(amphitheatre), VI.3.1-2, VIII.12.4-5, IX.21, IX.25.4-6, XI.36.2-3,
XI.38.2-6 (writing, papyrus), XII.15.3
Allusions, Digressions: Natural History   xix, xxii-xxiii, xxv, II.14,
IV.1, V.4.5-6, V.42.8, VIII.12.4-5, VIII.31.1-3,7, IX.24.8,
X.3.2-3, XI.14.5, XI.36.2-3, XI.38.2-5, XII.12 , XII.15, XII.24,
XII.25; cf. Landscapes
Allusions, Digressions: Secular History (pre 476)   xix, xxi,
xxvi-xxvii, xxix, I.4.9-14, III.1.1, III.3.3, III.6.3, III.23.2,
III.51.3-4,9, III.52.6, V.42.2-5, IX.19.2, IX.25.4, 10, X.11.2,
XI.1.9, 19, XI.39.1, 4, XII.13.1, XII.20.4
Appointments   xvi-xxi, xxvi, xxxi, xxxviii, l-lii, I.3-4, II.16, III.6,
III.13, III.17, III.23, V.4, V.40-1, VI.3, VI.5, VI.6, VIII.12,
VIII.15, IX.24-5, X.11, XI.1.16-18
Barbarian-Roman Relations   xi-xvi, xxv-xxviii, xxxi-xxxii,
xxxix-xliii, xlvii-l, liii, I.18, II.8, II.16.5, III.13, III.23, III.36,
n.24, VIII.28, IX.24.4-6, XII.5
Cities and Civic Life   xliii, xlv-xlvi, Preface, 5, I.25, I.27, III.21,
III.30-1, III.39, III.44, III.51, IV.6, IV.51, VIII.31, IX.15,
X.13.2, XI.14, XI.39, XII.8, XII.15
Civil Service   ix-xi, xiii-xv, xviii, xxii-xxix, xxxi, xxxiii, xli-xliv,
xlvi-lii, VI.3, VI.6, VII.42, XI.14, XI.36, XI.38, XII.13, XII.15,
XII.16
Coins, Weights and Measures   xxvi (n.45), I.10, XI.16, XII.16,
XII.24.6

Constitutional Position of Ostrogothic Rulers   xi-xii, xvi, xli-xlii,
II.1, VIII.1, X.11, n.4, X.22, X.31; cf. Accessions
Consulship   ix-xiii, xxv, xxxvi, xxxix, xlv, xlvii, I.27.2, II.1, III.6.6,
III.39, III.51, V.42, VIII.1.3, X.11.3
Diplomacy with Barbarian Kings   xii, xv, xxxix-xl, xlii, xlix, I.46,
II.41, III.1-4, IV.1, V.1, XI.1.13.
Diplomacy with the Emperor   xi-xiii, xv, xlii, xlvii-li II.1, V.40.5,
VIII.1, X.20-2, X.11, n.4, X.26, X.32, XI.1.10-11, XI.13, XII.20
Ecclesiastical and Religious Affairs   xi-xiii, xv-xvi, xxi-xxii,
xxiv-xxvi, xliii-xlviii, lii-liii, II.8, II.27, III.7, IV.22, VIII.15,
VIII.33.6-8, IX.15-16, IX.18.9, X.26, XI.2, XI.13.6, XII.13,
XII.20; cf. Jews, Magic, Papacy
Edicts   xiv, xviii, xxii-xxiii, xxx-xxxi, xli, l-li, II.24.5, II.25,
IV.10.2-3, VII.42, IX.15.7,11, IX.18-20, XII.13
Education   xiv-xv, xxiii-xxviii, xlvii, l, liii, Preface, 8, 14, I.46, 2-3,
III.6.3-5, III.52.7, IV.1.1-2, IV.6, V.40.5, VIII.12, VIII.31.6,
IX.21, IX.24.8, X.3.4-5, XI.1.4-7; cf. Rhetoric
Food Supply and Famine   xliii, lii, Preface, 5, II.20, II.38, III.41,
III.44, IV.5, VI.3.1,6, VI.6.6, IX.25.9, XI.2.4, XI.16.4, XI.39,
XII.12, XII.22.3-5, XII.24.2-4, XII.25, XII.26, XII.27; cf. Trade,
Transport
Fortifications   I.17, III.41, III.44, XI.39.2, XII.15.5; cf. Warfare
Jews   xliv, II.27
Landscapes   xix, xxi, xxiii, xlix, lii, VIII.31.5, VIII.33.3-5, XI.14,
XII.15, XII.22, XII.24
Law, Justice, and Public Order   xv-xvi, xxi-xxxiii, xli-xliii,
xlvii-xlviii, li-lii, Preface, 10, I.3.4-5, I.18, I.23, I.27, II.14,
II.16.5, II.21, II.32.4, III.7, III.13, III.17, III.18, III.20, III.23,
III.27, III.36, III.46, III.52, IV.10, IV.22, V.4, V.29, V.40.2-4,
V.41.3-4, VI.3.3-4, VI.5.4-5, VII.42, VIII.12.2, VIII.15, VIII.28,
VIII.33, IX.15-16, IX.18-20, IX.24.4-5, IX.25.10, X.5, XI.1.8,
XII.5, XII.20
Magic   xlvii, IV.22, IX.18.9
Panegyric   xviii-xx, xxiii, xxxvi, xxxix, xlvii, l, Preface, 9, 11, XI.1;
cf. Appointments

Papacy x, xiii, xxi-xxii, xxix, xliii, xlv, xlviii, lii, VIII.15, IX.15-16, XI.2, XII.20

Praetorian Prefecture ix, xiv-xv, xxi, xxxi, xxxviii-xxxix, xlii-xliii, l-liii, Preface, 4-6, I.3.6, I.4.6-8, II.16.4-5, II.24.2, III.20, III.27, VI.3, VIII.31.1, IX.24.11-12, IX.25.12, X.26.2, XI.16, XI.36, XI.38, XI.39.4-5, XII.5.1-2,9, XII.8, XII.13, XII.15.1,7, XII.16; see, in general, XI-XII

Public Buildings xix, xliii, I.25, III.30-1, III.44, III.51.4-10, IV.51, V.42.5, XI.39.2

Public Shows xix, xxi, xliii, xlv, I.27, III.39, III.51, IV.51, V.42, IX.21.8

Quaestorship ix, xiv, xxvi-xxix, xxxi, xxxvi, xxxix-xlvi, xlviii-li, Preface, 7-8, V.4, VI.5, VII.42, IX.24.3-5, IX.25.8

Rhetoric, Literature xiv, xviii-xxxii, xxxix-xl, xlvii, Preface, 1-3, 8-11, 15-18, III.6.3-5, V.4.4-6, VI.5, VIII.12, IX.21, IX.25.2-3,11, X.3.4-5, XI.1.6-7, XI.38.5-6; cf. Panegyric, Education

Senate and Ruler ix-xiii, xv-xvi, xxviii, xxxi-xxxii, xxxvii, xl-xli, xliii, xlvi-l, liii, I.23, I.27, II.1, II.24-5, III.6, III.21, III.31, III.36, IV.22, n.5, V.41.3, VI.6.2, VIII.15, IX.16, IX.21, X.11, X.13, XI.1.15, XI.13.3-4; cf. Appointments

Taxes, Levies, Services xxxviii, xlvi, li-lii, II.16.4, II.24-5, II.38, III.8, III.32, IV.5, VI.6.5, X.26.2, XI.14, XI.16, XI.36.4, XI.38.6, XI.39, XII.5.3-4, XII.8, XII.13, XII.15.6-7, XII.16, XII.22, XII.26, XII.27

Trade xxxviii, II.38, III.7, IV.5, V.1, VIII.31.5, VIII.33, XI.39, n.24, XII.12, n.3, XII.22, XII.24, XII.26, XII.27

Transport, Public Post xlix, lii, III.44, IV.5, VI.6.3-4, XI.14.1, XII.15.6-7, XII.22.2-3,5, XII.24

Warfare ix-xiii, xxv, xxxviii, xlii-xliii, lii-liii, I.4.11-12,14,17, I.17, II.8, II.38, II.41, III.1-4, III.32, III.41, VI.6.1, VIII.12.1, IX.18, pref., IX.21.4, IX.25.9-10, X.31, X.32.1, XI.1.9-13, XI.13.3-6, XI.16.4, XII.5, XII.26.2; cf. Fortifications

Women xiii, l-li, III.6.6, IV.1, IX.15.4-7, X.20-1, X.26.3, XI.1.5-19

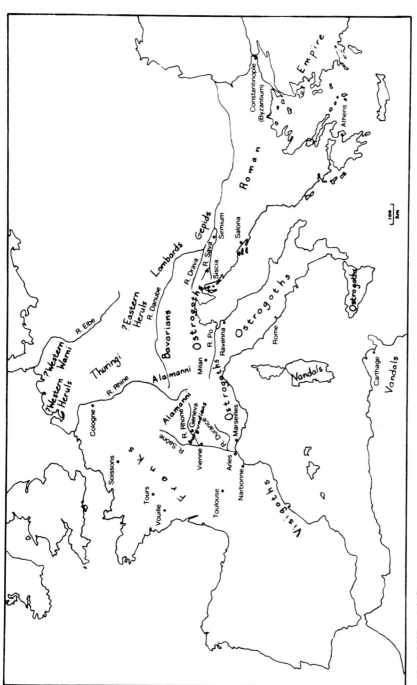

MAP 1. EUROPE. ca. 510 AD.

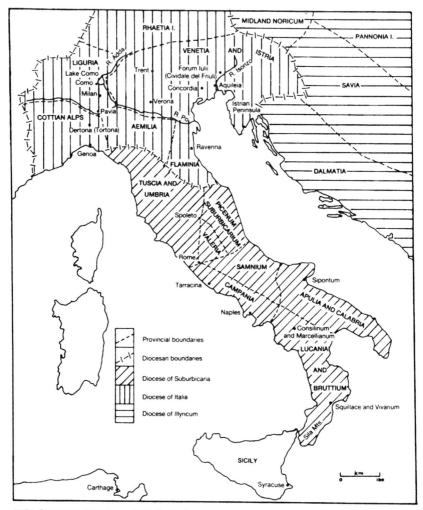

MAP 2. ITALY showing the late Roman administrative boundaries,
and places referred to in the text.